The Woman in the White House

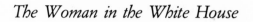

BOOKS BY NORMAN KING

Regis and Kathie Lee
Everybody Loves Oprah
Arsenio Hall
Madonna: The Book
The First Five Minutes
The Last Five Minutes
Donahue: The Man Women Love
Effective Advertising in Small Space
The Money Messiahs
Turn Your House Into a Money Factory
The Money Market Book
Two Royal Women
The Prince and the Princess: A Love Story
Here's Erma: The Bombecking of America
Dan Rather
Ivana
All in the First Family (with Bill Adler)

THE WOMAN IN THE WHITE HOUSE

The Remarkable Story
of Hillary Rodham Clinton

Norman King

A BIRCH LANE PRESS BOOK
Published by Carol Publishing Group

TO BARBARA:

The First Lady of *My* Life

Copyright © 1996 Norman King

A Birch Lane Press Book
Published by Carol Publishing Group
Birch Lane Press is a registered trademark of Carol Communications, Inc.
Editorial Offices: 600 Madison Avenue, New York, N.Y. 10022
Sales and Distribution Offices: 120 Enterprise Avenue, Secaucus, N.J. 07094
In Canada: Canadian Manda Group, One Atlantic Avenue, Suite 105, Toronto, Ontario M6K 3E7
Queries regarding rights and permissions should be addressed to Carol Publishing Group, 600 Madison Avenue, New York, N.Y. 10022

Carol Publishing Group books are available at special discounts for bulk purchases, sales promotion, fund-raising, or educational purposes. Special editions can be created to specifications. For details, contact: Special Sales Department, Carol Publishing Group, 120 Enterprise Avenue, Secaucus, N.J. 07094

Manufactured in the United States of America
10 9 8 7 6 5 4 3 2 1

Library of Congress Cataloging-in-Publication Data
King, Norman, 1926–
    The woman in the White House : the remarkable story of Hillary Rodham Clinton / Norman King.
        p.   cm.
    "A Birch Lane Press book."
    ISBN 1-55972-349-1 (hardcover)
    1. Clinton, Hillary Rodham. 2. Clinton, Bill, 1946–
3. Presidents' spouses—United States—Biography. I. Title.
E887.C55K567 1996
973.929'092—dc20   95-49281
                                                                                   CIP

Contents

The Woman in the White House

CHAPTER ONE

"Sister Frigidaire"

Hillary Victoria Rodham's family is the personification of the American Dream. Like millions of others, their saga is the old-fashioned immigrant story. By dint of hard work and grit, they rose to become an integral part of the great middle class that is the heart of America today and to which Bill Clinton would make his greatest appeal to become the forty-second President of the United States.

Hillary's paternal grandfather immigrated to the United States from Northumberland, England, when he was four years old and settled with his family in Scranton, Pennsylvania. One of his three sons, Hugh Rodham, wound up working for the Scranton Lace Company after graduating from Penn State on a football scholarship and majoring in physical education.

Fed up with carrying boxes around for low wages, he worked for a brief time in the Pennsylvania coal mines during the Great Depression, finally drifting to Chicago. While employed as a curtain salesman at the Columbia Lace Company, he met Dorothy Howell when she applied for a job as a secretary.

When America entered World War II on December 7, 1941, Hugh joined the navy. Because of his physical-education background he was selected to train sailors in what was called the "Gene Tunney Program"—a boot camp for recruits before they sailed off to war.

Dorothy Howell had grown up in Alhambra, California, with a Welsh father and a mother named Della Murray who was Scottish, French, and Native American. Life in Alhambra was dusty and dull, and Dorothy decided to move to Chicago, which, at that distance, seemed to be the epitome of Big City to her.

She met Hugh in 1937, and they were finally married in 1942. After the war, Hugh started a drapery business in Chicago, buying the fabric, printing designs on it, sewing it, and even hanging the curtains for customers. It was a one-man operation, even though he had an assistant. Although he badgered his help inordinately, there was an undercurrent of good humor in his manner—and nobody took Hugh at face value.

On October 26, 1947, Dorothy Rodham gave birth to their firstborn, Hillary Victoria. Three years later they moved to the suburb north of Chicago called Park Ridge. The suburban Hugh Rodham was tightfisted, hard to please, and always in command. Though it is not fashionable to be macho today, Hugh fit the pattern perfectly then. He epitomized the boot-camp instructor and developed a straightforward, curmudgeonly attitude that made him venerable and at the same time a bit remote. Hugh always voted Republican, only drove a Cadillac, and pushed his kids to be the best.

Both parents were traditionally conservative middle-of-the-roaders. Hillary's father worked hard to give his family the very best of everything. Her mother devoted herself to bringing up the family and keeping the home always in a state of efficient maintenance. Though Dorothy did not attend college, she was determined that her children would if at all possible—and that meant daughters as well as sons.

Hugh Rodham Jr. was the second child, born three years after Hillary, and Anthony was the third, born four years after that. As her brother Hugh once expressed it, the children were reared "with traditional Midwestern values: family, church on Sunday, respect your elders, do well in school, participate in sports."

It was Hillary who carried out the fourth attribute mentioned by her brother Hugh: "Do well in school." For her it seemed natural to excel in reading, writing, and even arithmetic. In addition, she seemed to surpass her peers at almost everything else she attempted. She was, in fact, the typical overachiever, always in intense personal competition with the other members of her rather traditional American family.

"My parents gave me my belief in working hard, doing well in school, and not being limited by the fact that I was a little girl," she said. "It really was the classic parenting situation, where the mother is the encourager and helper and the father brings news from the outside world. My father would come home and say, 'You did well, but could you do better? It's hard out there.' Encouragement was tempered with realism."

The security and support that she received from her parents proved fundamental to her own success in life. "The role fathers play in empowering girls is critical," she later observed. "That's one reason it's so troubling to have so many fatherless children [out there] these days."

Hillary Rodham grew up in a pleasant neighborhood where all the kids could play and freely ride on their bicycles. "Our parents never worried [about us]. They just said, 'Be home by five-thirty.' "

Dorothy recalled, "There must have been forty or fifty children within a four-block radius of our house, and within four years of Hillary's age. They were all together, all the time, a big extended family. There were more boys than girls, lots of playing and competition. She held her own at cops and robbers, hide and seek, chase and run—all the games that children don't play anymore."

Hugh and Dorothy Rodham were, by all accounts, traditional parents of the 1950s, quite content to adopt a somewhat relaxed life-style not particularly fraught with overall achievement and certainly not dedicated to *overachievement*. Thus, the exceptional talents of their daughter, Hillary, who started out from the beginning as a miniature whirlwind and who wanted to excel at everything, placed Hugh and Dorothy in a somewhat awkward position in regard to their neighbors.

Hillary never felt satisfied at letting things take their course. Even when she was small, she would be the one who organized the neighborhood kids into games and other activities. She started amateur sports tournaments and even put together a children's circus at one time. When she was a teenager, she formed a baby-sitting brigade to look after the children of migrant Mexican workers in rural Illinois. Dorothy later said, "Mothers in the neighborhood were amazed at how they couldn't get their boys to do much, but Hillary had them all running around."

"We all felt real secure," Hillary noted, explaining why she worked hard to help others who had less. Although not specifically born "rich," she pointed out, "I was raised to believe that I had obligations because I was a blessed person. To whom much is given, much is expected."

Even in elementary school Hillary was quietly working out her own destiny. Later on, when she discovered it had to do with what was called "public service," she put it this way: "I have a deep, abiding sense of obligation that makes it very hard for me to see the waste and the damage and the hurt that occur every day [in this world]. I can't help wanting to do something about it." She was always that way.

Her brother Hugh understood the whirlwind with whom he grew up. "Things appeared very easy for her. But only if you didn't know how hard she worked at them." Her brother Tony put it in a slightly different way: "She was always focused."

Those two elements of her character were at the roots of her success. She knew that much was expected of her, and she had the ability to concentrate on whatever she tried to do. Add one other most important element of her upbringing: "Do well in school." It was not surprising, with those givens, that she would succeed spectacularly.

Living in that not-quite-but-almost-posh two-story Georgian home on Wisner Avenue, Hillary made a name for herself from the beginning, even though as one of the "haves" she could easily have coasted through her younger years. Did she actually need to win all the Girl Scout badges there were? Perhaps not—but she did. As for the honors she won in grammar school, junior high, and high school—those were expected of the overachiever she became. But there were nonprestigious accomplishments, too. She worked at a public park every summer, in charge of sports equipment.

But it was in her education that she excelled—almost to the point of embarrassment for her rather low profile parents, who admitted to being "slightly uncomfortable" over the scope of her achievements. Her mother explained, "She was in that class of Baby Boomers, right after the Sputnik wars. There was a whole surge of competitiveness, and her class just excelled in scholastic achievement. It was the right time and the right place for intellectual stimulation."

Hillary always gave full marks to her mother and father. "I had a very positive childhood," she put it. "Two parents who really supported me and a good public school education. That determines how you respond when something happens."

But she knew that without the basic soundness of the country and the life-style about her, she could never have done what she did. "It was a very different time then," she explained recently. "There was a lot of security, a lot of stability, a lot of opportunities."

The move to Park Ridge was probably one of the best things that could have happened to Hillary and her brothers. "I've often kidded my father,"

Hillary said, "who has never been a fan of taxes or government, about moving to a place that had such high property taxes to pay for [a good] school [system]. But even though it was a very conservative, Republican community, there was just no griping during the fifties and sixties about paying for good education."

But Hillary did not take to suburban life happily at first. She was simply not used to associating with other children, since there was little chance for a social life in Chicago's apartments. Now she suddenly found herself with other kids, at the mercy of their aggressions and hostile intentions. She was just about four when one particularly obnoxious girl started picking on her and gained enormous prestige by making the newcomer burst into tears, almost on cue. Hillary sought refuge with her mother in the house.

This was a new experience for Dorothy. "You can do two things," she told her daughter. "You can ignore her"—and she quoted the old saw "Sticks and stones may break my bones, but names will never hurt me"—"or you can fight back."

Fighting back was a new concept to Hillary, who had never had to fend for herself against her peers. She took her mother's first advice and tried to ignore the girl. When that didn't work, she ran back into the house and sought solace again. Dorothy was surprised at her daughter's inability to stand up to her tormentor. "Hillary," she said, "you can stay inside here with me forever, if you want to, or you can go out there and face that kid yourself."

At first Hillary did nothing. Fighting was something new to her. When she had worked herself up to the *idea* of fighting, she left. Her mother watched out the window, positioning herself behind the curtain. She saw the tough little girl come up to Hillary, punch her in the chest, kick her, and push her down in the street. Dorothy sighed, thinking she would have to devise some other technique for helping her daughter. Then she saw little Hillary crawl to her feet. "Hillary stood up and went after [the other girl] and gave her as good as she got," Dorothy recalled. "It's just an idea we can always refer to—when somebody is beating on us, we go out and take care of things."

From that moment on, Hillary Rodham never worried about whether or not she could take care of people who were trying to hurt her. She found that she was an excellent take-charge person. It was not until her teen years that she began to realize that taking charge of others did have limitations and responsibilities. That realization came from her religious training.

There was a new youth minister at her church, the First United Methodist. The Reverend Don Jones, barely thirty, fresh from divinity school, right out

of Manhattan, came to know Hillary very well. He said of her, "She was
serious, but she was also gregarious. She wasn't the cheerleader type, but she
wasn't the shy bookworm, either."

Jones, now a professor of religion at Drew University, held a Thursday
night youth class, which the kids came to call "The University of Life." He
showed them prints of van Gogh's *Starry Night* and Picasso's *Guernica* and
talked about God and nature, war and violence. "I was used to relating
theology to pop culture, theology to art, theology to the world," Jones said.
"By the time I got to Park Ridge, I had read all kinds of things. I got them
reading, too." Among the writers Jones got the teenaged Hillary to read were
Paul Tillich, Reinhold Niebuhr, Dietrich Bonhoeffer, and Søren Kierkegaard.

A friend of Hillary's in those days, Rick Ricketts, whom she had known
since she was eight, recalled Jones's youth classes. "I remember when he
brought an atheist to the group for a debate with a Christian over the
existence of God. There was also a discussion of teenage pregnancy, which
got the whole congregation upset."

Religion was something Hillary Rodham never took lightly. During various
periods in her life, she would do occasional lay preaching in her church and
teach adult Bible classes. And she would make a habit, even when on the
campaign trail, of carrying a "tiny little Bible that has Proverbs, Psalms, and
the New Testament."

From the beginning of her training she often quoted what she termed the
"wonderful old saying" of the church's founder, John Wesley, about doing
"all the good you can." Wesley's rule was: "Do all the good you can, by all
the means you can, in all the ways you can, at all the times you can, to all the
people you can, as long as you ever can."

Her parents always stressed that in her family line, Methodism went "way
back to the days" of Methodist camp meetings. "My faith wasn't just my
parents' passing on to me what they wanted me to believe." What attracted
Hillary to Methodism was its "emphasis on personal salvation combined with
active applied Christianity" to serve as a "practical method of trying to live
as a Christian in a difficult and challenging world."

Throughout her life, in "the daily back and forth of living," especially in
rough times, Hillary has found prayer to be "a very important replenisher."
She was always drawn to the "approach of a faith . . . based on 'Scripture,
tradition, experience, and reason,'" the guideposts of Methodism. "As a
Christian," she said, "part of my obligation is to take action to alleviate
suffering. Explicit recognition of that in the Methodist tradition is one reason
I'm comfortable in this church."

Don Jones once took Hillary and the youth group she was a part of into downtown Chicago to hear the Reverend Martin Luther King Jr. preach. Hillary has vivid memories of that event. "Having my eyes opened as a teenager to other people and the way they live certainly affected me."

Jones recalled those days: "In Park Ridge then, you wouldn't know there were black people in the world. There were a lot of John Birchers in that church. . . . But Hillary was curious and wide open to everything—not that she liked everything and accepted everything at face value." Jones recognized Hillary as a "deeply religious person," even in her youth. "Hillary is so nonfrivolous, it's unbelievable," he said.

Hugh and Dorothy taught their own lessons to their children. To engender humility, they once took them to visit the Pennsylvania coal mines where Hugh's father had worked during the worst years of the Great Depression. The youngsters got the point. They understood what their father meant by "It's hard out there." At home, the children had the usual household chores to do for their pocket money. "We used to have dandelion-pulling contests—a penny a dandelion," Tony recalled. Nothing came easily for them.

In the Eisenhower era, America coasted politically. The country had been through a grueling war and had expended a great deal of its psychic energy on defeating Japan and Germany. The fifties was a decade of reaction against geopolitics, and that distancing from reality had spread to local politics as well. In a way, politics was a dirty word. It was generally conceded in conservative circles that "politics" had caused the trouble in Europe in the first place.

Particularly in the Rodhams' nonpolitical household, politics was rarely discussed, except on their summer outings at Lake Winona, near Scranton, Pennsylvania. There they frequently got together with one of Hillary's grandfathers and several uncles who were involved in local politics in Chicago. These were Republicans, of course. Chicago politics was anathema to all Republicans, since all political patronage was controlled by the Cook County Democratic machine. Hillary heard these discussions, though what impression they made on her is unknown.

In 1960's presidential election, John F. Kennedy beat Richard M. Nixon in a battle that should have been won by Nixon, at least according to the Rodhams. It was claimed that the Cook County machine had stolen votes from Nixon and awarded them to Kennedy, giving the Democrats their victory.

Hillary was thirteen and did not pay much attention to these rumors or even to the election itself. But the elevation of Kennedy to the White House did shake up the country. A new wave of excitement emanated from Washington, D.C. Kennedy's campaign had stressed a "missile gap," due, he said, to the previous administration's inability to focus on the Russian supremacy in weaponry. The new President urged the country into more space research—rocketry, missiles, and exploration. What Kennedy proposed was a war with the Russian scientists, a war that would put an American on the moon before the Russians got there.

Hillary and her brother Hugh used to spend hours in the basement, pretending to fly to the moon in a rocket ship. Now she was attending Emerson Junior High. An overachiever all through her grammar school years at Eugene Field Elementary, she wanted to prove herself a real contender.

"President Kennedy had just started the drive to the moon," Hillary recalled, "and this was, like, in 1961, and I was, like, fourteen or so. So I wrote a letter to NASA and asked them what you would do to be an astronaut. I told them something about myself."

Hillary soon received an answer from a NASA official who told her the sad truth: "We are not accepting girls as astronauts." To Hillary, his reply was "infuriating."

"I later realized that I couldn't have been an astronaut anyway," she said, "because I have such terrible eyesight." She had always been nearsighted and now wore glasses all the time. "That somewhat placated me."

Not much, though. Hillary knew that girls and boys were different. But she had done well in school—better than many of the boys—and was earning A's in most of her classes. Why should it be assumed that a girl like herself could not study to be an astronaut? An astronaut to perform needed training in mathematics and physics, not muscles.

Besides, she was very good at rough-and-tumble games as well as word games, playing on neighborhood pick-up teams with both boys and girls. She was great at field hockey and football. "She was a terrific forward on the hockey team," her brother Tony said, "until she went to high school and got too studious."

Hillary's teen years were, like those of so many of her peers, sometimes uncomfortable, with problems and mood swings. She dated, but she refused to go into any popularity contests with the other girls. She concentrated on her studies and became better and better at her schoolwork—better than she had even been before. She was getting her second wind. She could be a scholar, perhaps a teacher.

Hillary attended Maine East High School while Maine South was being built, then transferred to the new school, where she finished her high school years. She found she liked running for office, as well, indeed, as just running things generally. She was elected vice president of her junior class, but when she tried to become president of her senior class, she lost the election. She served as a gymnasium leader, a member of the student council, and a member of the National Honor Society.

She had always had straight blond hair, blue eyes, and high cheekbones, but now her hair darkened to brown. She never thought of bleaching it until much later. Her mother suggested that she might wear makeup, but Hillary refused. It was not the way she visualized herself. "I think she thought makeup was superficial and silly," her mother said, but then realized the real reason: "She didn't have time for it."

It was Hillary's brightness and her ability to communicate instantly, not merely to learn facts, that brought her to the attention of her teachers. Paul Carlson, who taught her history, could still remember in 1992 where Hillary sat in his class. "I had her twenty-nine years ago, room 338, seventh period, for freshman world history. She sat in the fifth row, in the seventh seat. She was a very fine history student. Very articulate."

Kenneth Reese, a teacher who served as student council adviser, remembered her as having the kind of character that promised success. "She was bright, articulate, and a young lady of conviction, who was willing to take an unpopular stand. . . . There were approximately 566 students in her graduating class, and she graduated in the top five percent."

Hillary was never one to hide her intellect. She looked askance at the girls who pretended to be dopes to attract the boys. "I would never do that!" she once said.

The high school newspaper made predictions for all the seniors. It was Hillary's fate, the prediction said, to become a nun and take the name of "Sister Frigidaire." Obviously she was known for her ability to freeze anyone with a glare from her blue eyes.

"At school, people sure expected a lot from Hillary's brother," Hugh remembered. Hillary's brother Tony was even more disenchanted with his older sister: "When she wasn't studying, she was a lot of fun. But she was always studying."

Martha Williams, a neighbor of Hillary's, recalled, "She won the Good Citizen Award from the Daughters of the American Revolution while she was in high school."

By now America—even, to a degree, Park Ridge—had become politicized by the ferment of activity commonly identified with the 1960s, or at least the country had become a nation oriented more to practical politics than to governmental noninterference.

"I had a wonderful government teacher who wanted us to debate the 1964 presidential election," Hillary recalled. "She made me represent Lyndon Johnson and my good friend, who was a Democrat, represent Goldwater." Hillary would look back on those years with nostalgia and think about the importance of such a debate.

"I wish school would do . . . what we did when I was in high school," she told an interviewer in 1992. "We had mock debates and mock elections. You took it real seriously. You had to go to the library and study up on people's positions in order to make your case for your debates.

"I think high schools and junior high schools ought to be doing that [now]. People should be assigned to play George Bush, Bill Clinton, Al Gore, and Dan Quayle. They ought to be told to go to the library. What was essentially good for us is that sometimes our teachers would assign us to the side that our parents were not on, so that if we came from a family that was supporting Goldwater or Kennedy, we'd be assigned to Johnson or Nixon. That was so smart."

Hillary was a teenage Goldwater supporter because her parents were Republicans, like most residents of the Chicago suburbs. In fact, many of them had moved out of Chicago—a definitely Democratic big city—to be with other people who thought the same way they did. She was the daughter of Republicans, and a Republican at that point in time by heritage. She had no reason to be otherwise. Kennedy's presidency—and his assassination— had not changed her political leanings at all. It seemed quite likely that they would never change.

The time was fast approaching when Hillary would be graduating from high school, and it was obvious that she was headed for college. Although her mother had never gone, times were different now. There was no reason— including money, since her father had set no limits on her expenses—why Hillary should not get the very best college education. Quite possibly she could go on and become a very good teacher herself.

Many of her peers gravitated to colleges in the area—Northwestern, the University of Chicago, the University of Illinois. But Hillary seemed to want something different. One day in the school library, browsing through some folders, she saw a picture that intrigued her. It showed a college set in a beautiful wooded background, with a lake in the middle. There were pictures of quaint Victorian classrooms and a tiny surrounding town. She thought the college might be the place for her.

"Wellesley," she mused. She had no idea that it was a Seven Sisters college, that its traditions were excellent for her, or that it was one of the top-rated schools in the country.

"I'm going to Wellesley," she announced to one of her teachers. And that opened the floodgates. Soon she was being lobbied by two young teachers who had just joined the high school faculty—one telling her to apply to Smith, the other to Wellesley.

"I don't know why I chose Wellesley," Hillary confessed later, "other than during my senior year I had two young teachers—one had graduated from Wellesley and the other graduated from Smith. They'd been assigned to teach in my high school, and they were so bright and smart and terrific teachers, and they lobbied me hard to apply to those schools."

She wrote away to both and was accepted at each.

"And then when I was accepted, they lobbied me hard to go and be able to work out all of the financial and other issues associated with it." She paused. "And so I went to Wellesley."

CHAPTER TWO

A Right-Thinker

Hillary had not visited the Wellesley campus on the outskirts of Boston before deciding to enroll there. It was, as she later pointed out, in another part of the country—the East. Her arrival was a revelation. "I just loved that place. I'm glad I went there."

A profile in *People* magazine described the freshman Hillary as "wearing Peter Pan blouses, box-pleat skirts, [and] loafers with knee socks." Her clothes reflected her conservative background, but in spite of her traditional upbringing, she had an open mind. "She arrived a Goldwater girl," *People* said, "and became a [Eugene] McCarthy girl."

Hillary admitted later that what she called her "instincts" were altered somewhat once she had settled in at Wellesley. "I was forced to think—a dangerous enterprise."

But there was a great deal more to it. She had always been able to think clearly, but her opinions had not so much been formed independently as they had been shaped by her family members and by others around her. What changed now was her environment. The changes in Hillary Rodham were still to come.

It was the middle of the 1960s, a decade that would forever alter the sociopolitical structure of not only the United States but most of the countries of the world. Change was everywhere. Even people protected from radical reformation—far removed from the ferment taking place on the campuses of America—felt those upheavals.

One of Hillary's soon-to-be close friends at Wellesley was Eleanor "Eldie" Acheson, the granddaughter of Dean Acheson, President Harry S. Truman's famous Secretary of State. Eldie was with Hillary during the first months of her sojourn on campus, and she could see how the atmosphere at Wellesley affected the young suburban woman.

"A ton of younger assistant professors and lecturers and instructors" had arrived at the school, Eldie said, all eager to put to the test "a lot of new ideas and some very aggressive, advocacy-oriented ways of teaching." In 1966 the old-fashioned method of throwing out factual knowledge to have it regurgitated by students in blue books was no longer acceptable. Dramatically different methods of teaching were now employed.

"Whatever the course," Eldie said, "one needed to draw a current application from it. How did it relate to where we are today in the United States of America and the world at large?" Relevance was the keynote of this new teaching.

In those changing times, Hillary changed. "What happens to everybody at Wellesley?" Eldie asked rhetorically. "They [become] right-thinking."

Not right-wing, but right-*thinking*—a precursor to the 1990s phrase "politically correct." Hillary was bright. She was psychologically sound. She came from a good, solid, established, middle-class world. It was not logical that she should change. But change she did. As Eldie said, she was in the right place at the right time—and she became right-thinking.

During her first months at Wellesley she met Jeff Shields, a young student from Harvard. Shields was fascinated by Hillary. "The thing I remember most were the conversations," he recalled. "She would rather sit around and talk about current events or politics or ideas than to go bicycle riding or to a football game."

Even though Hillary's conversations tended to be of a deep and serious nature, she did not turn people off. Diane Canning, another classmate, had a positive assessment of Hillary at Wellesley as a very popular and charismatic person. "Everyone knew her," Canning said. "She was quite active politically—even then—and very much a spokesperson for change."

Groups of women would cluster around her. She was a dynamo of talent, and in spite of her appearance—she had thick bottle-bottom glasses and rather unkempt, stringy brown hair and paid little attention to her clothes or the way she wore them—she was definitely a person to gravitate toward and cultivate.

She lived in what was called "Stone Davis," a Gothic dormitory that, after her billeting there, became a magnet for students who wanted to be considered "in" or "with it." Hillary was a trendsetter. Other students moved in to be near her.

Hillary's friends became *the* group of the period not long after her arrival on campus. Her built-in overachievement apparatus was obvious; so was the fact that she was light-years ahead of most of her contemporaries in intelligence.

She and her coterie of followers ate dinner in what might be described as a cloistered gazebo made out of stone and glass. That was "Stone Davis." What was not part of the architecture was Hillary's inquiring mind, her special brand of inquisitiveness, and her quick wit put an individual stamp on the coterie of which she was the leader. "You were surrounded by role models," said Jan Piercey, another classmate. "We came away just assuming that everyone had serious aspirations."

Everything about Hillary Rodham precluded a shift in values once she had departed from the close and friendly confines of her family. And yet the conservatism that had informed her earlier years was slowly being replaced at Wellesley by a more trendy type of academic liberalism. Some might term it "leftist," but it was at most a mild form of radical philosophy. Yet she was changing.

Hillary had always done daring things, at least within the confines of her moderate political milieu. For example, one day she invited a black girl to attend a Sunday service at church with her. Of course, she adhered to her Methodist upbringing. Political judgments might change in Hillary; religious beliefs never would.

"I knew I was testing myself as much as I was testing the church," Hillary wrote to her parents in Illinois in describing the event. That she told them at all attests to her awareness of her own shifting sensibilities. Her parents were not overly enthusiastic about the turns that were taking place in their daughter's attitudes. At best, they were simply resigned to what was happening on almost every campus in the country.

At Wellesley, Hillary majored in political science, with a minor in psychology. One of her favorite poli-sci professors was Dr. Alan Schechter. He remembered her clearly, even in 1992, recalling that she had always walked a very "fine line" politically.

"Hillary was never radical," he said. Schechter noted that she was a thoughtful, moderately oriented student. "She stuck with a liberal, remorse-oriented view of government."

Her way was essentially soft, he said. By her very nature she was not one to arrive at a startling conclusion on her own, to continue with the reasoning suggested, and to come finally to exactly the opposite conclusion of the line of thought she had begun. She reasoned slowly through the maze of possible contradictions and arrived at a logical point of view after testing countless theories and abandoning all those that she saw to be unworkable.

Politically speaking, she was the prototypical *tabula rasa,* the "clean slate." She had embraced the field of politics without any serious biases clutched to her. Thus, she was able to arrive at new hypotheses more easily than someone with prejudices that canted the thinking processes in stultifying ways. "She has no baggage" was the way Schechter put it. "She has never had to make those real enemies because she has never had to make those hard choices a politician has to make."

Overall, Schechter recalled, she was an "exceptional student, the best student I had taught in the first seven years I taught at Wellesley. She had strong analytical abilities. She could look at a problem objectively, and as a researcher, she was very thorough and detailed."

By 1967, Hillary Rodham had begun to feel that the Vietnam War was wrong. She was against U.S. participation in the undeclared conflict. By the time it became apparent that Richard M. Nixon would be the Republican presidential candidate in 1968, she had little faith in his promises to end the war.

If she had ever entertained any ideas of supporting him, she did not show it in any way. She was a practical person, always had been, and on the American campus in 1968 it was impractical to be a Republican.

In an atmosphere rife with anti-Republican sentiment and gung ho with Democratic aspirations, Hillary swam in the mainstream with her peer group. Also, since she was determined to do well in her political science studies, she adhered strictly to the line being advocated by her professors, which was a liberal point of view more moderate than radical.

In the summer of 1968, Hillary and her Park Ridge friend Betsy Ebeling rode a train in to Chicago to witness the excitement of the Democratic National Convention. "We saw kids our age getting their heads beaten in. And the police were doing the beating," Ebeling recalled. "Hillary and I just looked at each other. We had had a wonderful childhood in Park Ridge, but we obviously hadn't gotten the whole story."

That fall, Hillary threw aside all her Republican principles and went to work for Eugene McCarthy in his campaign for the Democratic presidential nomination. Hillary did not sacrifice too much of her academic time to politics. She had come to college to get an education. When Martin Luther King was killed, she slipped on a black armband and marched in Boston to protest his death. But her protest was token activism.

She put her energy into counseling freshmen. It was here that she excelled in a new capacity, teaching. Ann Rosewater, a longtime friend, described Hillary's experience in those counseling endeavors. "That put her in situations where she had to come to terms with a lot of people who didn't have the same experiences [that she had had]." And it opened her eyes to the fact that there were other people out there who might not be too different from her but might have a totally different idea of what life was all about.

By the time Nixon was elected President, Hillary was struggling to find the subject for her senior thesis. She finally decided on a critique of community-based antipoverty programs. She was critical of them because she did not feel that they did half enough for the people they were supposed to help.

The paper was titled "Aspect of the War on Poverty." As was her way, Hillary sailed through the writing of the thesis with little of the paranoia other students manifested during this critical phase of their education. "It was a straight-A thesis," said Alan Schechter. "The thesis was objective and highly pragmatic, not at all radical, and was directed to finding practical solutions as to what would work to fight poverty."

The Democratic loss in the 1968 presidential election brought about a ferment of activity on most U.S. campuses. At Wellesley the resulting uproar was an almost typical anti-Establishment cry for more undergraduate voice in educational affairs.

The agitation resulted in a meeting between representatives of the undergraduates and the Wellesley administration. In order to restore peace, the administration agreed to break with tradition and allow a graduating student, as well as the usual invited guest, to speak at the commencement program. However, there were two specific conditions attached to this concession: The speaker and her remarks must reflect a consensus of the graduating class; and the speaker must make "appropriate" remarks, remarks that would not embarrass the college.

During her senior year Hillary Rodham was elected president of College Government. And it was the student representatives who chose her to be the speaker, with the silent acquiescence of the college administration.

It was 1969. President Nixon had been in office for four months. The Vietnam War was still raging. Although Nixon had promised to "get the U.S. out of it," it was now seen by many as "Nixon's war" and not, as it might have been more accurately viewed, Kennedy's and Johnson's. Student protests continued, even though the 1960s were coming to a rather tattered and unseemly end. Obviously Hillary Rodham's commencement speech would reflect activism and a new order of things.

In discussing what was to be included in the commencement speech, almost every graduating senior had something to offer. The consensus was that it should address the events of the past four years: the escalation of the Vietnam War, the assassinations of Martin Luther King and Bobby Kennedy, and the riots in the cities, including the shame of the Democratic Convention in Chicago. A small committee of writers, including Hillary's friend Eldie Acheson and Dr. Alan Schechter, sifted through the morass of ideas and came up with a draft.

The guest speaker for the commencement was Senator Edward Brooke of Massachusetts, a black and a liberal Republican. According to Eldie Acheson, his address was without substance. "It was pretty much a canned speech, full of highfalutin words and concepts, but it could have been given anywhere, anyplace, and anytime." She went on, "He [Brooke] did not weave into its ideas or its content or its message anything about the four years we had spent at that school and what happened to the country in those four years. It was totally vapid."

When he was through, Hillary mounted the podium. She was small and seemed dominated by her mortarboard and cloak, but she was completely composed. Always able to think quickly on her feet, she knew where she and the student body were coming from, if the senator from Massachusetts did not. She felt that she had to protest. But she knew she must protest within the parameters of the institution from which she was graduating.

She embarked on an extemporaneous response to Brooke's boilerplate speech. "I am very glad that Miss Adams [Ruth Adams, Wellesley's president] made it clear that what I am speaking for today is all of us—the four hundred of us—and I find myself in a familiar position, that of reacting, something that our generation has been doing for quite a while now."

Her generation—the Baby Boomers, American men and women born just after the close of World War II—was forced to react, rather than act, because "we're not in the positions yet of leadership and power, but we do have that indispensable task of criticizing and constructive protest, and I find myself reacting just briefly to some of the things that Senator Brooke said. This has to be brief because I do have a little speech to give."

She was still speaking off the cuff. "Part of the problem with empathy with professed goals is that empathy doesn't do us anything. We've had lot of empathy; we've had lots of sympathy." It wasn't enough, she was saying.

She ended her ad-lib at this point and went on with the prepared speech. But she had administered her rebuke to Senator Brooke, and it lay in her use of the word "react"—a code word for "demonstrate." Most of the students caught the drift, although it was subtle. Senator Brooke was smiling.

"We feel that for too long our leaders have used politics as the art of the possible," Hillary declared. "And the challenge now is to practice politics as the art of making what appears to be impossible, possible. . . . We're not interested in social reconstruction; it's human reconstruction."

The speech-by-committee went on. It was a torturous talk, convoluted and wandering. "The issue of sharing power and responsibility, and of assuming power and responsibility, have been general concerns on campuses throughout the world. But underlying those concerns there is a theme, a theme which is so trite and so old because the words are so familiar. It talks about integrity and trust and respect."

Now the sounds of restlessness could be heard. There was a prolonged susurration under the words of the speech over the loudspeakers.

"Hillary had just sort of launched off on her own," Eldie Acheson recalled. "Some people, largely mothers, thought it was just rude and never got off that point. And another group thought she was absolutely right. It distracted a lot of people."

Alan Schechter loved it, as did most of the students. "She gave it to him, no ifs, ands, or buts about it," Schechter said later. Yet it was mild.

"Words have a funny way of trapping our minds on the way to our tongues," the earnest senior declared, "but there are necessary means even in this multimedia age for attempting to come to grips with some of the inarticulate things that we're feeling."

Discursive and abstract as it was, her speech was picked up by *Life* magazine, which included an excerpt from it along with her picture in a spread on college commencement speeches. Hillary's words were bland compared to some of the others.

For example, Stephanie Mills, of Mills College, said: "Traditionally, commencement exercises are the occasion for fatuous comments on the future of the graduates present. My depressing comment on that rosy future, that infinite future, is that it is a hoax. . . . Our days as a race on this planet are, at this moment, numbered, and the reason for our finite, unrosy future is that we are breeding ourselves out of existence. . . . I am terribly saddened by the fact that the most humane thing for me to do is to have no children at all."

For Hillary Rodham, however, the Wellesley speech was a triumph giving her national prominence.

Hillary's four years at Wellesley were a great success. She was well liked, even well respected.

As one classmate said, "She was an unusual young woman. She wasn't the same as other people in that everybody was usually more or less *of* something, and Hillary was really quite unique. She had a very strong personality. She wasn't everybody's cup of tea."

Eldie Acheson commented, "I've known a lot of people who are enormously gifted, but many of them are tortured by insecurity, have parents driving them, and there's sort of a mess associated with it. Hillary never had any of that."

Now she faced the prospect of life after Wellesley. For some time, Hillary had given much thought to continuing her education. Because she was so close to Boston, she was taken with Harvard Law School. She was also interested in Yale. One friend tried to convince her she should attend Harvard. This friend had her meet a distinguished law professor who taught there.

Introducing Hillary to the professor, the friend said, "She's trying to decide whether to come here [Harvard] next year or attend our closest competitor."

Hillary had sized up this professor as a character who might have escaped from the novel *The Paper Chase.* He now looked down at her and said; "Well, first of all, we don't have any close competitors."

Hillary smiled but said nothing. The professor continued, "Secondly, we don't *need* any more women."

"That's what made my decision," Hillary recalled. "I was leaning toward Yale, anyway, but that fellow's comment iced the cake."

CHAPTER THREE

Children and the Law

Hillary was accepted at Yale Law School and planned to enroll in the fall of 1969. But before that, she had an interesting summertime diversion. Her picture and the excerpts from her speech in *Life* magazine had intrigued Peter Edelman, an attorney who had served as Robert Kennedy's legislative assistant.

The League of Women Voters had asked Edelman to put together a conference composed of distinguished young and elder leaders to act as a think tank for future developments in politics and sociology. Edelman remembered Hillary's name from the *Life* feature, looked her up, and then invited her to the conference.

Surprised and excited, Hillary agreed to attend. She would be joining the group as, in Edelman's words, a "distinguished young leader."

During the time she spent with the League of Women Voters conference, Hillary met a number of influential people who would figure in her future professional life. Edelman was one of them, of course. He had recently married Marian Wright, an important veteran of the civil rights movement. She was the first black woman to pass the bar in Mississippi.

Hillary also met other important people, including Vernon E. Jordan Jr., only three years away from his prestigious appointment in 1972 to the executive directorship of the National Urban League after the sudden death of Whitney M. Young Jr. He had been a civil rights lawyer and organizer for the National Association for the Advancement of Colored People.

After the conference, plenty of summer remained. The new state of Alaska had been admitted to the Union only ten years previously, and Hillary decided to go there to see what it was like. A member of the sixties generation—that breed of backpackers, easy riders, and curiosity seekers—she took on odd jobs as she traveled through the civilized parts of the state.

One of the jobs she took was in a fish cannery. Never one to hide her attitudes or judgments, she informed the owner that the fish he canned looked black and might be unfit for human consumption. She was fired the next day.

At the end of summer, Hillary Rodham moved to New Haven and enrolled at Yale Law School. It was her plan to take the three-year course in four years, allowing herself time to assume extracurricular projects as part of her training for the law.

Her first year at Yale Law School was routine at best. In spite of her dogged adherence to study—she was definitely a grind in the minds of some of the other students—Hillary did not consider herself overly studious. But she showed her aptitude for textbook work and for research and came out with her usual good grades. And she managed to settle on a specific portion of the law that would become her main target of opportunity in the future.

A *Time* magazine was lying around in the Yale lounge in the spring of 1970, toward the end of her first year there, and she picked it up to read an article about Marian Wright Edelman, whose husband, Peter Edelman, had invited Hillary to the League of Women Voters conference. Soon after reading the article she forgot all about it.

Then, as Hillary herself put it later on, "in one of those strange twists of fate that enters all our lives if we're open to hear and to see them," she found the name of Marian Wright Edelman posted on the Yale bulletin board. Edelman, the notice said, would be coming to Yale to speak.

The coincidences—seeing the name in *Time* and on the bulletin board and knowing Peter Edelman—drew Hillary to the auditorium, and she listened to what Marian Edelman had to say.

Edelman spoke about her current job, which was in administering a new group temporarily called the Washington Research Project. Its purpose was to study ways and means of providing children legal rights within the existing system.

Hillary listened in her usual attentive fashion, and quite suddenly a thought struck her: "Children and the law." That was what Marian Edelman was talking about. That was what she had taken up as a career for herself. The idea appealed to Hillary. She decided that she wanted to know more about Marian Edelman's work. Could she possibly become a part of Edelman's project?

After the talk was over, Hillary went up and introduced herself and immediately requested permission to work with Edelman and her group on the Washington Research Project. Summer break would be coming up soon, and Hillary wanted something to do.

It was not possible to hire Hillary, Edelman said. There was no budget for her. However, she might be able to take Hillary on as an intern if she would work for nothing. Hillary did not like that idea at all. She needed some compensation to live.

Hillary had been learning how to get around within the academic-political system. She put her own talents to work and requested a grant for research within the government's civil rights programs. She received the grant and went to Washington to work for Marian Edelman.

Edelman was impressed with her style and her abilities and in turn sent her to Walter Mondale's Senate subcommittee, which was studying the plight of migrant workers. It was a sort of déjà vu for Hillary, who had once organized Park Ridge youngsters to serve as baby-sitters for the children of just such laborers.

She spent the summer talking to workers and their families. Most of her attention went to the children. A long list of hardships experienced by migrants filled Hillary's notebooks. They included the uprootedness of the migrant life-style, the lack of proper housing facilities, the low-grade sanitary conditions, the bad diet suffered by the young, and the dearth of proper educational opportunities.

She thrived on the work, even in the bleak world of the migrant workers. She felt she was doing something—however little it might be in the long run—to help elevate those people's lives.

Hillary's interest in children continued to grow. On her return to Yale for her second year, she volunteered to work in the Yale Child Studies Center. There she joined Sally Province, who was studying the general effects of infant distress, ranging from physical abuse through psychic depression.

Hillary was eventually able to obtain permission from her faculty advisers to do an extra year of study concerning the rights of children under the law. Her interest in this rather specific area of the law soon came to the attention of Joseph Goldstein, then her professor in family law. At the time he was editing a volume called *Beyond the Best Interests of the Child* with Anna Freud and Albert Solnit. He invited her to help with the research.

This work became one of the first to name and describe the inadequacies of the legal system guiding the court system in cases of child abandonment, neglect, or abuse. The point of the volume was to give judges, who according to law are supposed to consult "the best interests of the child," some kind of standard or standards to be applied. The thesis of the book was that the best interests of the child can never be judged without consideration of all the other elements in the case.

In conclusion the book proposed a brand-new standard: "the least detrimental available alternative." That is, the standard should weigh the interests of the child in each of the several options given by the litigants. The one that proved to be, on analysis, the least bad would be the one approved by the court.

Goldstein himself told a reviewer that his book did not propose the intrusion of the court into the lives of families. Rather, he hoped to create standards under which the rights of children could be protected with the least amount of dislocation. He said, "The proof that we set useful guidelines is that the book has been translated into Japanese, French, Swedish, Danish, and other languages, where the cultures of child raising are all different."

In her work at Yale and in New Haven, Hillary found that the book's point made good sense. For example, she volunteered to work with New Haven's new Legal Services. Here she found a number of real-life situations that helped her not only in her research for the Goldstein volume but in her future work with children.

In one case she saw a black woman in her fifties who, as a foster parent, had raised a child of mixed black-white parentage while the claims of each parent were being contested in court. Caught in a classic impasse, the woman lost custody of the child. The law decided that the parents had given up all claims to their offspring by their actions but that the best interests of the child could not be dealt with by the foster parent, who wanted to adopt the child.

The reasons? The foster parent was now in her fifties. She was single. And she was not well-off financially. Because of those three points, the courts took the child away from the one person who could provide a sense of stability in life and gave her to another foster home to await possible adoption. To Hillary Rodham this case reflected the worst kind of bureaucratic nonsense. And yet the decision was valid under the law.

Hillary also found time to work with Penn Rhodeen, a staff attorney at the New Haven Legal Assistance Association, which was then involved in a series of legal battles with the state of Connecticut over the treatment of foster children. In addition, she volunteered at New Haven Hospital, where she worked with doctors on cases of child abuse.

The "best interests" of the child, she found, were not always clear-cut or even possible to serve. "For some young children," Hillary said, "abuse may be the only attention the child got; so when you remove it, there is an extraordinary guilt: 'I must have done something *really* terrible because now they do not even *want* me.' "

But there was a more subtle case of abuse when a parent sought the sterilization of retarded children or sought abortions when the pregnant daughter wanted the child. In most of the cases in New Haven, Hillary found that it was not the pregnant child who wanted the abortion but the *parents* of the pregnant child.

In addition to the Goldstein volume, Hillary became involved in another book project, Kenneth Keniston's *All Our Children,* which was published in 1978. It was through Marian Edelman that Hillary got the job. "Marian, Pat Wald, and Hillary did the research for the chapter on legal protection of children," Keniston said.

Pat Wald was Patricia McGowan Wald, a member of the editorial board who in 1977 was appointed assistant attorney general in charge of the legislative office of the Department of Justice. She later became a member of the American Bar Association's committee for the development of a set of guidelines for children's rights.

The chapter in the Keniston book dealt with children's rights to education, not only in situations in which parents keep children out of school for religious or other reasons, but in instances in which school authorities suspend or expel children for disciplinary or medical reasons. It also dealt with children's rights to medical care, in conflict with parents who do not believe in such care or who impose extreme treatments—sterilization, shock treatments, lobotomies—on children. "The first right of a child is to a parent, where that is possible," Keniston said, summing up the main theme of his work.

In her third and fourth years at Yale, Hillary became an editor of the *Yale Review of Law and Social Action,* a publication now defunct. It was an ad hoc journal of its time. One of its covers, for example, showed a cartoon of police officers as pigs. The subject of the issue was the Black Panthers.

Daniel Wattenberg wrote that one of the covers showed "rifle-toting, hairy-snouted pigs with nasal drip marching in formation emitting 'oinks' and thinking to themselves, 'niggers, niggers, niggers. . . .' Another shows a decapitated and dismembered pig squealing in agony. It is captioned, 'Seize the Time!' "

An article from the *Review* calling for groups to take over a lightly populated state and to seize control of the government said: "Experimentation with drugs, sex, individual life-styles or radical rhetoric is an insufficient alternative. Total experimentation is necessary. New ideas and values must be taken out of heads and transformed into reality."

Much of this material was no more than the rhetoric of the time. It was her work with the children that she loved the most.

Nor was Hillary one to hide facts from herself. "There was a great amount of ferment and confusion about what was and wasn't the proper role of law school education," she said. "We would have great arguments about whether we were selling out because we were getting a law degree, whether in fact we should be doing something else, not often defined clearly but certainly passionately argued. That we should somehow be 'out there,' wherever 'there' was, trying to help solve the problems that took up so much of our time in argument and discussion. . . . Those were difficult and turbulent times."

It was in her second year at Yale that Hillary met Bill Clinton. She told Regis Philbin and Kathie Lee Gifford in 1992, "The first thing I ever knew about him, and this is the truth, was when I was walking through the student lounge at Yale to get a Coke between classes. I heard this voice say: 'And not only that, we grow the biggest watermelons in the world.' "

Hillary continued, "And I said [to a companion], 'Who is *that?*' "

Her friend told her. "That's Bill Clinton. He's from Arkansas. That's all he ever talks about."

"I kind of, you know, looked [him over]." She paused. "He was good-looking. And I thought—you know, I kind of filed that thought away. And after a while, I got to meet him, and we were in a class together."

About the details of the meeting itself, Hillary was vaguely amused. *"He* tells a story which is really kind of funny. He says that I began to look at him, and he began to look at me, and that is true. We *were* kind of stalking each other.

"Finally, one day," Hillary said, "he was standing outside the law school library. And I was in, trying to study, but I was kind of keeping my eye on him. And he kept kind of looking at me, and finally, I went up to him, and I said, 'You know, if we're going to keep looking at each other, we ought to at least know each other's name.' " And they introduced themselves.

Not everyone agrees with the story as Hillary told it. Jeffrey Glekel, a friend of Clinton's, had a slightly different version.

"One evening in the Yale Law School library I spotted Bill studying and attempted to convey to him the advantages of joining the *Yale Law Journal*." Glekel was pitching the various attractions of working on the publication, and Clinton was listening patiently but somewhat absent-mindedly, yet asking all the proper questions.

Glekel said he "somehow sensed that Bill was far from convinced that the *Law Journal* was the place where he should be concentrating his energies." Finally, Glekel realized that Clinton's concentration was wavering. "It was becoming clear to me that Bill's focus was somewhere other than the *Law Journal*. . . . He appeared to be glancing over my shoulder with increasing frequency while we continued to discuss whether or not he should participate in *Journal* activities."

Turning around, Glekel noted that his classmate Hillary Rodham was seated at a nearby desk with a businesslike stack of books and notepads in front of her. She saw Glekel looking at her. Then, decisively, she rose, walked over to them, and spoke directly to Clinton. "Look," she told him, "if you're going to keep staring at me and I'm going to keep staring back, we should at least introduce ourselves."

The Arkansas version is something else again. Listen to Clinton: "This guy [obviously Glekel] was trying to talk me into joining the *Yale Law Review* and telling me I could clerk for the U.S. Supreme Court if I were a member of the *Yale Law Review,* which is probably true. And then I could go on to New York and make a ton of money."

Clinton told him he didn't want to go to New York. He was going to return to Arkansas. "It didn't matter to anybody [in Arkansas] whether I was on the *Yale Law Review* or not. And they were trying to get Southerners, they wanted geographical balance on the *Law Review.* . . . I just didn't much want to do it."

Clinton was staring at Hillary Rodham, without knowing her name. She was at the other end of the library. "The Yale Law School library is a real long, narrow [room]. She was down at the other end, and . . . I just was staring at her. . . . And she closed this book, and she walked all the way down the library . . . and she came up to me and she said, 'Look, if you're going to keep staring at me and I'm going to keep staring back, I think we should at least know each other. I'm Hillary Rodham. What's your name?' "

Clinton couldn't remember his own name. "I was so embarrassed," he went on, winding up the Arkansas version. "But that's a true story. That's exactly how we met. It turned out she knew who I was. But I didn't know that at the time, either. But I was real impressed that she did that. And we've been together, more or less, ever since."

Time magazine had a shorter version. After Hillary noticed Clinton at the student center, she didn't see him again for some time. Then he literally ran into her as she was registering for classes. "He joined me in this long line," she said, "and we talked for an hour. When we got to the front of the line, the registrar said, 'Bill, what are you doing here? You already registered.' "

Even Harvard economist Robert Reich, a Rhodes scholar with Clinton at Oxford, claimed the honor of introducing Hillary and Bill. Jim Moore, author of *Clinton: Young Man in a Hurry,* once questioned Clinton on the many versions of their meeting.

"He hastened to assure me," Moore wrote, "that he and Hillary did, indeed, meet in the law library at Yale, and since Reich was a friend of both him and Hillary—his Rhodes scholar companion set up their first date."

Clinton recalled, "Bob knew Hillary pretty well, and he arranged for us to go out. We've been together ever since."

Actually, Reich was close enough to Clinton to hear from Clinton what he *really* thought about Hillary. "He admits that when he first began courting her, she scared him," Reich told *Maclean's* magazine.

People magazine quoted Clinton: "I remember being genuinely afraid of falling in love with [Hillary]. She was a star."

Who *was* this Bill Clinton, anyway? That was what Hillary wanted to find out.

CHAPTER FOUR

The Man From Hope

The question was always: How did Bill Clinton come to be called Clinton when his mother's name was Virginia Cassidy and his father's name was William Jefferson Blythe III? For Bill Clinton called himself Clinton all through his early school years, although he did not change his name legally until he was fifteen. Actually, the name derives from his stepfather, Roger Clinton.

Clinton's biological father, William Blythe III, was driving down Highway 61 near Sikeston, Missouri, in 1946, four months before Bill Clinton was born, when his tire blew out and his car crashed into a ditch. Thrown from the car and knocked unconscious, Blythe drowned in only a few inches of water.

In his twenties, Clinton visited the site of the accident. Years later he told Bill Moyers, "I was driving north from Arkansas to Chicago, and I just was near the town in Missouri and the space of highway where I knew he died, and I had never been there. So I decided to go and check it out. And I did. . . . He was thrown out of the car, face down in the ditch. I was looking at the way the road was and wondering what it might have been like and wishing he'd landed the other way."

Virginia Cassidy was a nurse trainee at Tri-State Hospital in Shreveport, Louisiana, when she met William Blythe, an auto salesman from Sherman, Texas. They married in 1942, and Blythe soon enlisted to serve in World War II. After the war he landed a job as a traveling heavy-equipment salesman in Chicago, whence he commuted to see his wife in Hope, Arkansas. It was during one of his frequent drives to Hope that Blythe was killed.

On August 19, 1946, Virginia Cassidy Blythe gave birth to William Jefferson Blythe IV, who would later become known as Bill Clinton. The mother and child lived with Virginia's parents, Eldridge and Edith Cassidy. The Cassidys' next-door neighbor Mary Baker said, "They all worked, and the three of them, including Virginia, took turns taking care of him. He was the first great-grandchild in the family."

Bill Clinton grew up in Hope, a farming town thirty-two miles northeast of Texarkana. His lower-middle-class family couldn't afford indoor plumbing. When he was two years old, Virginia left him with the Cassidys in order to pursue her career as a nurse anesthetist at Charity Hospital in New Orleans.

His grandparents taught him how to read and count. According to Clinton, "I was reading little books when I was three. They [his grandparents] didn't have much formal education, but they really helped imbed in me a real sense of educational achievement, which was reinforced at home."

Even as a child Clinton had the uncanny ability to meet and befriend rich and powerful people. While in Hope, he came to know Thomas R. "Mack" McLarty. McLarty would become an influential Arkansan and chairman of Arkla, Inc., a colossal natural gas conglomerate, and would come back into Clinton's life, when Clinton assumed the presidency of the United States, as his chief of staff.

Bill helped out his grandparents, who owned a small country store in a predominantly black neighborhood, as he grew up under their tutelage. One of his myriad friends at the time was Joseph Purvis, who went to kindergarten with him in the fifties. Purvis said of those days, "My mother, Martha Houston Purvis, and Bill's mother were very good friends. I have seen pictures of our mothers with Bill and me in our respective strollers.

"Hope, Arkansas, in the late forties and early fifties was not a place of great financial wealth, and the result was that everyone was pretty much in the same social strata. On reflecting over some forty years, however, I can see that we were rich beyond our wildest imaginations, in that Hope was a town with a great community spirit and a great deal of love.

"For nearly all of us, it meant that you grew up with both parents and also had your grandparents, cousins, and others there around you. Everyone in the town knew everyone else, and everyone there seemed to look out for everyone else's children. Thus, in many ways, the town was like one large neighborhood.

"I remember quite vividly that in the 1951–52 school year we went to Miss Mary's kindergarten. This kindergarten was run by two old-maid sisters, Mary and Nannie Perkins. Their kindergarten was run in a small white clapboard schoolhouse with a ministeeple and bell that was located in their backyard on East Second Street in Hope.

"This school had a large, open room for classes and something of a cloakroom in the back. I also remember that everyone had to bring [his] own 'pallet,' as it was called then, because after lunch recess, we were all required to come in and lie down on our pallets to take a nap. How I hated those naps!"

Purvis especially recalled a dramatic incident in young Clinton's life.

"We were all playing high jump with a jump rope in the yard around the schoolhouse during the recess. This was played by two boys each grabbing an end of the rope, stretching it straight across, and everyone taking turns high-jumping over the top. As you cleared a particular height, the rope was raised to whatever level the holders thought appropriate.

"The general attire for boys at that time was a T-shirt, blue jeans, and either army boots or cowboy boots. On this one particular occasion, I remember Bill was wearing cowboy boots, because when it came his turn to jump over the rope, his heel caught on the rope and he fell hard to the ground.

"I remember Bill wouldn't stop crying, and Miss Mary or Miss Nannie had to call his grandparents to come pick him up and take him home from kindergarten. Imagine my shock when I got home from school and found out the *reason* Bill had been crying was that the fall broke his leg in three pieces."

Another one of Bill's kindergarten pals was George Wright Jr., who said Clinton wanted to be everyone's buddy. "And he was!" Wright declared. "He never forgets names! I remember him, even when he was younger, as an extrovert, fun-loving, and having a good sense of humor."

Clinton's ability to make people believe he liked them and was interested in them would serve him well as a politician. This knack garnered votes. It also secured him the good graces of wealthy, powerful people, whose friendship and patronage paid off for Clinton.

When Bill was four years old, his mother married Roger Clinton. Even though Roger was a drunkard with a mean streak, Bill found much in him to admire.

"He was a wonderful person, but he didn't like himself very much. He had a prolonged bout with cancer. And I think in the course of fighting it through somehow, he gained some peace with himself that enabled him to reconcile with all the rest of us. He was a marvelous person and he was very good to me. It really was a painful experience to see someone you love, that you think a lot of, that you care about, just in the grip of a demon."

Bill Clinton may have believed Roger was a wonderful guy, but he could not stand it when Roger got drunk and beat Virginia. During one binge Roger became so drunk he fired a gun into the wall of the Clinton living room and was promptly carted off to jail. Bill did not like Roger's drunken jags, but as a little boy he was powerless to do anything about it.

When the Clinton family moved to the town of Hot Springs, Arkansas, his mother enrolled Bill, who was seven, in the second grade of St. John's Catholic School. The family was Baptist, not Catholic, but Virginia believed St. John's would educate him better. (He would later attend another Catholic school—Georgetown University in Washington, D.C.)

When he entered the fourth grade, Virginia enrolled Bill in Ramble School, the public school at Hot Springs. While attending Ramble School, he became fond of Elvis Presley songs.

According to David Leopoulos, a classmate, Clinton and Leopoulos "spent many hours playing Monopoly and listening to Elvis records. We had most of Elvis's records memorized and would hum them during our dog-eat-dog football games. We also spent time together in total silence. He would be there in person, but his mind was somewhere else. At first it was frustrating, but I soon got used to it. He still does it today."

Virginia and Roger Clinton had a son, Roger Jr., when Bill reached the age of ten. Sometimes Bill would baby-sit his half brother, as Virginia spent so much of her time working as a nurse anesthetist.

At the age of fourteen, Bill could no longer live with his stepfather's drunken, vicious beatings of Virginia. Day in, day out, he saw his mother's bloody, swollen face and had great difficulty controlling his temper.

One day, as he listened to Virginia's screams while Roger bashed her face to a pulp in their room, Bill exploded. "I just broke down the door of their room one night when they were having an encounter and told him that I was bigger than him now, and there would never be any more of this while I was there." Bill separated his mother and half brother from his stepfather, whose fists were covered with Virginia's blood. "You will never hit either of them again," Bill said. "If you want them, you'll have to go through me."

In obtaining a divorce from Roger, Virginia said in a deposition that he "has continually tried to do bodily harm to myself and my son Billy."

Roger Jr. persuaded Virginia to remarry his father Roger Sr. a year later. Bill was against it and made no bones about telling her so, but she overruled him. Not only that, but to make her happy, Bill changed his last name, which had been Blythe, to Clinton.

"Overall I was a pretty happy kid," Clinton recalled. "When my stepfather married my mother, they moved to Hot Springs, they both worked, we had a comfortable living. I had a little brother when I was ten. I had a normal childhood. I had friends, I did things, I was absorbed in the life of a child in a beautiful place where people were good to me, and I learned a lot in school.

"I had a good normal life. But at times it was really tough. I had to learn to live with the darker side of life at a fairly early period. But I wouldn't say it was a tormented childhood. I had a good life, and I've still got a lot of the friends of that childhood."

In high school Bill demonstrated his leadership abilities. He was president of the Beta Club for outstanding academic work and became a National Merit Semifinalist. He belonged to the Calculus Club, the Bio-Chem-Phy Club, the Junior Classical League for advanced Latin students, and Mu Alpha Theta, an advanced math club. His clubbiness would come in handy as he pursued his political career. His acting skills would also help. In high school he played a starring role in *Arsenic and Old Lace*.

He also loved music. At one time he even considered becoming a professional musician. In high school he played in the Band Key Club, the Marching Band, the Concert Band, the Stage Band, and the Pep Band. He became first chair tenor saxophone in the All-State First Band. A high school musician could attain no higher honor. He played for the Stardusters stage band and won trophies and awards. He obtained First Division ensemble and solo medals and citations. He was also the top band officer, called the "band major," as well as the assistant band director as a student officer of the State Band Festival.

He involved himself in assorted community clubs, such as the Kiwanis Key Club and the Elks Club. He made no enemies, and nobody uttered an uncharitable word about him.

At the age of seventeen, Bill attended Boys' State, a camp where high schoolers learned about politics by enrolling in fictitious parties and trying to become elected to office. It was 1963, a year that would change Clinton's life. His buddy Mack McLarty was elected governor of the make-believe state. Not to be outdone, Bill sought office as a delegate to Boys' Nation. Why be a mere state leader when he could become a national leader? He was elected and won a trip to Washington, D.C.

It may sound surprising, but the amiable, perpetually smiling young man was somewhat shocked that he won. "I didn't know if I could run a race like that because when I was a student politician [in high school], I was about as controversial as I have been in my later life. I was not one of these guys who won all of his races. And I wasn't always universally popular."

While in Washington, Bill visited politicians' offices. One of the people he met was Arkansas Democratic Senator J. William Fulbright, who was then chairman of the influential Senate Foreign Relations Committee. He also met his idol, President John F. Kennedy.

At the moment he shook the president's hand, Bill Clinton decided what he wanted to do. Up till then he had vacillated between choosing a musical, a religious, or a teaching career. Now Clinton knew his calling—politician.

Carolyn Staley, a lifetime friend, described how that meeting with Kennedy changed Clinton's life. "Virginia said she could see in Bill's eyes upon his return home that he was clearly on a path to public service through elected office."

Clinton explained his idolization of John F. Kennedy. "I decided to be a Democrat, starting in the presidential election of 1960, when John Kennedy excited me with a promise to get the country moving again. I think he gave people the sense that they could make a difference. And he did it without ever promising that all the problems could be solved—just that tomorrow would be better than today. He convinced me that he and Lyndon Johnson wanted to do something about civil rights problems, particularly in the South, my own region."

To pursue his political career, Bill decided to attend Georgetown University in Washington, D.C. "By the time I was seventeen, I knew I wanted to be what I'm doing now [being a politician] . . . and I knew that if I was in school in Washington I would have many opportunities to learn a lot about foreign affairs, domestic politics, and economics. . . . I just started asking people, including staff members of our congressional delegation, what was the most appropriate place. The consensus was that the School of Foreign Service at Georgetown was the most appropriate and the most academically respected and rigorous."

Bill's high school counselor, Edith Irons, recalled advising him to attend Georgetown when he told her he was interested in becoming a foreign diplomat. "I gave him the catalog for Georgetown and told him I would order more catalogs and send them to him as they came in. I explained that it was *most difficult* for a Southerner to get into the Ivy League schools and that I would explain to him the steps he had to take at a later conference." She told him that Georgetown was a good choice because of its proximity to the nation's capital.

Clinton applied to Georgetown and was accepted. Attending the conservative Jesuit-run university in the heart of Washington, D.C., necessitated a certain amount of adjustment for Baptist Bill Clinton.

"Bill and his mother went to Georgetown for his orientation," Edith Irons recalled. "A Jesuit priest had shown them around the school, and they came back to his office. He said, 'What foreign languages do you speak?'

"Bill answered, 'None, sir.'

"The priest exclaimed, 'What in the name of the Holy Father is a Southern Baptist who can't speak a foreign language doing in the *Mother* of all Jesuit schools?!' As Bill and his mother headed back toward the car, not a word was spoken. Then Bill finally walked over to her, put his arms around her shoulders, and said, 'Don't you worry, Mother. They will know what I'm doing here when I've been here a while.'"

Clinton determined to prove himself. He would have to hold a part-time job at Georgetown, and he wanted to work in politics, so he decided to seek a job in the U.S. Senate. Senator Fulbright, whom he had met through Boys' Nation, seemed a likely employer. However, Clinton thought it tactless to barge in on him and ask for a job outright.

What Clinton did illustrated the way he generally went after something he sought. He asked Arkansas Chief Justice Jack Holt to do him a favor by recommending him to Senator Fulbright. Holt knew Clinton as one of the boys who had helped him run for office. It was time now for Clinton to call in his marker.

Holt telephoned Lee Williams, Senator Fulbright's administrative assistant. In return, Williams called Clinton and told him he had two choices of part-time jobs—one that paid $5,000 a year and one that paid $3,500. Clinton said he wanted both. "You're just the guy I'm looking for," Williams replied. "Be here Monday."

Thus began Clinton's job as administrative and research assistant for the chairman of the Senate Foreign Relations Committee. In his studies at Georgetown, Clinton received a 3.57 grade point average in 1965 and achieved honors on the spring dean's list.

Dru Bachman, one of Clinton's friends at Georgetown, said of him, "Everyone at Georgetown knew of Bill Clinton. He was the campus politico, a self-confessed overachiever in a school cradled in the heart of the most political city in America, with a student body almost totally indifferent to politics. In those days, it was *not* stylish to run for class office. It was even less stylish to openly court every friendly face with a handshake in search of a vote.

"But that was exactly what Bill Clinton did with a sunny naïveté that knew no different. It *was* very stylish to attend polo games and embassy parties and to treat academics as a minor inconvenience, particularly for those of us in the School of Foreign Service.

"And that was *not* what Bill Clinton did. Somehow he just never bought into the pseudosophisticated pose assumed by so many. He openly admitted to being a small-town boy who had come to the big city to soak up every ounce of information and experience he could find, and he proceeded to do just that with a hunger and gusto bewildering to those with far less self-assurance."

Bachman also remembered Clinton's ambition. "Many of us worked in the popular saloons on M Street, or, better still, didn't work at all. Bill toiled away on the Hill for Senator Fulbright and probably visited every white-columned building and monument that the city had to offer. Typical adolescents that we were, most of us had no sense of time or urgency, much less an agenda.

"Bill exhibited all the signs of someone who was on the way to somewhere else and in a hurry to get there. If he had not been so totally amiable, genuinely kind, open, and friendly, he would have been heartily disliked by one and all, but he had absolutely no pretense about him, and that, of course, made him irresistible."

For six weeks in 1967, as Roger Clinton Sr. lay dying from cancer in Duke University Hospital, Bill visited him on weekends. Bill reconciled with his stepfather.

"It was beautiful," Bill Clinton said. "I think he knew that I was coming down there just because I loved him. There was nothing else to fight over, nothing else to run from. It was a wonderful time in my life, and I think in his."

Roger Clinton died soon afterward.

Bill Clinton returned to his studies at Georgetown. He had in fact never left them, despite the long trips to visit his dying stepfather. A classmate, Tom Measday, recalled, "He was very well spoken, very dedicated to what he was doing, very hardworking, and very political. He knew everybody."

Clinton's professors urged him to apply for a Rhodes scholarship. Even though he didn't believe he had the slightest chance of getting it, he worked hard at his studies and enlisted Senator Fulbright's support. Fulbright, himself a quondam Rhodes scholar, responded to Clinton's request for help by recommending him for the scholarship. To this day Clinton feels Fulbright was the man most responsible for his securing the prestigious Rhodes award.

A fortuitous event also helped Clinton in his pursuit of the scholarship. Before his final interview, Clinton was waiting at the airport and happened to see a *Time* magazine. He read an article about the world's first heart transplant. Clinton called it the "luckiest thing in the world," for one of his interview questions happened to concern the very same subject.

Clinton's mother sat by her phone all day waiting for him to inform her of the results of the Rhodes Committee's decision. "I never refused to do an anesthetic before in my life," she said. "But this was on Saturday, and they had an emergency, and the doctor called me, and . . . I said, 'I'm sorry. You'll have to call someone else.' . . . It was around five o'clock in the afternoon, and he called and he said, 'Well, Mother, how do you think I'll look in English tweed?' "

As a Rhodes scholar, Clinton won the right to attend Oxford University in England. He went there for two years, from 1968 to 1970.

Trouble came Clinton's way at Oxford in the guise of Vietnam as he studied for his bachelor of philosophy in politics. Clinton was against the Vietnam War. He felt it was a "poor boys' war," one fought by men who could not afford college and hence deferments or who could not call on political connections to avoid going. He was not alone. During his stay in England, opposition to the war mounted in the United States.

Clinton later gave several different answers as to whether he participated in antiwar protests. He told the *Arkansas Gazette* in 1978 that he played no part in the demonstrations, only observed them. In a letter in 1969 he wrote, "I have written and spoken and marched against the war. . . . After I left Arkansas last summer, I went to Washington to work in the national headquarters of the Moratorium, then to England to organize the Americans . . . for demonstrations October 15 and November 16."

Clinton's draft status at the time was not clear. When he graduated from

Georgetown and went to Oxford for graduate study, he apparently did not get a draft deferment, even though some graduate students could obtain them if they met certain complex criteria created by the Defense Department. While Clinton was at Oxford the draft board sent him a notice of induction. The reporting date had passed. Clinton phoned the board to find out what to do. The board gave him a deferment for the remainder of the year.

Clinton returned to Hot Springs in the summer of 1969. Believing that the draft board would not grant him a deferment for his second year of study at Oxford, he decided to enroll in the University of Arkansas Law School and sign up with the Reserve Officers Training School there. This would gain him a few more years of deferment, since he would be training for the military while studying at law school.

Then Clinton changed his mind. He opted to return to Oxford, nullified his ROTC agreement, and became available for the draft. Around this time the government set up a draft lottery, which was based on birthdates. The higher your lottery number, the less chance you had of getting drafted. Clinton was lucky. His lottery number, 311, was high enough that he would never be drafted. Clinton's cloudy explanations of his draft status and his complex maneuvering earned him a reputation as "Slick Willie" years later during his run for the presidency.

At Oxford, Clinton met one of the few people who came to detest him. Cliff Jackson happened to be a fellow Arkansan and a Fulbright scholar as well. At first, like everyone else, Jackson became Clinton's friend. The friendship soured years later when Clinton ran for President. By then Jackson had become a Reagan Republican, and Clinton was a full-fledged Democrat. Jackson did everything he could to sabotage Clinton's bid for the White House, making public a letter Clinton had sent him in which Clinton admitted he had received a draft induction notice. Jackson would be a thorn in Clinton's side through the entire election year.

In contrast, Clinton's best friend at Oxford, Strobe Talbott, always had kind words for Clinton. In 1992, as a senior correspondent for *Time* magazine, Talbott would write an article defending Clinton's antiwar protests.

Talbott recalled that at Oxford Clinton was competitive but not ruthless. "Part of his success, I think, derives from his ability to be extremely competitive without turning people off. He doesn't come across as being vicious or mean and hungry; and, as a result, he doesn't frighten people or antagonize people. At least that is my impression from Oxford days, and that squares with my impression of how he has conducted himself since then."

In 1970, Clinton had to choose between finishing at Oxford and accepting a scholarship to Yale Law School. He picked Yale because he wanted a law degree, though he entertained some regrets about not graduating from Oxford.

At Yale an unstoppable force met an immovable object: The liberal Bill Clinton met the conservative professor Robert H. Bork, an expert on constitutional law. Clinton disagreed with most of what Bork taught him in class. Years later, when Bork was nominated to the U.S. Supreme Court by President Ronald Reagan, Clinton remembered those lectures at Yale. He submitted written testimony to the Senate Judiciary Committee suggesting that they should reject Bork's nomination because of his interpretations of constitutional civil and individual rights.

Clinton harbored no personal grudge against Bork. "I liked him. I respected him. But I also believe that he meant what he said, and I thought that when he . . . basically went up there for those confirmation hearings and they tried to paper over all this stuff he'd said . . . I didn't find that persuasive, because I had been in his class many years ago. But, anyway, I like him fine. I think he was a good, challenging teacher; but I took him at his word. I think he did mean everything he said; and I think . . . the Senate should have made their decision based on the assumption that he did."

It was also at Yale that Clinton met Hillary Rodham, the person who would play a role in his life that would profoundly affect his future.

CHAPTER FIVE

Is There Life After Yale?

The carefully programmed, logically controlled, and career-oriented Hillary Rodham did not need the intrusion of romance into her life. Until her unexpected meeting with Bill Clinton, she had managed her life with skill and independence. And Bill Clinton had expressed his own very real fear of falling in love with Hillary. Kris Rogers, a fellow student of Hillary's at Wellesley as well as at Yale, put it this way: "They were both very strong personalities. They were both ambitious—they both had aspirations to make a mark on the world. And what is often the case with those types of couples is that they either work wonderfully or fail miserably; there's no in-between. And so we were all kind of holding our breath, wondering if it was going to work or not."

Hillary Rodham must have worried how her career would be affected if she became romantically involved with the young man from Arkansas. No matter what reservations either might have had, the two spent a great deal of time with each other. Hillary could frequently be found at nearby Fort Trumbull Beach, where Bill lived with his two Oxford roommates, Doug Eakeley and Don Pogue. Pogue was then going with Susan Bucknell. Later, the two married and settled down in Connecticut.

"Before the first semester ended," Susan recalled, "Hillary became a frequent visitor to Fort Trumbull Beach. When I first met her, I was impressed by her directness, her own commitment to public policy, her intelligence, and also her affection for Bill."

Susan could sense Bill's reluctance to become seriously involved with Hillary. After all, Hillary knew he was adamant about returning to Arkansas after graduation. He wanted to be a politician in his home state. He had always wanted to make his home and his living there. Yet the two of them soon seemed inseparable.

"It was fun to be with them as a couple," Susan said. "They enjoyed and respected each other and recognized each other's potential. As women grappling with the Women's Movement, and as young women trained for professional careers, we were searching for men who would support and respect our potential."

Susan Bucknell felt that Bill and Hillary shared similar attitudes even though their backgrounds were diametrically opposed. They did believe in an equal partnership as the basis of a solid relationship. And yet the future did not look clear for the two of them.

"There was also a delightful sense in which they complemented each other. I can still hear Hillary's humorous and fond admonition [to] Bill when he would wax a little too eloquent on some idealistic vision. I always had a sense that this was a couple who would have made it across the West in a covered wagon."

Don Pogue saw a great deal in Hillary Rodham that he did not see in Bill Clinton. "I think Bill's favorite professor [at Yale] may well have been J. W. Moore. Moore taught procedure. More than that. Moore *was* procedure. There was a national law of procedure to a large part because Moore wrote it. Crusty and cigar chomping, Moore had a dominating grasp of the subject. He was an awesome intellect. Bill was attracted to such people—which brings us to Hillary."

Pogue thought of Hillary as more than just plain smart. Being just smart was akin to being good. But Pogue sensed a subtle difference between being just good and being *very* good. Hillary, he thought, was just that—*very* good.

"Bill and Hillary really were a good match," he observed. "She was more midwestern, schooled in straight, analytical thinking. He noticed subtle differences. They shared an open, warm approach to people—it seemed a good harmony."

Professor Burke Marshall knew both Bill and Hillary. Described as a "civil rights giant" by Garry Wills, Marshall had served as assistant attorney general in charge of the Justice Department's Civil Rights Division in the crucial years 1961–64 under John F. Kennedy and Lyndon B. Johnson. He wrote a great deal of the important civil rights legislation of the era.

Now teaching at Yale, Marshall once said about Hillary, "She was even then forceful, very smart, very articulate. Some very good lawyers ramble, but that's not Hillary. Her mind is an organized mind." No small praise from one of the sharpest and most astute lawyers involved in the civil rights struggles.

As for Bill, Marshall had this opinion: "He was a very good student. He's very, very smart. But I'd never have thought Bill Clinton was law-firm material. He was obviously going to be a candidate."

The romance between Hillary and Bill continued along with her outside voluntary work. Their relationship became more firmly established as time went on. In Hillary's third year at Yale, she and Bill moved in together. They rented a typical Victorian-style New England house with a pillared porch, just off the campus.

"I loved being with her," Clinton said, "but I had very ambivalent feelings about getting *involved* with her."

He told Hillary the truth about his feelings for her. "You know," he said, "I'm really worried about falling in love with you, because you're a great person, you could have a great life. If you wanted to run for public office you could be elected, but I've got to go home [to Arkansas]. It's just who I am."

In 1972, Hillary and Bill flew to Texas to do campaign work for Sen. George McGovern, the Democratic presidential aspirant. Hillary's job took her to San Antonio, not far from the Mexican border, to register voters for the Democratic National Committee. Clinton worked at McGovern's state campaign headquarters in Austin.

Sarah Ehrman, a member of Senator McGovern's staff and later a director of issues and research for the McGovern campaign, met Hillary in San Antonio. "I was profoundly impressed with her intelligence and grasp of the issues and her strength and toughness. We were together only for a week, but we became fast friends."

Neither Hillary nor Bill had opened a schoolbook during the entire semester they were working in Texas. However, they returned to New Haven in time to take their finals. Neither had gone to one class. The professor had written the text that was required reading. They simply boned up on the text. And they both passed.

Later, when things settled down after McGovern's defeat by Nixon, they became partners in the annual moot-court competition at Yale. Doug Eakeley noticed that Hillary's legal skills were different from but complementary to Clinton's.

"Hillary has the same wonderful personal warmth and commitment to public service that Bill has. But coming from the Middle West, she was more direct and outspoken than Bill, the gentle Southerner. They made a wonderful team, as evidenced when they became the finalists together in the mock-trial competition sponsored by the Yale Law School Barristers' Union. A former U.S. Supreme Court justice presided, and I vividly recall seeing Bill and Hillary interrogating witnesses in a splendid (and coordinated) display of forensic skill."

Bill was superb at presenting—himself, his client, his ideas. But his glitter was mainly on the surface. He was a man who definitely thought, fought, and swayed you on his feet.

Hillary was superb at getting down to the core of the issue, at figuring out what direction things should take, which points should be made and which ignored. She was best at getting the background together and the whole case stitched up in presentable fashion.

He was on the surface, brilliant, sparkling, able to maneuver anyone. She was deep down, serious, logical about everything, able to produce a brilliant case in toto. Brilliant as they both were, they did not win the prize that day.

During Christmas break in 1972, Hillary invited Bill to her home in Chicago. "He came home with her one Christmas," Hillary's mother recalled. "I don't think her father was too impressed," she continued ruefully. "I thought he was interesting. He was sincere and had traveled a lot. I remember asking him what he was going to do after Yale, and without blinking, he said:

" 'I'm going back to Arkansas—to help the state.'

"I thought, Gee, that's great for him. Least he knew what he wanted."

The truth of the matter was that none of the Rodhams had any idea of what life in Arkansas was like. "We always had this picture of the barefoot, hillbilly type," she admitted. Li'l Abner was a national stereotype of the awkward, overgrown, childish Ozark clodhopper.

Also, Clinton's surface charm seemed to elude most of Hillary's family, including her two brothers, who remembered another visit.

"I was cutting the grass," Tony recalled, "when Bill showed up." Tony was eighteen then. "He climbed out of the car, came right over, and started *helping me cut the grass*. We had a nice little chat, and, of course, I had something else I wanted to do—so Bill immediately volunteered to help finish the job with the grass. I think Dad came out of the house and put a stop to it."

Hillary's brother Hugh had little to say about Bill except that his Arkansas accent seemed just "a tad strange." But the two brothers finally agreed that "if he was good enough for Hillary, he was certainly good enough for us."

By that time, Hugh had graduated from Penn State, where he had played football like his father, and had then spent two years with the Peace Corps in Colombia. Tony was going to Iowa Wesleyan College.

The fact that her family remained fairly neutral about Bill probably motivated Hillary in a backhanded way to like him all the more.

In 1973, Clinton invited Hillary to take a trip down to Arkansas to see *his* homeland. "I first came to Arkansas to visit Bill in 1973, to visit his family and see the state," she said. "And I was very taken by how beautiful it was."

Clinton met her at the airport in Little Rock, a city almost in the middle of the state, located on the Arkansas River. (You pronounce the river "Arkansas" just like it's spelled, but the state is "Arkansaw.") He drove her along Highway 7 through Hot Springs National Park—the long way home—impressing her with the natural endowments of the countryside. "It was just beautiful," she recalled.

If Clinton thought the sight of his world would stampede Hillary into moving there to be near him, he was mistaken. And if Hillary thought that Clinton would give up on his home state and move to one of the big cities to practice law, she, too, was mistaken.

In 1973, both graduated from Yale. Clinton packed up and returned to Arkansas. Hillary found herself at loose ends, without a specific course to follow. Yet she knew everything would sort itself out for her soon. Meeting Bill Clinton at Yale had been something she had not counted on. She knew that going to Arkansas was not exactly what she had in mind for her future.

"In 1973," she said, "when we both graduated from Yale, he came right home to Arkansas to teach in a law school." As for her, "I was very unsure about where I wanted to be." Musing about it later, she said, "I certainly was not ready to move completely to Arkansas yet, because I just didn't know whether that would be a decision that Bill would stick to. I really didn't know what to expect."

It was hard for Hillary to get Bill out of her mind after those golden years at Yale when she had known him so well. And yet Hillary's ambition was still in the ascendant.

At this time of indecision, Marian Edelman offered Hillary a permanent job as a member of the staff of what had previously been her special "project." Under Edelman's auspices the Washington Research Project had metamorphosed in or by 1973 into the Children's Defense Fund. The CDF was intended to provide a voice for America's voiceless and voteless youngsters. Part think tank, part lobby, the nonprofit, nonpartisan organization cut across both race and class.

Mainly, the Children's Defense Fund engaged in research, public education, monitoring federal agencies, assisting with the drafting of legislation, and providing testimony before lawmakers, all for the sake of legal assistance for children. Financed by private foundation grants, the CDF worked with individuals and groups to change policies and practices that resulted in neglect or mistreatment of millions of children and advocated a strong parental and community role in decision making.

Hillary would be an attorney on the staff of the organization and a member of the board of directors. She would be doing both research and development, trying to help both children and adults become aware of the rights they had under the law.

Six months later, she was just beginning to settle into the job. Then, in early January 1974, the telephone rang. The caller was an attorney named John Doar. He said he had been hired by the House of Representatives to assist the House Judiciary Committee in preparing impeachment proceedings against President Nixon, at that time struggling to escape the tentacles of the Watergate scandal.

Doar was the head of the committee's legal staff. A good friend of Burke Marshall, who was still dean of Yale Law School, Doar said he had telephoned Marshall with a plea: "I need about five young lawyers who don't mind working real hard, who will do the grunt work." Off the top of his head, Marshall gave Doar some names—among them, not surprisingly, both Bill Clinton and Hillary Rodham.

Later, Marshall admitted his first impression of Hillary was that she was a "run-of-the-mill Democrat." But he also remembered her as a "good lawyer, a hard worker, part of the team."

Offered the job on the legal staff, Clinton turned it down, Hillary quickly accepted and immediately settled into the work. She felt it was a good cause. President Nixon was high-handed, a conservative, and secretive in his dealings—not her favorite type of politician.

Each of the neophyte lawyers worked from eighteen to twenty hours a day. The staff had been assigned the task of drawing up three articles of impeachment, charging President Richard M. Nixon with obstruction of justice, abuse of power, and contempt of Congress in denying any involvement in the June 17, 1972, burglary of the Democratic National Committee headquarters. The point was to amass enough evidence to prove that the staff of Nixon's White House had tried to cover up any involvement by the President in the robbery.

Hillary's main objective was to establish the proper legal procedures to follow in the course of the inquiry and the subsequent impeachment. That meant she would be taking care of subpoenas and making sure all the proper legal steps were taken in agreement with the Constitution.

She drafted procedures for conducting formal presentation aspects of the inquiry, what sort of rules of evidence would be involved, and the kinds of objections that could and could not be used, as well as defining the scope of the cross-examination.

In addition, she worked with C. Vann Woodward, a historian assigned to research historical parallels or lack of them in other presidencies. And she listened to the famous tapes.

"The most tedious work was transcribing [them]," Hillary said. "I was kind of locked in this soundproof room with these big headphones on, listening to a tape. It was Nixon taping himself while he listened to his tapes, inventing rationales for what he said. So you would hear Nixon talk and then you'd hear very faintly the sound of a taped prior conversation with Nixon, [his top aides Bob] Haldeman, and [John] Ehrlichman.

"At one point, he actually asked Manuel Sanchez [his valet], 'Don't you think I meant *this* when I said *that*?' "

"I mean, it was surreal, unbelievable, but it was a real positive experience because the system worked. It [the impeachment inquiry] was done in a very professional, careful way."

On arriving in Washington, Hillary had looked up Sarah Ehrman, whom she had met during the McGovern campaign in Texas, and Ehrman put her up in her town house in southwest Washington. "I barely ever saw her," Ehrman recalled. "I just remember driving her at seven A.M. to the Watergate committee offices in an old converted hotel. We used to laugh and laugh about the absurdity of the life she was leading."

Another member of the legal staff was Fred Altshuler, from San Francisco. He remembered the ordeal vividly. "We worked seven days a week, twelve hours a day. Within that context, Hillary was among the cream of the crop. She was extremely hardworking. We were approaching it in as clinical a fashion as we could. We viewed our role as pure lawyers."

What interested Altshuler about Hillary was her straightforward objectivity. "She kept politics out of it," he said.

Hillary looked back on those months in Washington with a kind of awe. "It was an unbelievable experience. I got to hear all the tapes, all the other evidence."

But Nixon would never be brought to trial in the House of Representatives for impeachment by the Senate. On August 9, 1974, he resigned the presidency, and Vice President Gerald Ford—who had been selected by the President to fill the vacancy created by the resignation of Vice President Spiro Agnew—moved into the White House.

Hillary was enervated by the ordeal. She had been working in Washington with the legal staff for eight months. She wanted a break from the grueling chore of paperwork and the endless transcribing of taped material—which had turned out to be her main job.

In addition to all her hard work, Hillary had used her personal time in Washington to good effect. She had visited the better-known law firms in town and had talked to a number of top people about a job.

"We were quite interested in bringing her on," said Steven Umin, a partner at the prestigious Washington firm of Williams and Connolly. "Over the years I've probably talked to at least three hundred–odd prospects, and I remember Hillary's interview—it must have been in the early 1970s—quite vividly.

"She was a real sixties kind of woman," recalled John Labovitz, a partner at Steptoe and Johnson, "very sure of her own persona and her abilities. And she was already the Washington type. She knew how things worked here, and she knew her way around the Hill."

William Wilson Jr., a Little Rock lawyer, said, "Hillary would have been a cleanup lawyer back in New York, or anywhere. She is quick and gets right to the point. She doesn't meander. More of a blitzkrieg than an invasion-of-Normandy type of lawyer. There is no wasted motion."

Edward Bennett Williams wanted to hire her, yet she did not sign up with Williams and Connolly after Nixon's resignation. She had a commitment elsewhere.

CHAPTER SIX

Southern Social Mores

Hillary had reached another turning point in her life. She had navigated an earlier crossroads successfully when she had opted to go to Wellesley College. And she had made the right move in continuing her education at Yale Law School. Her third right choice was to go to work for Marian Edelman at the Children's Defense Fund.

She knew that she could always go back to the CDF. Edelman had made that clear when Hillary left to work on the House Judiciary Committee for John Doar. She would feel safe and secure there. She had decided to hew to the area of children's rights in her law career, or at least use it as an anchor in the future. Right now she was hesitant about returning. Would her immediate reappearance there not look like a retreat?

She had been hearing from Bill Clinton—a letter or two since she had been working for the committee. She knew he had taken a job teaching law at the University of Arkansas Law School. The campus, located in Fayetteville, was in the northwest part of the state, technically in the Ozark Mountains.

Teaching was a temporary measure, he had told her. He needed a steady income while he pondered his political moves. He had said that when he returned home after his graduation from Yale Law School, he had stopped his car on Interstate 40 and telephoned Dean Wylie Davis at the University of Arkansas Law School. Through a Yale professor he had heard that the school had two teaching vacancies.

He told Dean Davis that he would like to try for one of them. Davis immediately informed him that at twenty-six he was much too young to be a law teacher. Clinton told him he would do anything the dean wanted him to do and that he had always been too young for everything he had ever done before.

The dean agreed to interview him. After a brief conversation, Davis hired Clinton to become a member of the faculty. He was impressed not only with Bill Clinton as a person but with his excellent credentials: Georgetown University, Oxford, and Yale Law School.

Clinton had been teaching all the time Hillary had been working for the Children's Defense Fund and for the House Judiciary Committee. He had been thinking of running for Congress from the Third District in Arkansas.

It was tempting to Hillary to think of joining one of Washington's prestigious law firms. It would be hard work, but it could prove rewarding. She would be doing what she did best in the capitol of the country. And yet . . .

Unbeknown to Clinton, Hillary simply reached over to lift the receiver and dial the University of Arkansas Law School in Fayetteville. During her first visit to Arkansas, Bill had taken her to the Fayetteville campus and introduced himself and Hillary to Dean Davis. Somewhat expansively, Davis had invited her to apply for a job teaching for him.

Now she was talking to Dean Davis once again. Yes, he remembered her. Quickly Hillary filled him in on her current curriculum vitae and began a sales pitch on her own personal abilities and talents.

Then she reminded him that he had once told her that if she ever wanted to teach, he would give her a job. "Were you serious?" she asked him.

"I sure was, and I am. I'll hire you right now."

She would teach criminal law, and she would be hired at the rank of assistant professor. That was enough for Hillary. In a way, it was a sign that the road to Arkansas was open.

Now she needed transportation to Fayetteville. Sarah Ehrman had a car and was a friend of whom she could ask a big favor. Sarah was appalled at Hillary's intention to move away from Washington, the power base of all political activity in the country—and to move in a southerly direction, of all things.

"In August 1974, Hillary told me that she was going to Arkansas to take a job teaching as an assistant professor of law at the University of Arkansas Law School in Fayetteville. And there was much consternation in my face, I'm sure, when I heard the news because this young woman had a tremendously bright future in law in the Northeast and could really have done anything she wanted."

Ehrman pointed out how much more important in law it was to be a small fish in a big pond than to be a big fish in a small pond. The big ponds were the big cities; Ehrman pointed out that Hillary could be anything she wanted to be in New York, in Boston, in Chicago.

"But she decided that she was going to go down to teach law in Fayetteville and just see whether she and Bill Clinton could make a life together down the road. She had a lot of stuff with her—books and paper and clothing and all sorts of things, including a bicycle, and she couldn't figure out how she was going to ship it down to Fayetteville."

Of course, that was the reason Hillary needed Ehrman. She recalled, "I offered to drive her to Fayetteville from Washington, D.C., which was about a two-and-a-half-to-three-day drive."

In spite of Ehrman's dismay at Hillary's seemingly suicidal move, she complied willingly. And "we had an absolutely marvelous time!"

Every so often, on the pretext of resting from the drive, Ehrman would pull over to the side of the road to admire the scenery—and to excoriate Hillary for her idiocy in opting for Fayetteville and Clinton. "Hillary," she would say finally, "are you crazy? Are you sure you want to go to Fayetteville, Arkansas?"

Hillary would listen and smile and say something in a low-key way, quite unlike herself. It was obvious to Ehrman that Hillary was still undecided about Bill Clinton. At least that was something.

"And it went that way all the way down through the Blue Ridge Mountains," Ehrman said, "the Great Smoky Mountains, into Tennessee and across the Mississippi to Arkansas. And we spent that wonderful time together talking, gossiping, and exchanging ideas and getting to be fast lifelong friends."

Hillary did not change her mind. She had decided to look around at Fayetteville, to watch Bill Clinton in his natural habitat—and to play the waiting game.

When they finally arrived in Fayetteville, a small college town, it was a Saturday, the day of the Texas-Arkansas football game. The entire town swarmed with college-age kids running around and yelling the cry of the Arkansas Razorbacks, "Soo-ee, soo-ee, pig, pig, *pig!*"

Ehrman shook her head. "For God's sake, Hillary, are you crazy? You're not going to stay in *this* town! Why are you doing this?"

Hillary said nothing for a long moment. Then she turned to Ehrman and let a faint smile pull at the corners of her mouth. "I love him."

It was August. As Hillary might have suspected, it was not difficult to find Bill Clinton once she had crossed the Arkansas border. For he was hard at work running his first campaign in Arkansas. As he had hinted, he was indeed standing for the office of representative of the Third District in Arkansas in the U.S. House of Representatives.

Hillary immediately settled into her niche at the university. It was summer, but she had to prepare for the upcoming semester. She was going to teach criminal law, civil procedure, and a seminar in her own favorite subject, children's rights.

But as soon as her daily work was finished, Hillary joined Clinton at his headquarters to help him win the election. The Third District, discouragingly enough, was heavily Republican. John Paul Hammerschmidt, who had been in Congress since 1966, had been elected on the antiwar backlash. He seemed a shoo-in. Nevertheless, Clinton thought he could beat him.

Hillary was stunned at the absolutely anarchic lack of discipline at Clinton headquarters. Instinctively she stepped in and began turning things right side up. Soon enough she was barking out commands. The words "Hillary said" became a cry that everyone heeded. A semblance of order began to appear.

A casual telephone call to Park Ridge brought about a dramatic change in the campaign composite. Hillary's father had retired some years before. Her two brothers were both at home—one after graduating from Penn State and the other just finishing up at Ohio Wesleyan.

They decided to spend a month or two in Fayetteville on the campaign trail with Clinton. It was one of those sudden decisions. The next moment, the whole clan was there: Hugh Sr., Dorothy, Hugh Jr., and Tony. They took over an apartment in town. But it was Hillary who gave the orders—and those commands were obeyed.

Hugh Sr. answered the phones. Dorothy supplied all the food. Hugh Jr. and Tony made the signs and put them up all over the countryside. "We'd go out and nail them on anything that didn't move and some things that did," Tony recalled.

The family got along fine together. Hillary's brothers had always been very compatible. They were two of a kind—big, boisterous men who loved to joke and slap other people on the back, political animals without being politicians. They were good with Clinton's constituents. They were almost exactly like him in their outgoing, rip-roaring way.

No matter how good they were—or how good Hillary was at masterminding the campaign—Clinton lost the election. His draft record had become an issue in the campaign, and he was running against an incumbent Republican who was considered virtually unbeatable. Even so, Hammerschmidt beat Clinton with only 51.5 percent of the vote. No Democrat ever did any better against him.

Hugh Sr. and Dorothy headed back for Chicago. Hugh Jr. and Tony stayed on in Fayetteville. They both signed up for classes at the University of Arkansas, taking education courses. It had been Hillary's suggestion that they make use of the university facilities—Hugh Jr. because he was a good student and Tony because he was there with Hugh.

With the excitement of the lost election finally subsiding and the aftereffects of the loss beginning to manifest themselves in second thoughts and second hopes, Hillary found her life had returned to normal. She could now attend more fully to the business of settling into a totally new and very different environment. "I loved Fayetteville," she said, "and I loved Arkansas. I didn't know why, but I just felt so much at home."

The people were more friendly than on the East Coast or even in Park Ridge. "Once I got there, I made friends. I quickly became very comfortable." There were many reasons for her to feel comfortable in Arkansas. "I liked people tapping me on the shoulder at the grocery store and saying, 'Aren't you the lady professor at the law school?'"

The law school itself was a wonderful environment in which she could flourish. "There was no air-conditioning [at the law school], and it was as hot as it could be," she said. "It was a great group of faculty people, people who became my closest friends as soon as I moved to Arkansas."

There she made some of the best friends she ever had in her life. "It was an adjustment in the sense that I'd never really lived in the South and I'd never lived in a small town, but I felt so immediately at home."

The presence of her happy-go-lucky brothers helped. They rapidly became favorites on the university campus. Known as "the boys," Hugh and Tony were everywhere, and wherever they were, there was a sense of ribald fun and excitement. When you heard their laughter, you knew things were happening nearby.

Fayetteville's small-town atmosphere intrigued Hillary. One day a student missed her class. Hillary decided to telephone to see if he was all right. The information operator for his home number responded by informing her that the student was not at home.

"Excuse me?" Hillary said. She didn't quite understand what the operator meant.

"He's going camping," she told Hillary.

Hillary was stunned. "You call information and you get a person who knows the person you're trying to find?"

It was all so unlike any experience that she had ever had that it resembled some fictional Eden.

Dean Wylie Davis was very much taken with Hillary Rodham. He knew that she had the talent to make it big almost anyplace she decided to go, including the big metropolitan areas, and that he was lucky to get her. "I didn't anticipate that Hillary would be coming on, either," he confessed. "That was serendipity—enormous—she was really great, too. She was great in criminal law—she was great in everything she did."

Professor John Pagan, one of Hillary's colleagues, echoed Dean Davis's assessment. "She would have been as successful if she had been in New York, San Francisco, or Chicago. The only difference is that she would probably have made five times as much money."

Perhaps it was true that she would have been successful at anything she tried. She took to teaching and was obviously good at it. Clinton would teach a class with dispatch and care. However, he would always be looking over the shoulder of the student or students he was addressing and thinking about serving somewhere in a position of influence and power. But Hillary was right there with the students.

Woody Bassett, later one of Clinton's Arkansas campaign managers, had both Clinton and Hillary as teachers at Arkansas Law School. "Bill was a good teacher, he did it so effortlessly, speaking without notes at all. But it was pretty clear this was just a stopping-off point for him. Tell you the truth, I'm not sure Bill *prepared* all that hard." Hillary struck Bassett as different. "She was extremely well-prepared and much more blunt than Bill, a much more aggressive questioner and more analytical."

At the end of the law-school term the students were asked to evaluate their professors. Hillary was dismayed at the number of unflattering comments she got on their papers—about her appearance. "Students would write things like, 'Please stop wearing those big old granny sweaters,'" Diane Blair, a fellow teacher at the law school, recalled. "We used to take long walks around the campus and have these intense conversations: 'Does it matter? *Should* it matter? Should I *change?*' "

Hillary adamantly refused to make herself over cosmetically. It smacked too much of transforming herself into a sex object. And that was strictly not acceptable. The long walks and talks soon ended, and she did not change her style of dress or makeup.

Her activist mind soon turned to something she could do to help the members of the community. She took time out from her busy teaching schedule to set up a legal aid service for the poor. It was a move that gave her a lot of good press and brought her to the attention of important people who would help her later.

One Arkansas community tried to close a youth commune that had been formed nearby. Hillary immediately rushed to the defense of the commune. "The judge *loved* that case," she recalled. "It was the first time he ever wrote on constitutional issues."

Another case involved an itinerant woman preacher in a nearby town who continued to be jailed every time she was arrested for obstructing traffic or blocking the access to storefronts. Finally, the judge who kept jailing her decided to have her committed to a mental home.

The jailer who knew the woman had had enough. He telephoned Hillary. "This woman is not crazy," he told her. "She just loves the Lord."

Hillary collected a group of student aides and drove over to the town. There she conversed with the woman, who was languishing in jail. In the conversation, Hillary discovered that she had a family in California.

"People need the Lord in California, too," Hillary told the woman.

Then she talked to the judge. She suggested it would be a lot cheaper to pay for a plane ticket to California than to support the woman in an Arkansas mental home. The judge got the point. Hillary was discovering there was more than one way to achieve justice in the community.

Although she had followed her heart to Arkansas, as she had put it to Sarah Ehrman, she made no immediate move to cement a permanent relationship with Clinton. In fact, Hillary was still a conflicted woman. "I kept struggling between my head and my heart," she admitted later.

The lure of a solid law practice in a big city was always there, overpowering such conventional considerations as a home and children. Hillary owed it to her parents to make something of herself in the world of jurisprudence. She owed it to her teachers and her mentors to continue in the law. And she owed it to Hillary Rodham to continue in the direction she had set out for herself— and thus far had so successfully maintained.

But there were Clinton's ultimate aims in life to be considered, too. "Bill's desire to be in public life was much more specific than my desire to do good," she decided at one point. "I just knew I wanted to be part of changing the world."

She knew her desire was unfocused, a sentimental dream, perhaps. It would take time, talent, and a great deal of hard work to make a success of it. Yet the presence of Bill Clinton so close to her at the law school kept reminding her of what her heart was saying, what her own needs were demanding of her. She had made up her mind to go to Arkansas to be with him, to be close to him.

As Gail Sheehy wrote in *Vanity Fair,* they did not live together at that time in Fayetteville "because of the local mores," which were quite different from the customs prevalent in more sophisticated cities. But they were always together. One of Hillary's newfound friends in Fayetteville was Ann Henry, who recalled, "Occasionally Hillary would join me and Diane Blair for poolside visits about political, social, and personal issues. Through our normal interactions and personal affinity, we became good friends." Ann remembered Hillary and Bill fondly. "[They] were guests at both large and small parties, because Bill, especially, loved kicking ideas around and talking politics and history."

It was college and law school all over again. But it was the way both Hillary and Bill enjoyed themselves the most. Hillary was the intellect. Bill was the backslapping politician. They were both deep-down, rock-bottom serious about public life.

There was still a vague doubt in Hillary's mind about her future. If she finally decided to give up all her grand dreams of becoming a power in one of the big cities to settle down in Arkansas with a man whose interests were strictly on the public life of a politician, then she would have forever closed off any hope of becoming something more than a schoolteacher and a politician's wife. Yet there were advantages to making a life *with* someone.

Fred Altshuler had been impressed by Hillary's flair during the nine months they had worked together on the House Judiciary Committee's legal staff.

"It was definitely not on her radar scope to go to Fayetteville, Arkansas," he said. "It was not what she had worked for. She anticipated something more, and I think she had a hard time with it. She really stood out. She had incredible energy. She had fantastic skills as a lawyer."

Susan Bucknell, who knew both Hillary and Bill at Yale, realized the struggle that was going on in Hillary's mind. "Caught between her own career aspirations and a [romantic] partnership, Hillary struggled with the decision to move to Arkansas. She was fearful that it might prove less than a satisfying environment for her. However, she made the decision to go, fully determined to embrace both her partnership with Bill and [with] Arkansas. One of Hillary's great strengths is indeed her ability to be practical and focus on what really matters."

The warning bells would not stop ringing. Hillary said, "I have always tried to listen to that voice deep inside of you—the voice that tells you right from wrong. It's so easy to find yourself editing feelings and beliefs based on what people may think. You only have one life to live." Pause. "I knew my relationship with Bill was very important to me."

Torn in two by the struggle between her heart and her mind, Hillary took her vacation time in 1975 to visit her home in Park Ridge to see her mother and father and then return for a brief visit to the East Coast, where a number of her friends were working.

Hillary's friends were unanimously in favor of her leaving Arkansas forever and making it big in the legal profession, perhaps even as a justice on the Supreme Court. Still undecided, Hillary returned to Fayetteville in August 1975. Clinton met her at the airport, gave her his usual amiable greeting, escorted her to his car, and let her in. He got behind the wheel and turned to her with an expansive grin, then started up the car and hit the highway. Clinton was the first to speak.

BILL: Hey! You know that house you liked so much?
HILLARY: What house?
BILL: That little glazed-brick house.
HILLARY: Bill, I don't know what you're talking about!
BILL: You know. Remember when we were driving around the day before you left and there was a For Sale sign and you said, "Gee, that's a nice house"?
HILLARY: Bill, that's all I said. I've never been inside it.
(More exchanges on the ride through town.)
HILLARY: What's all this got to do with us?
BILL: I'll tell you what it's got to do with us. I bought it.
HILLARY: You bought it? That's got to do with you, not *us.*
BILL: I can't live there alone. Besides, I bought an antique bed and got some flowered sheets.
HILLARY: Bill—!

(They turn into a driveway leading up to a glazed-brick house.)
BILL: So I guess we'll have to get married now.

Looking back at her actions, Hillary soon perceived a silhouette of her own unconscious psychological machinations. What she had done, in effect, was indulge in probably the oldest of all traditional love maneuvers. She had absented herself from the presence of her beloved—even though he was unperceived by her conscious mind as her beloved—and had brought him up against the possibility of losing her. And so he had capitulated.

His surrender took the pressure off her own obvious inability to make up her mind—or what she *thought* was her inability to make up her mind. While subconsciously she had brought him to heel, consciously she had simply taken a few days off to travel.

The date was finally set for October 11, 1975. Realistic consideration of the impending marriage brought Hillary and Bill face-to-face with a problem encountered when they first began going together, their respective religions.

They were both Protestants. Nevertheless, for these serious, no-holds-barred people, the differences in their chosen sects would have to be addressed. As Hillary put it, they both had "strong feelings about our respective [religious] traditions." Clinton was a Southern Baptist. Hillary was a Methodist.

"We spent a lot of time talking about our religious faith and beliefs," Hillary said. They decided to stay within their own original denominations. Hillary would remain with the United Methodist Church. Bill would continue to attend the Immanuel Baptist Church.

Separate, but together, as Hillary put it. "We, of course, think the most important thing is your personal relationship with God, and the denomination you belong to is a means of expressing that and being part of a fellowship." They would, of course, visit each other's churches from time to time.

They decided to be married in Fayetteville, in a private family ceremony at the house Bill had bought on California Drive, with a big reception the next day at Ann Henry's place. At that reception all of Hillary's and Bill's academic and political friends would congregate.

"Hillary delegated all details to me," Ann Henry recalled. "So we washed windows, ordered food, and got the yard in shape for the big party. Hillary's mother, Dorothy Rodham, came to visit Fayetteville around Labor Day of 1975, and came to our home for lunch."

The house Bill had bought was unpainted. While Bill Clinton was a consummate politician, he was not cut in the same mold as another Southern politician, Jimmy Carter, who had carpentry and painting skills at his command as well as the old sweaters to wear while practicing them. But there were always "the boys"—Hillary's two energetic brothers—and other friends. While Clinton rushed about with his usual good humor surveying the work, "the boys" and the FOBs—the Friends of Bill—managed to get the house painted and ready for the nuptials.

In the meantime a local bakery prepared a three-tiered cake, to be decorated only with a cream-colored icing and pale yellow roses. Hillary and Bill had decided there would be no typical bride and groom on top of the cake; that was just a bit too corny and conventional.

The wedding itself was plain, discreet, and private. Only immediate members of the family were present. Roger Clinton Jr., Bill's half brother, was best man. Hugh Rodham Jr., Anthony Rodham, Hillary's mother and father, and the groom's mother, Virginia, attended.

Hillary and Bill exchanged rings that were family heirlooms. As a concession to the 1970s, Hillary did not become Mrs. Bill Clinton, but retained her maiden name and would continue to be known as Ms. Hillary Rodham.

The reception the next day was one of the biggest bashes of the Fayetteville season. There were members of the law school and university faculties, state and local dignitaries, politically active businessmen and their wives, and students. Every politician in the entire Third District had been invited.

"I had borrowed my mother's white handmade cutwork tablecloth," Ann Henry said, "which was used in both our home receptions, to use on the main table. We had a champagne fountain out on the porch, where ferns and hanging baskets were hung for color." Another table held cheese sandwiches and small pieces of smoked meat, finger foods for the guests who would be milling around the house and yard.

"Somebody played our grand piano during the whole evening," Ann Henry recalled. "I don't remember who it was."

Luckily, the weather held. It was a Saturday. The evening was balmy, with a cool October breeze.

The honeymoon that followed was something else again—and yet in its very exuberance it seemed to be a typical Rodham-Clinton affair. Because both bride and groom were busy at the university, they had to cut short their time away from home. It was Dorothy Rodham who suggested that since they couldn't go on a real honeymoon, they might take a trip to Mexico.

Mexico translated into Acapulco. The ten-day package deal was so good that the whole family decided to go, too: High Sr., Dorothy, Hugh Jr., Tony—and even Hillary and Bill.

"We had a marvelous time," Tony reported later. "Acapulco for ten days!" Plenty of laughs. Plenty of fun. Plenty of eating at the restaurants along the coast. It was a honeymoon for six!

CHAPTER SEVEN

Her Own Woman

Although Hillary Rodham's marriage to Bill Clinton seemed to everyone to be the traditional conclusion to their relationship with one another, many of Hillary's closest friends were not at all happy with her decision.

"I was disappointed when they married," said Betsey Wright, an Arkansan who had met the two of them during their work in Texas on the McGovern campaign in 1972 and who would be a key figure in future Clinton campaigns. "She has been absolutely critical to Bill's success, but, then, I had images in my mind that she could be the first woman president."

So did others. They based their attitudes mostly on the fact that as a married woman Hillary Rodham Clinton—even though she called herself strictly Ms. Hillary Rodham—would be somehow consumed by the energies of her husband as a public figure and the ordeal of running for reelection every year or so.

They were wrong. Hillary had no intention of allowing herself to be overwhelmed by her husband's career needs. As for Clinton, he certainly had enough sense to realize that Hillary was "her own woman."

Once back from their honeymoon, the Clintons individually settled down to their work. Hillary taught at the university, and so did Bill. But he had already begun to run for office again. His first loss had not deterred him.

At the reception party after his wedding, he had talked briefly with his fellow politician Jim Guy Tucker, who was attorney general of the state of Arkansas. In Arkansas, the attorney general was second in command. He ran on the party ticket along with the governor. Tucker knew Clinton from the time Clinton had invited Tucker to speak before one of his law classes.

After Tucker's talk to Clinton's class, the two men had flown together to Little Rock. During that flight they had discussed the job of attorney general.

"I told him I thought attorney general was just an absolutely terrific job to have, and we talked about the duties of the office," Tucker said. He knew enough about Clinton to see that he had "an activist view of the law" and understood how the law could be used to accomplish public policies and goals. "He was obviously very bright and capable of understanding what you can and cannot do with the law."

In the Henrys' yard, when Clinton and Tucker talked once again, Tucker intimated to Clinton that he would be running for the House of Representatives next year. He suggested that Clinton might like to become a candidate for the vacated post of attorney general.

The year 1976 was one of hope for most dedicated Democrats. The Republicans were left with the Watergate mess, which had been blown up into a well-publicized, full-fledged scandal in 1973. President Nixon's Vice President, Spiro Agnew, had been forced to resign because of illegal financial dealings during his term as governor of Maryland. Nixon had then appointed Gerald A. Ford as Vice President. Ironically, when Nixon himself eventually resigned, Ford became the first President in American history not to have been elected by the people.

The Republicans were in disarray. It was time for the Democrats to make history. Clinton had promised to work on Jimmy Carter's campaign in Arkansas; Hillary had been asked to help orchestrate Carter's primary fight in Indiana. She flew there in early 1976 to work for Carter's ultimately successful campaign for the presidency.

By the time she returned to Fayetteville, Clinton had become involved in his own run for attorney general. During the summer Hillary helped all she could with his political work. The primary election was the contest, for by filing deadline, no Republican had entered the race. The three contenders were Clinton, George T. Jernigan, a former secretary of state, and Clarence Cash, who had been assistant attorney general for several years and wanted to move up.

Jernigan and Cash had the inside line on the state's political environment, but Clinton was a fresh face and ran a hard campaign. His victory proved impressive. He polled more than 55 percent of the vote, winning the position without a runoff. Jernigan received 24 percent and Cash about 20 percent of the vote. Clinton was scheduled to take office in January 1977. At that time he would be almost thirty years of age. He and Hillary would have been married fifteen months.

The Clintons left the house on California Street in Fayetteville and moved to Little Rock. It was with some sadness—tempered, of course, with elation at Clinton's new elected job—that they took their leave of their jobs at the law school.

In comparison to the Ozarks-oriented town of Fayetteville, Little Rock was the big time. Yet the people there were not markedly different from those in Fayetteville. Little Rock took to Hillary as easily as Fayetteville had. She was still viewed the same way as when she arrived in Arkansas in 1974, "a young Chicago-bred, Yale-educated lawyer with a hotshot reputation for thinking on her feet."

While her husband took the oath of office in January 1977 and prepared for two years of dealing with the enforcement of law in the state of Arkansas, Hillary looked around for some kind of legal work. Starting at the top, she was pleasantly surprised—but not astonished—to land a place at the prestigious Rose Law Firm, certainly the best in Arkansas. Founded in 1820, it was one of the oldest law firms west of the Mississippi River.

U. M. Rose, whose name is now given to the firm, was among the founders of the American Bar Association and acted as its president in 1900. Rose is one of two Arkansans whose statues are in Statuary Hall in the U.S. Capitol. Six Arkansas Supreme Court justices have come out of the Rose Law Firm. One Rose lawyer, A. F. House, served as head counsel for the Little Rock School Board during the historic Little Rock Central High School desegregation case in 1956 and 1957.

Conflict-of-interest questions frequently arose because the Rose organization was so ingrained in the Arkansas establishment. Generally, the firm specialized in complicated business litigation. Thus, many of its clients were corporations, including General Motors, E. F. Hutton, Arkansas Poultry Federation, the Winthrop Rockefeller Foundation, and Tyson Foods.

Contrary to some reports in the press, it was not her work in establishing a legal-aid clinic at the University of Arkansas Law School that led the Rose firm to recruit her. According to partner George Campbell of Rose; "Herb

[Rule] was the one responsible for getting her." Rule was the bankruptcy expert. "Hillary was just a law professor—that's all. But she was a very bright woman."

Clinton and Rule, a former member of the Arkansas House of Representatives, had been friends since Rule's campaign for the 1974 congressional seat. "I was the point person on recruiting," Rule recalled, "and I got the word [from Clinton] that she was coming [to Arkansas], and I tracked her down. She had an interest and talents that would indicate that she would make contributions beyond the mustiness of law." Three years later, when the Clintons moved to Little Rock, she joined Rose.

Hillary was able to establish herself immediately as a skilled intellectual. Her work with the Children's Defense Fund had given her a good introduction to jurisprudence. In a short time she settled down into an area of the law called "intellectual property." That area has always been a rather arcane and remote territory, involving such esoteric items as copyrights, trademarks, and licensing.

She was a natural. Joseph Woods, an attorney in Oakland, California, had worked with her on the House Judiciary Committee during the attempt to impeach President Nixon. When the firm he represented in Oakland needed help representing a computer software producer who was complaining that someone had used its software improperly, Woods turned to Hillary Rodham at Rose immediately. Woods said, "She is certainly the person I thought of for that work."

She did not submerge herself in intellectual property, even though it was a very lucrative and friendly field. She would take other cases that came along—representing the Little Rock Airport Commission or even doing personal-injury work, divorce, sexual assault, and child-custody matters. But her primary interest still seemed focused on children's rights, whetted by her work at the Children's Defense Fund just after graduation from Yale.

"There were very few women trial lawyers in Arkansas when she first pitched her hat in the ring," Stephen Engstrom, a Little Rock attorney, said. "Putting the issue of gender aside, she ranks among the top of Arkansas's trial lawyers. She just hasn't backed away from a fight."

Her ideas about children's rights had been solidifying since she initially expressed interest in them. In 1974, she wrote an article titled "Children Under the Law" for the *Harvard Educational Review*. But it was "Children's Rights: A Legal Perspective," which appeared in *Children's Rights: Contempo-*

rary Perspectives, edited by Patricia A. Vardin and Ilene N. Brody and published by (Columbia University) Teacher's College Press, in which she expanded her original concept into a cohesive argument for the implementation of the legal rights of children.

What thoroughly irritated her legal mind was the fact that children throughout history had never enjoyed any true legal rights. Children were still in effect "the empire of the father," as William Blackstone, the authority on Western law in the eighteenth century, said.

That is, children were subject to a father's guardianship until they attained legal age. So were women, in Blackstone's time. However, history had treated women with greater kindness than children. They had become competent legal individuals and are so in America today. Children had not made such good progress. As Blackstone wrote: "Infants have various disabilities; but their very disabilities are privileges." Those disabilities were the source of the privilege of maintenance.

Hillary argued in "Children Under the Law" that Blackstone's thesis held for a time when young people were apprenticed at the age of seven or forced to work in the fields and young women bore children very early in their lives. In fact, the law was mainly concerned with the successful passing on of estates belonging to the propertied classes.

"The phrase 'children's rights' is a slogan in search of definition." she declared. "Invoked to support such disparate causes as world peace, constitutional guarantees for delinquents, affection for infants, and lowering the voting age, it does not yet reflect any coherent doctrine regarding the status of children as political beings.

"Asserting that children are entitled to rights and enumerating their needs does not clarify the difficult issues surrounding children's legal status. These issues of family autonomy and privacy, state responsibility, and children's independence are complex, but they determine how children are treated by the nation's legislatures, courts, and administrative agencies."

Her main line of thought focused on the "artificial and simplistic" device of turning a child into an adult at the age of either eighteen or twenty-one. "The capacities and the needs of a child of six months differ substantially from those of a child of six or sixteen years," she said.

However, certain rights of children were recognized by the law, including the right to drive a car, the right to drop out of school, the right to work, the right to marry (although before a certain age marriage could be voided in the absence of parental consent), and the right to vote. Supreme Court rulings even recognized the right not to salute the flag in the public schools, if so doing would violate religious beliefs, and the right to don a black armband to protest the Vietnam War.

Yet in other areas, Hillary said, the courts did not keep up with the current life-style. "This attitude is especially prominent in regard to the labeling of certain behavior as delinquent"—for example, the so-called status offenses, including truancy, sexual promiscuousness, running away, and incorrigibility—which, she wrote, "represent a confused mixture of social control and preventive care that has resulted in the confinement of thousands of children for the crime of having trouble growing up."

The young children, not those who were approaching maturity, always suffered the most. "Older children have organized themselves politically with some success, especially on the issues of the eighteen-year-old vote, civil liberties of school students, and anti-war activities, but they too have relied heavily on the support of adults."

Reform schools, juvenile courts, and child labor laws came about only after a great deal of agitation and the relentless application of political pressure. For example, children of a certain age could not be hired for work in spite of ability, need, or desire. Their rights were ignored by the fact that all children, regardless of age within a certain span of years, had to attend school. These rights, Hillary said, should be attended to but have not been.

Hillary saw two steps in granting these rights to children. The first was the extension of adult rights to children, in view of the children's needs and interests. And the second was a guarantee that critical needs would be met if such rights were granted. A blueprint of such needs might include adequate nutrition, healthy environment, continuous loving care, a sympathetic community, intellectual and emotional stimulation, and other prerequisites for a healthy adulthood.

She then explored some court cases relating to children, including *Brown v. Board of Education,* in which the courts held that the constitutional rights of black schoolchildren were violated by segregated education and emphasized the critical importance of education both to children and to the general public.

But the most famous children's rights case was *In re Gault,* a landmark case on procedural rights in the juvenile court, which she discussed in more detail. *Gault* held that in juvenile court, children were entitled to due process guarantees formerly granted only to adults in criminal court. These guarantees included four important rights: (1) the granting of reasonable opportunity for parent and child to prepare a defense, (2) the right to representation by counsel, (3) the right not to testify against oneself so as to lead to self-incrimination, and (4) the right to confront and cross-examine witnesses appearing against one. The Supreme Court restricted children's rights to these four points, and it limited the guarantees to juveniles facing commitment to a state institution. Yet the Court did declare that "neither the Fourteenth Amendment nor the Bill of Rights is for adults alone."

In *Wisconsin v. Yoder,* an Amish family contested the state's right to require their children to attend high school. The family claimed that compulsory school violated their religious freedom and that of their children. One of their three children testified that she did not wish to go to school. The other two children did not testify.

The majority opinion upheld the rights of the family—and parents—to keep their children out of school. Justice William O. Douglas, for the minority, agreed that the child who had testified should remain out of school. However, he pointed out that the other two children had not been heard. He was looking at the rights of these two children as well as of the one who had been heard. The child who testified was obviously in agreement with her parents; the other two might not be.

In *Wisconsin v. Yoder,* Justice Douglas assumed that the children were intelligent and mature enough to express an opinion on their interests. Essentially, Hillary pointed out, Douglas had "reversed the presumption of incompetency." He had, instead, looked for factual evidence to contradict the presumption of competency but had found none, thus arguing that *all* the children should be given full rights as parties to a lawsuit.

This was an important point. And it led Hillary to a later article on the subject of competency of children.

In "Children's Rights: A Legal Perspective," Hillary developed and fine-tuned the arguments that she touched upon in 1974. She introduced the article by discussing the rights of children in relation to the family of which they were a part. Then she continued with the rights of children without families, children's rights in institutions, and children's rights in society.

"Because children now remain in the family for longer periods," she wrote, "during which they are still dependent but becoming more and more adult, the opportunities for intrafamily disputes have increased dramatically." She noted that some parents feared being sued by their children for forcing them to do simple household chores like taking out the garbage.

She proceeded to discuss children's rights and responsibilities. A correlation always existed between rights and responsibilities. A society might deny a legal right to a certain citizen considered incapable of taking care of himself or herself. But by the very fact of being denied that right, the individual was left unable to safeguard his or her position in that society. And the same cause and effect operated on children, who were basically without rights under the law. She wrote:

"This presumption of incompetency has profound significance not just because children are reliant on adults to exercise their rights for them, but because a child denied the opportunity to exercise responsibilities is effectively denied the opportunity to mature into a responsible adult."

She then moved on to her key point. "The first thing to be done," she declared, "is to reverse the presumption of incompetency and instead assume all individuals are competent until proven otherwise."

She was, of course, taking her cue from Justice Douglas in the *Wisconsin v. Yoder* case. And she continued: "It is not difficult to presume a newborn child is incompetent, in the sense of exercising responsibilities and caring for himself or herself."

However, she pointed out, it might be impossible to prove that a twenty-year-old was totally incompetent—and just as difficult to presume a sixteen-year-old incompetent. She admitted that it would be difficult to write laws for the various ages within the eighteen- or twenty-one-year span so as to calibrate competency chronologically. But treating all children—newborn babe and gangling teenager—as the same, all incompetent, "ignores psychological and social realities."

And she went on, "If we were able to fashion laws that decided on the basis of available knowledge which children were competent and which were not, we could begin assigning responsibilities as well as rights and expect both to be fulfilled and enforced."

Of course, society was not able to fashion such intricate laws to safeguard the rights of its citizens. There must be another approach. "Since children," she wrote, "with or without rights, will remain dependent on adults to secure the assistance they require, they deserve competent and effective advocates. Interested adults should be alerted to the work that must be done to inform the public and decision makers about children's needs, interests, rights, and responsibilities and to secure positive action."

Meanwhile, in her own private life, Hillary found that her husband was making a number of speeches in his tours of the state as attorney general. Probably no other attorney general within memory had ever done so much traveling as Bill Clinton had. But there was a method in his peripatetic politicking. He wanted to be known to everybody.

The *Log Cabin Democrat* in Conway, Arkansas, wrote an editorial about him that called him one of the state's "fast-rising politician stars." It also said that he was "an attractive, articulate political leader," adding:

"His record as attorney general has been studded with examples of hard work, consumer concerns, and a generally aggressive stance that has led him into a variety of situations with seeming zest.

"He is young and popular, and certainly must be getting a considerable amount of rather flattering encouragement to seek higher office." Of course, the newspaper meant as governor, congressman, or senator.

In 1977, Clinton published his own "Attorney General's Report," lauding the achievements of his time in office. The *Arkansas Gazette* said that he described his activities "in glowing terms." Clinton used campaign funds rather than state funds to pay for the printing and distribution of the panegyric. He had learned that he would be under intense scrutiny as a public servant, no matter what he did.

When he had won the job of attorney general in the 1976 election, he had already planned to make the run for governor in 1978. His opponents did not share his free-and-easy views on the marijuana laws, his liberal views on gun control (he was for it, in a state where possession of a gun was a fundamental right), or his views on capital punishment. (He was against it.) Most of all, he was attacked for his extremely liberal views on women's rights. (He was for them.)

When Bill Clinton had announced for the attorney general's post, a reporter had raised his hand and asked him, quite pointedly, "Will the fact that your wife has retained her maiden name hurt you politically?"

"I hope not," Clinton answered. Why should the wife of an attorney general need to prove herself as an old-fashioned woman on the distaff side? She should be her own woman.

Even the *Arkansas Gazette* sided with the Clintons: "It was important for her to maintain the [professional] recognition she had built as Hillary Rodham."

Now things were different. With the pot a lot bigger than before—the governorship as opposed to the attorney generalship—the candidate's wife became the focus of an intensive barrage of attacks by antifeminists. Her last name became a major issue, especially when she joined him on the campaign trail and worked hard on his election strategy. When she spoke, Hillary was frequently attacked for her views—her use of her maiden name, though married, her selection of a profession over homemaking, and her stand on children's rights.

It was Hillary's strategy to place her husband among the South's "compromise progressive candidates," maintaining that the new Southerners reflected the area's rising aspirations and more flexible attitudes in government and politics.

Clinton defeated four opponents in the primary, garnering 60 percent of the vote and carrying seventy-one of seventy-five counties. He defeated his Republican opponent, Lynn Lowe, the GOP's state party chairman, 338,684 votes to 195,550. The winner, thirty-two years of age, was touted nationally as the youngest governor in the United States.

Hillary Rodham—of Park Ridge, Illinois, the Rose firm, and the *Harvard Educational Review*—was now the first lady of Arkansas.

CHAPTER EIGHT

Diamonds and Denim

Hillary Rodham's assumption of the role of first lady of the state of Arkansas was the most unexpected move in her already eventful and diversified life. That this sophisticated, well-bred, advantaged woman from the grassy environs of Park Ridge would eschew the summits of the law business for a life in Arkansas was something that no one could have guessed even a few years prior to her arrival on the steps of the governor's mansion.

She had made her way and earned accolades most of the time through Wellesley, Yale Law School, and Washington and was now in the top echelon of the Arkansas political hierarchy. As a member of the prestigious Rose Law Firm, she became known for her astute legalistic talents. And yet the impression of her was mixed.

Still addicted to the styles of the sixties—shapeless clothes and wildly disarranged hair—and wearing thick horn-rimmed glasses for her very poor eyesight, Hillary Rodham was an anomaly as she entered the halls of the governor's mansion in Little Rock. She still insisted on being called Hillary Rodham, not Hillary Clinton.

She was widely suspected, frowned upon, if not totally *dis*liked, and kept at arm's length. Even during the election she and her husband had been getting letters, most of them addressed to him, questioning the fact that Hillary did not call herself Mrs. Clinton and asking him, "Doesn't your wife love you?" and "What's wrong with your marriage?"

Arkansas was not quite as modern in its attitudes as Massachusetts, where Eldie Acheson, Hillary's friend from Wellesley, understood quite well what Hillary was doing as well as what her Arkansas public was up to. To Hillary, Eldie said, using her own name even after marriage was simply a part of women's liberation. "It was," she added, "an act of self-worth."

Eldie realized that there were problems to be surmounted in sustaining Hillary's somewhat high-handed attitude. She recognized the complications her mind-set brought about during Hillary's first months as first lady. "Many people felt she was one of those pointy-headed, overeducated Yale types who had come back with Bill to Arkansas to spread the word to the uninitiated," Eldie said.

The public generally disliked her from the beginning. "Who the hell does she think she is?" summed up the opinions of many of the women in the state.

John Brummett, an editor on the *Arkansas Times,* saw it the way many men did. "A lot of Bible Belters felt it was a sign of wimpishness on [Bill Clinton's] part, that he couldn't persuade her [to use his name]. There was also a feeling she was a little bit uppity and alien."

That attitude prevailed during the first months of her reign as first lady. And it did not alter thereafter in any significant way, since Hillary made no attempt to change her style or even minimize her air of exclusivity.

One anecdote that circulated about the first lady in the fall of the year was enough to draw a picture of someone who seemed to be inhabiting an alien planet peopled with far lesser humans than she was accustomed to. The setting was the football field at the University of Arkansas, where the Razorbacks were playing an exciting game. Screams of "Soo-ee, soo-ee! Oink, oink, oink!" filled the air. The governor was in his special box, waving his arms, standing, shouting, then sitting down again, overcome with emotion. The cheerleaders were cheering; the fans were howling. Chaos. Hillary was seated next to the governor. She was holding something in her hand. Oblivious to the excitement surrounding her, she was reading a book.

Although Hillary never seemed to bother much with appearances, she did give some thought to furnishing the small area of the governor's residence where she and her husband were to live. The so-called mansion sits in all its Georgian-style splendor on a well-landscaped, finely kept estate with a fountain out front and trimmed sculptured gardens surrounding the brick building. Yet it is really not a mansion at all. Nor is it a relic of American history. While it might seem to have been built in 1750 or thereabouts, the two-story house was actually constructed in 1950, only forty-odd years ago.

The mansion was designed to be not a comfortable abode of well-to-do people but an imitation country home to be visited and ogled by the general public. In fact, its public rooms are the most visited square footage in the state. The area reserved for the privacy of the governor and his wife is a cramped and confining two bedrooms, a den, and combined living room and dining area. No more room is allotted the governor and his family than would be available in a modest-sized ranch house.

According to Jill Brooke in *Metropolitan Home,* "The few rooms that the Clintons call home reflect the taste of a younger generation whose emphasis is on comfort, not formality; whimsy, not ceremony. They're fun, and real." "Fun," for example, was the pillow embroidered with the words "Raise and Spend," a jocular reference to FDR's famous dictum: "Tax and tax, and spend and spend."

The den, in particular, received the full Hillary Rodham treatment. When she first surveyed the interior of the living quarters, she was appalled at the lack of bookshelves on the walls. From her home in Illinois through her years in college, she had always been surrounded by books. Not to have any books in view seemed degrading. Immediately she ordered bookshelves built all around the den, and quite soon those shelves were bulging with books of all kinds, from legal tomes to light fiction.

"Hillary and Bill combine an American spirit that's still on the frontier," Christopher Hyland, one of their friends in Little Rock, explained. Hyland, a wallpaper designer, went on: "It says, 'We're young, we're moving forward.' These are rooms that reflect their life as it is. Hillary has a twinkle in her eye when it comes to design, but her mission is to provide warmth."

The warmth, of course, was tempered with the need for comfort. Hillary certainly understood the risks she was running in playing her own role as first lady of Arkansas. And she did not in any way intend to change. Not surprisingly, her role model was Eleanor Roosevelt.

Bill Clinton was inaugurated as governor of Arkansas on January 10, 1979, a bitterly cold day. The ceremonies took place in a packed House chamber of the Capitol in Little Rock. Hillary Rodham was wearing a necklace that contained the 4.25-carat Kahn diamond, a twenty-thousand-dollar jewel, borrowed for the occasion from the state of Arkansas. It had been mined at the Arkansas Crater of Diamonds State Park. That state park, incidentally, holds the only diamonds ever discovered in North America. That is the reason the diamond is one of the state of Arkansas's symbols, represented on the stage flag.

After the swearing-in ceremony, the governor and his wife moved to the steps of the Capitol for his inaugural speech. Only two hundred of the faithful showed up to hear the speech in the piercing cold. In it the governor promised to move Arkansas into "a new era of achievement and excellence" and "a life that will be the envy of the nation."

Clinton promised to focus his administration on education. Arkansas was known, with one exception—Mississippi—as the state that spent the least amount of money on education per pupil and on the salaries of teachers. The young governor promised to put an end to that. He also said he would provide for "better accountability and assessment of students and teachers, a fairer distribution of aid, more efficient organization of school districts and recognition of work still to be done in programs for kindergarten, special education, and gifted and talented children."

The inaugural ball was held at Robinson Auditorium in Little Rock, with the theme of "Diamonds and Denim." The diamond connection was obvious, and so was the denim. Theoretically, the Clintons were trying to combine an urban sophistication with the old-fashioned down-home values of the area. Guests could come in formal clothes or in denim—or in a combination of both. They were told to be natural and comfortable.

Hillary herself wore a made-over gown, the basic dress she had worn at her wedding. She had taken it to Connie Fails, a Little Rock dress designer, and discussed making it over. "She brought her wedding dress and another gown," Fails said. And she quoted Hillary: "Bill likes the way I look in this [the wedding gown], and I like the way I feel." And so Fails had used the wedding gown as the foundation, altering the sleeves, omitting some of the trim, and adding more in other places.

Fails recalled, "It's pretty conservative, with a nice elegance about it." The dusty rose panne velvet dress had a fitted bodice, set-in sash, and tiered skirt. The modified leg-o'-mutton sleeves were puffed from shoulder to elbow, then fitted to the wrist. The gown carried out Hillary's wish that her Inaugural Ball dress be "something Arkansas made, Arkansas related."

Clinton had made a risky decision when he invited former governor Orval Faubus to the inaugural ball. Faubus was anathema to the blacks because he had tried to prevent the desegregation of Little Rock's Central High School in 1957; his name was synonymous with racism.

The party was a smash. John Robert Starr wrote that it was "a triumph of public relations and political fence-mending," although he did not condone the inclusion of Faubus's name in the guest list.

True to his promises, the governor did introduce an outline for his education plan within five days of his inauguration speech. It contained two very controversial and inflammatory proposals: (1) a legislation providing fair dismissal procedures for teachers and requiring all new teachers to pass a standard competency examination before being certified; and (2) a bill calling for mandatory achievement tests for all students in three grades each year to enable parents, educators, and state officials to make decisions about educational directions.

This move brought about a firestorm of objections. Clinton had made a tactical mistake. He had neglected to smooth the way for passage of his educational proposals in the state senate. Many of the legislators came from areas with small school districts, and their constituents were opposed to reorganization of any kind. Seeing that he could never get the measures passed, Clinton withdrew the bill. It was a major failure for a new governor.

The bill's withdrawal was a blow to Hillary. Because of her interest in children's rights, she was concerned with the educational system in Arkansas, which was in serious trouble. She was ready and waiting to help push Clinton's educational reforms through. It was not to be. At least not in 1979. Certainly she did not let this momentary setback discourage her. She continued to assess future improvements in the system all during the governor's first term. In 1979 he named her to head the Rural Health Advisory Committee, a forty-four-member board established to develop a program to deliver health care to people in isolated communities.

In this capacity she met not only with health officials but toured the state, talking with local and state politicians and proposing possible changes that might improve the health care that was already available. In spite of the fact that she was purposely low-keyed in her approach, it was hard for anyone to forget her once she had decided to move on something. And it was obvious that her close connection to the governor made her presence a formidable one.

It was a struggle to keep her profile low, but she tried to make her moves without creating waves at every attempt. A friend, Joan Campbell, put it candidly by saying, "She's very much a partner with him [the governor] on the political scene."

Tommy Robinson, a Republican representative, was on the scene at many of her battles with other legislators. "As someone who worked in the governor's first administration," he once said, "I know of times when Mrs. Clinton made the tough decisions that others did not have the courage to make."

Trying to justify her impact on those in office, Hillary said in response to comments such as Robinson's: "If I were a man, they would probably say what a great, strong person this fellow is, how commanding he is, and all the rest. . . . I'm not reluctant to say what's on my mind, and if some people interpret that one way instead of another, I can't help that."

The storm of criticism against her did not undermine her will at all, but it did give her pause. How could she combat it without putting herself—and her husband—in an untenable position? "There are no guideposts, no signposts, to understand it," she said. "I think we're between generations in a very significant way, and change is always difficult, always going to be resisted. We have to figure out ways of making change into a friend instead of an enemy."

She went back to her role model, Eleanor Roosevelt, again. "I've got *My Days,* [a collection of] Eleanor Roosevelt's newspaper columns, next to my bed because it's important for me to put this experience I'm going through into some kind of historical context."

She may have been copying some of the moves of Eleanor Roosevelt, but she made them in a political era light-years beyond the 1930s and 1940s. "Women in professions across the line," she pointed out, "not just politics or married to people in politics, have faced challenging issues. I think it's important to see the threads that run through women's lives"—whether they were coping with life-threatening diseases or with aging parents.

As she saw it, "The issue is not what people say about me, but what it represents in the way that women are being divided among themselves. Instead of pitting ourselves against one another or claiming that one choice is the only choice, we need to be supporting the many options in our life. Women feel guilty enough without imposing more on them from the outside. Rather than ignore women's advances of the last twenty years, we need new policies to help us live in this stressful world."

Although she was trying to keep her professional work distinctly separated from her life as the first lady of Arkansas, she found it daunting and not always possible to make the proper separation. She said, "I think that any responsible choice that a woman makes, if she does it with commitment, is going to be difficult. My friends who are full-time homemakers are not 'sitting around.' Like my career friends without families, they're fully engaged in what they view as the most important work that can be done.

"Then there's the vast majority of us who are trying to balance family and work. The first thing I think one has to do is to give up any idea of perfectionism, which is hard, particularly for women who have been achievers. You have to be tolerant of yourself and what you're capable of doing in twenty-four hours. Then you have to set priorities."

As a reward for working on the Jimmy Carter campaign in 1976, when she was in charge of field operations in Indiana, Hillary Rodham was appointed to the board of the Legal Services Corporation in Washington. She served as a board member between 1978 and 1981, making trips to Washington several days a month. The Legal Services Corporation is a federally funded program that allocates hundreds of millions of dollars to help the poor with their legal problems. The money goes to legal aid clinics for the poor, especially in urban areas. The organization is an independent, private, nonprofit, and nonpolitical corporation. It provides legal assistance in criminal cases but by law cannot help litigation in noncriminal cases.

She proved quite skillful in increasing the program's yearly appropriations. And she also increased its activities everywhere she could. During her time in office, the agency allocated tax dollars to contribute to political campaigns, to hire lobbyists to fight an initiative in California to cut taxes. She helped wage a successful war to prevent budget cutters from abolishing the corporation itself.

One of the Legal Services Corporation's most controversial suits was filed during her tenure. It sought to ask the government to pay for a sex-change operation for a Connecticut individual. Another suit sought to give back two-thirds of the state of Maine to Native American tribes that had claimed ownership.

In 1980, two Democrats from Arkansas, Senator Dale Bumpers and Representative Ed Bethune, said that Legal Services Corporation attorneys "look for too many cases which can effect an economic or social outcome."

Clint Lyons was director of field operations of Legal Services at the time. "If you looked at the map of Legal Services programs in 1976, you could see dots up and down the East Coast. Through Hillary's term, the dots spread to the point that legal services for the poor became a reality in every jurisdiction in the country."

Hillary proved extraordinarily successful in establishing clinics in areas that most needed them. "The biggest obstacles early on were some local bar associations," Lyons said. "But Hillary took a very practical approach to problems. Before we went in and opened a new clinic, she always insisted that we sit down and talk to local bar officials and community leaders and try to neutralize their opposition, or better yet, get them on our side."

In 1980, two years after Hillary Rodham had become the first lady of Arkansas, she gave birth to a seven-pound baby girl, Chelsea Victoria. The baby was expected on March 15 but arrived somewhat early, on February 27. Hillary was thirty-three years old and had been married just over five years.

According to Carolyn Huber, a family friend, Hillary was undergoing stress at the time in the litigation of a child custody case for the Rose Law Firm. Clinton had been in Washington and was just returning to Little Rock and the mansion. Fifteen minutes after he set foot in the house, Hillary began experiencing labor pains.

He rushed her to Little Rock's Baptist Medical Center. The Clintons had taken a course in the Lamaze method of delivery, but it was not to be. Chelsea was delivered by cesarean section because of her position in the womb.

As Gail Sheehy put it, "Bill emerged from the delivery room in green scrubs, cradling a seven-pound baby, saying he was 'bonding' with his new daughter." The governor, according to newspaper coverage, "walked all over the area last night holding the baby in his arms." Diane Blair, Hillary's friend and a political science professor at the University of Arkansas Law School, described Clinton as acting in general the way he might if "he had just invented fatherhood."

The newspaper reported Chelsea's birth in neo-chic fashion: "Governor Bill Clinton and Hillary Rodham had a daughter."

Needless to say, the wording of the notice—implying that two unmarried people had a baby—did not sit well with the electorate, although at the time neither of the Clintons worried about it. Bill felt secure in the governorship. After all, no Arkansas governor had been defeated in a reelection attempt in twenty-six years. He was sure he would win.

Throughout his tenure as governor, he had been a strong supporter of President Carter. But Carter had been saddled with the Iran hostage situation, with Iran holding fifty-two Americans as captive enemies of the state. An abortive attempt to free the hostages in a paramilitary rescue operation turned into a political and media fiasco. Lives were lost, aircraft destroyed.

Not only that, but thousands of Cubans had been fleeing from Castro and had sailed for Florida. The Federal Emergency Management Agency began placing these refugees in Fort Chaffee, in northwest Arkansas. They were unhappy in Arkansas and wanted to go to Miami. Several hundred escaped and had to be rounded up. Clinton sent two hundred National Guard troops to Chaffee and asked President Carter to order the Cubans to stay on the base. On June 1 there was a riot at Chaffee.

There were also those who believed Clinton had surrounded himself with too many college and law-school friends, too many Yale-Harvard types. In addition, the populace was angered at an unexpected increase in auto-license fees, in spite of the fact that Clinton had earmarked the money for highway improvements.

Some Arkansans thought Clinton was "too big for his britches" and too far removed from his roots to be a good governor. And others felt Hillary Rodham was too uninterested in her appearance as a woman. She seemed to be more hippie than professional, more dowdy and uncaring than feminine. And she did not even use her husband's name.

When Ronald Reagan was swept into the presidency in 1980 and Carter out of it, Arkansas experienced a coattail effect. Clinton was unseated in favor of his Republican opponent, Frank White. This was the first time in twenty-six years that an incumbent governor had been beaten in Arkansas. To Clinton's 403,241 votes, White got 435,684.

It was a grim blow to the young governor, who considered himself everybody's favorite. He took it badly but tried to maintain a hopeful front. Hillary Rodham and Bill Clinton appeared on the steps of the Capitol with Chelsea the morning after the election. Clinton declared:

"Hillary and I have shed a few tears for our loss of last evening, but we accept the will of our people with humility and with gratitude for having been given a chance to serve our state. . . . I grew up in an ordinary working family in this state, was able to go through the public schools and become attorney general and governor and serve people in the way that I had always wanted to since I was a boy."

But that was only an expedient, politically correct persona for Bill Clinton to exhibit. Inwardly he was crushed and dispirited. The decline into which he sank in the following months was precipitous and dangerous. There was no one who did not think he would try a comeback. But the big question still remained: Would he succeed?

As for Hillary, an even more serious question occupied her. Her professional reputation was growing. How would her husband, in his failure, view her success? And how would this situation affect their marriage?

CHAPTER NINE

Reaching Out

His defeat at the polls was a tremendous setback for Bill Clinton. But her husband's loss proved an even more stinging blow to Hillary Rodham, who had worked hard on his campaign. She had thought he would win despite the wave of Reaganism and the cry for "change" throughout the country in the wake of Jimmy Carter's administration.

In spite of the impressive voting figures—nearly 840,000 Arkansas had cast ballots—Frank White had won by more than thirty-two thousand votes. While hardly a landslide, the difference was enough to show a weakness in the passed-over governor's popularity.

Yet not all the newspapers were enthusiastic over the change. The *Arkansas Gazette* published an article titled "Clinton's Leave-Taking," noting, "It was a poignant scene as Clinton appeared before a joint session of the legislature in a crowded House chamber, his wife, Hillary, holding their ten-month-old daughter, at his side. Just two years earlier he had taken the oath in the same chamber as the nation's youngest governor, one whose intellect and personality were soon to capture national admiration and credit for the state. Now he was beaten, leaving the state government after a narrow upset loss in November, asking the people to 'remember me as one who reached for all he could for Arkansas.' "

The story then commented on the governor's farewell address. "It was an upstream speech, moving against the current of political fashion. But, as the governor remarked, Arkansas remains fifty-first—last—in the payment of state and local taxes: We pay less taxes than the people in any other state in the Union, not to mention the District of Columbia. Accordingly, we are at or near the bottom in the level of public services in nearly every category, from teacher salaries to higher education to unemployment compensation. There is but one answer—broadening the tax base—and the state will have to come to it, sooner or later, meantime settling for the barest minimums in the services expected in the American society."

The story closed with a farewell to Clinton. "It is sad to see Clinton go, departing public life for an indeterminate period before the comeback campaign . . . that everyone knows is certain. We have always thought of Bill Clinton as something special. No one in Arkansas in modern times has been elected governor so young with so much promise. If circumstances joined with certain errors in political judgment to deny him the customary second term, inevitably Clinton has learned lessons that will service him in the future."

Clinton had dedicated himself to serving the public as a leader. The voters' rejection after only two years in office could destroy the man to whom Hillary had committed her life. Largely because of Hillary's insistence, the Clintons took time out to travel to Israel in 1980. They joined a group organized by the Reverend Worley Oscar Vaught, the pastor of Bill Clinton's Immanuel Baptist Church in Little Rock. The trip was both a religious pilgrimage and a voyage that would give the onetime governor a change of scene and perhaps boost his morale a bit.

During the trip the Clintons visited most of the traditional tourist sites, including Galilee, Masada, the Western Wall, and, of course, the Old City of Jerusalem. The visit reinforced their support for the people of Israel. According to Sarah Ehrman, their friend from the McGovern days, "Bill and Hillary understand the profound effect that Israel has on American Jews and around the world and share a feeling for the security and stability of the State of Israel."

In his own way the Reverend Vaught helped solidify the Clintons' attitude toward Israel. "I have believed in supporting Israel as long as I have known anything about the issue," Clinton said later. "It may have something to do with my religious upbringing. For the last several years until he died, I was very much under the influence of my pastor.

"He was a close friend of Israel and began visiting even before the State of Israel was created. And when he was on his deathbed, he said to me that he hoped someday I would have a chance to run for President, but that if I ever let Israel down, God would never forgive me. I will never let Israel down."

It was the first time Hillary had heard her husband speak about running for the presidency of the United States, but it was no surprise to her. She thought that the therapy of travel had helped restore her husband's buoyancy and good feeling about himself. But once back in Little Rock, things seemed to go downhill.

It would be almost two years before the ex-governor could consider running for that office again. Husband and wife discussed briefly a run for the chairmanship of the Democratic National Committee, but there were some pitfalls in that job that might expose him to the strong political influences of Washington, D.C. Even Hillary knew that her husband did not want to move to Washington. He had his heart set on working in Arkansas.

Although Clinton could certainly have joined the Rose Law Firm, he did not want to operate too near Hillary, who was making great strides in her work there. Besides, he knew that he might not be quite so good a researcher and litigator as his wife. The idea of holding a lesser position in the same organization did not sit well.

Instead, he joined the Little Rock law firm of Wright, Lindsey, and Jennings—second only to Rose in Arkansas—where he established himself as a specialist in commercial litigation. However, he never hesitated to let it be known that this was a temporary post and that he would be back on the political circuit as soon as he could.

It was not the greatest therapy for Bill Clinton. He was not born to be a litigator. He was a servant of the people, a politician, pure and simple. To him working at the bar was a step down. Close friends said he was going into a period of depression and withdrawal. Typically and foremost an optimist, he seemed to have turned bitter about what he considered "unfair treatment" from the people he had served. He seemed without purpose or hope.

He said later in a speech at Yale, "When I decided I didn't want to give up and I wanted to go on in politics, I realized I had to be in better communication with the voters. I began to drive around the state and talk to people."

During 1981 he covered almost the entire state. In conversations with people who opposed him, he apologized for not listening to their problems and complaints. He spent seemingly endless hours with the people of Arkansas. Sometimes Hillary would join him. At other times, Betsey Wright, his campaign manager, and Bruce Lindsey, his law partner, would go along.

On one of his tours Bill Clinton stopped at an ancient service station in the countryside. It was, as he put it, a "kind of a political watering hole."

The attendant recognized him. "You're Bill Clinton, aren't you?"

"Yes, sir."

"Well, I cost you eleven votes, son," said the man. "And I loved every minute of it."

"You did?"

"I did. It was me and my two boys and their wives and six of my buddies. We just leveled you."

"Why did you do it?"

"I had to. You raised my car license."

Clinton pointed across the road. "Remember when that road right there was on the front page of the biggest newspaper in the state—because cars were buried in it and I had to send tractors down here to get those cars out?"

"I don't care, Bill. I still don't want to pay it."

"Let me ask you something else. Would you ever consider voting for me again?"

The attendant looked at Clinton. "You know, I would. We're even now."

Though Clinton was determined to win back the voters, it was not a happy time for him or Hillary, who worked hard at Rose while she managed the Clinton home. Clinton no longer seemed to be in control of his own life. Rumors began to filter into the newsrooms around Arkansas that Bill Clinton was having an affair with this woman or that woman. And the rumors persisted. Hillary heard them, too. There was little she could do about them except hope that they were untrue and would subside. Luckily the reporters and newspaper editors decided to ignore the stories and not write them up.

Later, Bill Clinton revealed that the most persistent rumors concerned Gennifer Flowers. He said in January 1992 that he had met her in the late 1970s when he was attorney general. She was "one of a number of young people who were working for the television stations around Little Rock." But she had left Little Rock and had gone to another state. For some years, Clinton said, he did not hear from her or know what she was doing. "Then she came back . . . sometime a few years [later] and went to work again in the state."

The Gennifer Flowers rumor first surfaced in the middle of 1980, Clinton said. "She was contacted and told about it," he said, and "she was so upset" she telephoned him. How could she be mentioned as having had an affair with him, she asked. During at least one of her telephone calls, Hillary listened to the conversation.

In 1992, she recalled the situation for a "60 Minutes" interview. "We reached out to them," she explained, referring to a number of women rumored to have had affairs with her husband. "I met with two of them to reassure them. They were friends of ours. I felt terrible about what was happening to them."

Hillary was specific about Gennifer Flowers. The woman was terribly concerned, she said. She felt that her life was ruined. She was probably right.

But Bill Clinton was every bit as upset, if not more so. He even asked a number of his close friends, "What am I supposed to do about these women who throw themselves at me?" His friends told him what to do. Resist the temptation and think about the effect an affair—or affairs—would have on his family and his political future.

Clinton spent two years at Wright, Lindsey, and Jennings. He could have built a more affluent life in private practice than in politics. Hillary had been elevated to full partner at Rose in 1979 and was the chief contributor to the Clintons' net worth, bringing in approximately $400,000 annually. As governor of Arkansas, Clinton made $35,000 a year. Yet Bill Clinton wanted only to get back on the hustings and run for office again. So he traveled the state, listening to repeated criticism of his performance as governor. He reached two conclusions about what he would do if he ran again.

First, he decided to confess to his errors and apologize, something politicians usually avoid. He would enter the race with that message. Second, he realized that he had tried to do too much during his first two years in office. Next time he would set a simple agenda, and at the center of that agenda would be improving education in the state of Arkansas.

Meanwhile, Hillary Rodham was getting her act together in a decisive and exceptionally telling manner. She devoted her time at Rose to juggling the emotional demands of family law and the economic concerns of commercial litigation. She also found time to work with other Little Rock lawyers on a variety of pro bono matters, ranging from criminal law to a high-profile case concerning the redistricting of schools in Little Rock and two neighboring suburbs.

Aiston Jennings Sr., the name partner of Wright, Lindsey, and Jennings, known as the "dean of the Arkansas trial bar," was impressed with Hillary during a child custody case in which he opposed her. "It obviously involved people of wealth and was hotly contested," he recalled. "There was a lot of evidence against my client that was not favorable, but what I think was the principal thing she did was to use depositions very effectively to search out additional evidence in her favor. She did not sit on her laurels because it looked better for her to begin with."

Vincent Foster, who worked closely with Hillary from the time she joined the firm, had a number of things to say about her. "Those kinds of cases are very tough," he pointed out. "She took domestic matters on, but it was not something that we were trying to encourage or promote at the law firm. So while she continued to do some family law quietly, she really was trying to build her commercial litigation practice."

Foster noted a particularly effective victory of Hillary's in that area, a 1982 breach of contract action involving the purchase of Little Rock's radio station KLRA by the Rose Law Firm's clients for three million dollars. Notably, the loser was Aiston Jennings.

Jennings noted wryly, "Well, she was still a young lawyer at the time, but she was not particularly green!" Hillary was, in fact, thirty-five then.

Foster recalled, "There was some human drama to the case because Aiston was close friends with the owner of the station. Plus, we were very excited because we were trying a case against Aiston. And we were even more excited to win."

Carol Arnold joined Rose in 1981. She became a Rose partner, then moved on to become a partner at Seattle's Preston Thorgrimson Shidler Gates and Ellis. "Hillary helped recruit me," Arnold said, "and she was also very supportive of new lawyers and new female lawyers in particular. She made opportunities for people who worked with her."

With Thomas Mars, then a Rose associate, Hillary handled a child custody case in Arkansas Chancery Court. "This was a real tough case emotionally," Mars said. "It involved a father who was living in Connecticut who wanted to get custody of his kids. I remember [Hillary's] closing remarks, which must have started at about nine at night. It was very moving, and the judge ruled in our favor right away. And getting custody for a father isn't always easy."

When Clinton was ready to start the run for the statehouse again, she was prepared to go along with him to help. She had given a lot of thought to what had gone wrong during her husband's two years in the governor's mansion. There were specifics, and Hillary jotted them down.

1. The increase in auto license fees
2. The Cuban riot at Fort Chaffee

3. The Yale-Harvard syndrome in the governor's mansion
4. Clinton's arrogance
5. Hillary's use of the name Rodham instead of Clinton
6. Hillary's casual appearance

This last reminded Hillary of her Arkansas Law School days, when she had been shocked to learn that the students thought she dressed sloppily. What mattered to them did not matter to Hillary, but perhaps it was time to reconsider some of her precepts.

She realized that she might indeed have had a great deal to do with her husband's defeat in his reelection campaign. Now she came to a decision. She would make it impossible for her husband's friends to complain about her dowdy and hippielike appearance. She would make a concession to the office to which her husband aspired and present herself as a more viable first lady.

In January 1982, Clinton entered the gubernatorial race exactly as he had proposed to do. He produced a one-minute commercial "mea culpa" message confessing his own faults and apologizing. "If you'll give me a chance to serve again," he told the public, "you'll have a governor who has learned from defeat that you can't lead without listening."

He also vowed that he would set a simple agenda, the central element of which would be education. He would raise Arkansas from its position at the absolute nadir of the nation. Clinton was referring to a 1978 study of Arkansas's schools by Kern Alexander, an education professor from the University of Florida, which had concluded that they were the worst in the country.

New education standards would have to be set, he told the electorate. In spite of the fact that he had been forced to withdraw his program for educational reform during his first term, he said he was determined to improve Arkansas's educational image. And he did have Hillary at his side. She had headed the Rural Health Advisory Committee during his first term, but her main expertise involved children and, peripherally, education.

John Brummett, of the *Arkansas Gazette,* had never been particularly excited about Hillary Rodham. "She didn't seem to care too much about the First Lady role when she started," he wrote. "That Hillary has sort of disappeared." At first, though, "she didn't make any concessions to the trappings of the office of governor. She looked hippie-ish."

But quite suddenly a stunning new Hillary appeared. "The heavy glasses were replaced by contact lenses," he wrote, "the brown hair was streaked blond, baggy dresses gave way to stylish suits, and lipstick and eye shadow brightened her face."

Brummett concluded, "There's the first-term Hillary and the comeback Hillary. It's a fairly stark difference between the two."

According to a friend, "Hillary just decided it was time to start wearing makeup and get her hair fixed right. It's that old thing of getting lighted up within."

Hillary herself played down the change. "I have been trying to wear contact lenses since I was sixteen, but I could never get the hard lenses to stay in my eyes. I'm really near-sighted, so I had a choice—either try to wear hard contacts and not see or wear my glasses. So, obviously, I wore my glasses." Technological advances, however, had been made in the lens industry.

As for the fashionable styling of her hair, Hillary said, "I like to experiment with my hair. I mean, I don't even know what it's going to look like this time next year. I just think you should have some fun with your life and not take yourself real seriously."

But the change that must have been the hardest to make was her name. Overnight Ms. Hillary Rodham became Mrs. Hillary Clinton. "I gave [Ms. Hillary Rodham] up. It meant more to them [her husband's constituents] than it did to me."

The *Arkansas Gazette* wrote, "Mrs. Clinton is almost certainly the best speaker among politicians' wives, probably the only one who can fully engage an audience on her own merits, rather than just as somebody's wife.

"She is an Illinois native, perhaps a little brisker, a little more outspoken than the traditional Southern governor's lady. . . . The name change indicates that she's working at softening her image a bit. . . .

"And succeeding, apparently. She has become a good hand-shaking campaigner in the traditional Arkansas style."

In the second round, Clinton won 431,855 votes, or 54.7 percent, to Frank White's 357,496.

He was back. And he would remain in Little Rock, as governor of Arkansas, for the next ten years.

CHAPTER TEN

The Chairperson

It was as if Bill Clinton had never left the governor's mansion. In his January 1983 inaugural address, he said his first and most important duty would be to put people back to work. He then turned to his main objective:

"Over the long run, education is the key to our economic revival and our perennial quest for prosperity. We must dedicate more of our limited resources to paying teachers better; expanding educational opportunities in poor and small school districts; improving and diversifying vocational and high technology programs; and perhaps more important, strengthening basic education. Without competence in basic skills, our people cannot move on to more advanced achievement."

Already on the books was an Arkansas Supreme Court mandate to increase education funding on a statewide basis. Eleven school districts had filed a lawsuit against the state, claiming that the distribution of education funds was unequal and hence unconstitutional. The supreme court agreed. The majority opinion, stating that the disparity in property tax revenues among different parts of the state was not sufficiently compensated by the state's partial equalization formula, found funding so unequal that it was unfair.

Clinton's reform package began to take shape when he appointed a fifteen-member commission to devise a set of minimum standards for schools. The standards were to take effect in 1984, with all districts required to meet them by 1987. Those districts that failed would be required to consolidate with districts that met the standards.

The fifteen members of the commission were teachers or administrators, mostly from the small communities in the state. But the governor's coup was the appointment of the chairperson: Hillary Rodham Clinton. And the selection was a calculated risk for the reelected governor.

For it was not the old Hillary Rodham who appeared in the limelight now. It was the brand-new Hillary Clinton. New name. New hair. New contacts. New clothes. A softer, gentler Hillary Clinton.

It was Hillary Clinton's first starring role in Arkansas. With the exception of the Rural Health Advisory Committee, her work prior to 1983 had been confined to her profession as attorney. She was a working wife engaged in a profession outside the home. She had never appeared with her husband in his work as governor except for making speeches during his campaigns.

Now, on her own, she was to discharge an important public duty. Like the other members of the vital committee, she would serve without pay. That Hillary and her husband had discussed her work on the committee was obvious from an early statement of his:

"This [selecting Hillary to chair the committee] guarantees that I will have a person who is closer to me than anyone else overseeing a project that is more important to me than anything else. I don't know if it's a politically wise move, but it's the right thing to do." Exactly the right note: the hint of deference to the public reaction to such a move; at the same time, a resounding affirmation of his wife's qualifications not only as someone close to him but as someone who knew what she was doing in the pursuit of educational standards.

"I've gone to school a large part of my life," Hillary said. "I've been involved in classroom activities and visiting with teachers as a volunteer." She added that most of the expertise in producing the committee's report and recommendations would come from the members of the committee. She would be the leader and organizer, not the most active of those producing input.

Coincidentally, a report by the National Commission on Excellence in Education appeared at just about the time Hillary assumed the chair of the Arkansas Education Standards Committee. Titled "Nation at Risk," it spoke of a "rising tide of mediocrity" in the schools across the country. The first step Hillary took was to assure the public that the committee would study Arkansas's school system with that report in mind.

A look at Arkansas's educational statistics proved disheartening. Hillary found that the typical Arkansas student ranked far below the national average in reading and math scores on the Science Research Associates standardized tests.

Some 76 percent of the state's students, in 162 high schools, were offered the courses that the Commission on Excellence report suggested, but none of the state's 371 districts demanded that students take all the subjects the commission said should be required.

The report recommended not only a longer school day but a longer school year. In Arkansas, few schools were in session for more than the state requirement of 175 days per year; the commission called for 220.

The governor talked to the committee during their first meeting, telling them that their work would be "as important as any to be done in public life in the next few years." He promised that once the committee had submitted its report he would call a special session of the legislature for the money to pay for their recommendations. His target, he noted, was to get a draft of new standards by the 1983–84 school year.

The committee enthusiastically endorsed the governor's recommendations. It was their intention, the committee members said, to make vital changes in Arkansas education. "I would be happy if what we came out with caused absolute panic—even in my own house," Hillary said.

Funding would be the biggest problem. No one knew where the money was coming from to implement whatever the committee finally decided on.

Normally the Arkansas legislature met only sixty days every two years, but under the constitution, the governor could call a special session at any time he deemed necessary. As the committee did its work, the governor made plans for a special session of the legislature to consider education funding and a new formula for allocating money to for the schools; the old formula had been invalidated by the supreme court's finding.

As head of the education commission, Hillary traveled all over the state, holding hearings and meetings with parents and teacher associations. So did the governor, taking every opportunity to gain support for educational reform on a grass-roots level. "We have today a historic obligation to equalize funding and to improve education," Clinton stressed.

The strategy was to prepare the public for some kind of tax increase that would undoubtedly be highly unpopular. The public in general believed in education—if it didn't cost money. Even the people involved in education were suspicious of any new moves. They were worried about how any changes would affect them. But the governor persisted in wooing them all.

In pursuit of its basic objective, the commission proposed a so-called minimum-competence test for eighth-graders, a test that would allow them to be promoted to the ninth grade. Students would also be tested at the third-grade level for minimum competence in reading and mathematics and in the sixth grade in reading, math, language arts, social studies, and science. On all three levels the tests would affect promotion.

But the students were not the only targets of the commission's proposals. Arkansas teachers would also be required to conform to a standard of excellence. The commission felt that the students could be only as good as those who taught them. And if the students had to prove themselves, the teachers should, too. So it was proposed that all teachers be required to take the National Teacher Examination regardless of how long they had been in the teaching profession.

Some of the other major components of the new standards included:

1. A maximum class size of twenty students in kindergarten; an average of twenty-three and maximum of twenty-five in grades one through three; an average of twenty-five and maximum of twenty-eight in grades seven through twelve, with an exception for classes such as band or choir
2. A specified thirteen and a half units that must be taken for graduation: four of English; five of mathematics and sciences; two of social studies; one of practical arts or a third unit of social studies; a half unit each of physical education, health education, and fine arts
3. Lengthening of the school year from 175 days to 180 by 1989–90
4. Provision of one counselor for every 450 high school students and every 600 elementary students

The teacher-testing requirement would provoke the greatest controversy in getting the commission's recommendations passed by the state.

"She did a magnificent job," John Brummett wrote in *Working Woman,* speaking about Hillary Clinton's work as chairperson of the Education Standards Committee. "I'm not one of her biggest fans, but I give credit where credit is due. She worked hard and competently and built political consensus for reducing class size, increasing accountability—it was masterful."

Hillary's Standards Committee completed its report and released it to the public on September 6, 1983, less than a year after Governor Clinton had appointed the committee. She held a press conference as she issued copies of the report.

"Our schools are not doing as good a job as they must," she said. "While there may be many causes for our dilemma, there is only one solution. We Arkansans have to quit making excuses and accept instead the challenge of excellence once and for all."

She pointed out that a school that produced illiterates or semiliterates committed educational fraud. "There is a feeling of urgency and a need for changes in education. If we do not seize the opportunity we have now, we will go backward."

The media reaction was all positive. Ernest Dumas, a columnist on the *Arkansas Gazette,* wrote that the committee should be praised for "not limiting its vision and not being oppressed by the practicalities of Arkansas's low station." However, he was not sanguine about the possibility of getting Hillary Clinton's standards passed by the politicos in control of the statehouse.

"Not that the standards are radical. The requirements on curriculum, graduation, faculty staffing, and length of school terms are in line with what are generally required across the country. . . . But most Arkansas school districts don't meet those requirements now, and the standards may be beyond the reach of fifty or more tiny districts. . . .

"What is innovative and refreshing about the recommendations of Mrs. Clinton's committee is that the state for the first time will not only measure paper staffing and classrooms but how well every school actually performs in educating children. . . .

"The criticism will be that schools often will resort to devoting exorbitant attention to teaching the tests. But the result will be that everyone in the educational system, from the teachers to the state Education Department, will have a stake in every child's development. It will not be bad if the schools must redouble their attention to the needs of each child."

The recommendations were enthusiastically endorsed in principle by the state Board of Education. On October 4, 1983, Governor Clinton formally proposed a tax increase to provide the new funds that would be needed to implement them. The cost would range from $158 million to $175 million.

"To put it bluntly," Clinton said, "we've got to raise taxes to increase our investment in education. Arkansas is dead last in spending per child, and the

Arkansas Supreme Court has just ordered us to spend more money in poorer districts to improve education there."

The governor went on, "I hope to be able to convince you that we have to raise this money for education if we ever hope to get out of the economic backwater of our country, that this expenditure can bring greater economic opportunities to us, and that my program will do just that."

Clinton was dealing with a state that had always been *poor.* Arkansas had the lowest proportion of residents with college degrees, only 9.8 percent. The state had long based its economic-development strategy on using depressed wages and low taxes to attract industry from the North. Accustomed to being near the bottom of most quality-of-life rankings, Arkansas had coined a jocular phrase: "Only Mississippi kept Arkansas from ranking fiftieth of all fifty states."

During Clinton's first year as governor, in 1979, the state's per capita income was $6,183, the next to lowest figure in the United States; Mississippi was last. That year the national average was $7,820. Even now the state had not moved perceptibly upward. Nevertheless, he was asking for support from the public and the legislators to bring about the recommendations of Hillary's commission.

"We have been given an opportunity that we have never been given before and that, if we fail to seize, we will probably never be given again." Clinton added. "And I ask for your personal commitment because it will personally benefit you, your children, your grandchildren, and the future of the state we all love so much."

The teaching community in Arkansas reacted strongly to the implication that their competence was in question. Ermalee Boice, assistant executive director of the Arkansas Education Association, said, "House Bill 47 will single out Arkansas as the only state that believes that its teachers are so bad they have to pass a literacy test. I think Arkansas can do without that. I will guarantee to you that if this bill passes, you will lose more good teachers than you will weed out bad ones."

Hillary Clinton disagreed. She maintained that teacher testing would clearly benefit all teachers in the system. She said to the senate, "I think we have to hit head-on the widespread public belief that we have a lot of incompetent teachers because I don't think we can build a constituency for education unless we do confront that. . . . I think it will clear the air of a lot of misconceptions and inaccuracies about our teachers."

Interestingly enough, the original draft of the Standards Committee contained no suggestion that there should be teacher testing. The issue was addressed only in vague terms, such as recommendations that all teachers be certified and that teachers acquire additional educational experience in their subjects.

The original draft of the Standards Committee stated, "The problem of teacher accountability begins in higher education, and we think teacher education is inadequate in many respects. The governor is quite probably looking at teacher accountability in the context of his overall recommendations."

The governor's package included the following proposals for raising the required $179.4 million:

1. Raise the state sales tax from 3 to 4 percent ($91 million the first year and $161.7 million per year thereafter)
2. Raise the tax on natural gas
3. Raise the corporate income tax from 6 to 7 percent for corporations with income over $100,000 per year
4. Tax membership in country clubs and other private clubs
5. Eliminate all but $200 a month of the 2 percent total sales tax collections for retailers
6. Tax services now excluded from the sales tax
7. Place the sales tax on cable TV bills

Most of the proposals failed to pass in the legislature. However, because of a quirk in Arkansas law, it took only a one-third majority of both houses to approve a sales-tax increase, but two-thirds to approve other kinds of tax increases. So, of all the proposals, only the sales-tax increase was approved.

The toughest part of the package to pass was the teacher-testing provision. The Arkansas Education Association did everything it could to prevent that piece of legislation from going through the house. The AEA had supported a filibuster in the Arkansas senate and had stopped a vote on the house version of the testing bill. It had also distributed letters to the senate quoting the Educational Testing Service advising the governor that the proposed use of teacher tests was improper and "perhaps illegal."

In turn, the governor was outraged and publicly announced that if the AEA defeated the teacher-testing bill he would kill his own proposed one-cent sales tax increase, thereby leaving teachers without raises and schools without funds to implement the new standards. "There will be no tax increase without a testing bill," he proclaimed.

Dr. Kai Erickson, the executive director of the AEA, called Clinton "irresponsible" and accused him of being "hot and overreacting."

Clinton said, "The AEA leadership apparently cares nothing about teacher raises, more money for standards, or more money for higher education." He accused the head of the AEA of being concerned "solely to protect a few teachers who might be incompetent." He was resentful that the AEA had failed to support any of his tax bills. In response, the AEA held that the teacher-testing proposal was a "witch hunt."

Finally, at the end of October 1983, Hillary and the governor celebrated the passage of the crucial bill through both houses. And on November 4, the tax increase was approved. Even though the sales tax paid for the new education reforms, the increase would leave Arkansas as usual in fiftieth place as the state with the lightest state and local tax burden. But Hillary's education package was now law.

"You've done a lot to assure a better future for the young people of this state," Clinton told the General Assembly, "and for the rest of us, too."

He regretted that the only tax bill that had succeeded was the sales tax, but was grateful for the fact that it had been passed. "This is a beginning, not an end, to the work we must do," he said, and pledged a more equitable tax system for his constituency, citing the state's low tax as an example of what was wrong with the system.

Despite the passage of the teacher-testing bill—actually the regulation called for all public school educators, including principals and superintendents to take the test—the Clintons were still subjected to hostility and demonstrations by teachers across the state. There were times when Hillary Clinton would bristle with anger as she walked through the corridors of a school, with the hisses and snide comments of teachers echoing in her ears. It was even more embarrassing when she was in the company of friends who were still in the teaching profession.

John Brummett of the *Gazette* pointed out that the struggle of the governor and his wife to pass the bill had strained to the utmost any relationship of cooperation between the Clintons and the seventeen thousand members of the AEA. He added there was "harsh public bitterness and nasty private name calling, totally the result of Mr. Clinton's insistence on requiring teachers to take a basic skills test in exchange for the nice raises most of them will likely get from his tax program."

"I was exceedingly disappointed when they testified against some of the standards," Clinton told Brummett, "disregarding the fact that I'd appointed three people to the Standards Committee [whom] they wanted. And I was equally disappointed when they made no concerted effort in support of any of the revenue bills."

At an AEA convention in Little Rock in November 1983, Ermalee Boice of the AEA told the teachers that they and the Clintons were "at war."

The governor spoke to another group the same day, predicting that the teacher tests would "show that an overwhelming majority of our teachers are well prepared to do the job they have been hired on to do, and that will bolster public support."

As a reaction to the Clinton-AEA battle, the Arkansas Association of Professional Educators, a rival organization with about four hundred members, asked its people to promote actively their willingness to take competence and subject-area tests. The association declared, "The too-much-publicized campaign of the AEA against teacher testing is doing irreparable harm to our profession."

The Clintons were ready to give the rebellious teachers a taste of their own medicine. On November 19, the governor was scheduled to speak to a group of eight hundred AEA delegates at its convention in Little Rock. Clinton's mother had been tipped off that he would be given the silent treatment by the audience. There would be no welcome, no applause, and the teachers would studiously ignore him.

She related the story later to the press. "He came in the back door, walked directly to the stage, made his speech, did not go up and down the aisle to visit with people, did not open it [the speech] to questions and answers, and totally ignored [AEA President] Peggy Nabors. And he just made his speech and left by the same way. . . .

"I'll never forget it as long as I live. . . . I was with a group of people, and we were walking out of this meeting. And I usually keep my mouth out of Bill's affairs. . . . But there was a professor walking right behind me, or a teacher . . . so help me, his words were, 'I ain't gonna take no damn test!' I couldn't help it. I turned around, and I said, 'Sir, that's a double negative, and that means that you will take the damn test.' "

Even the National Education Association soon followed suit in condemning the testing law. It said it would work for repeal or amendment of the law and would legally challenge it. The NEA criticized the law first as being "an educationally unsound testing statute that will not contribute to educational excellence in the Arkansas public schools" and then as a measure that demeaned "the education profession, deceives the public, and is detrimental to the teaching and learning process."

The Educational Testing Service announced in November 1983 that it would not allow its National Teacher Examination to be used to evaluate teachers who were already on the job, since it was designed only to test new teachers, fresh out of college. "It is morally and educationally wrong to tell someone who has been judged a satisfactory teacher for many years that passing a certain test on a certain day is necessary to keep his or her job," said Gregory Anrig, president of the Educational Testing Service.

"We don't need their tests," Clinton shot back. "We can get them from some other state or school district."

In March 1984, the NEA issued a report on the teacher-testing issue. It was, as might have been expected, a nasty, negative, stinging response aimed at putting Clinton on the defensive. Yet the governor said he could continue to work with Arkansas teachers who wanted to improve education. Many teachers in the state, he said, had given him a good deal of positive feedback about the education programs. But the report caused the governor to rebut it.

Clinton placed the blame for the discontent of the Arkansas teaching community squarely on the shoulders of the Arkansas Education Association. He said that the AEA had established "a deliberate, organized, and systematic opposition to the testing provision, to blind people to the fact that if you flunk the test it just identifies a group of people who have to go through a development plan."

He added that Arkansas should look at what other states, even other countries, were doing in the area of teacher testing. "We need to be able to say with confidence that we are going to have a nationally competitive system for certifying teachers, that we are going to have as modern, as adequate, as sensible an approach to our teacher education program as exists anywhere."

In March 1984, Clinton announced that he had selected a firm to implement the teacher-testing program. Instructional Objectives Exchange, a firm in Culver City, California, would administer a basic skills test between March 15 and April 30, 1985. The cost would be about $300,000. The test would be given.

In the give-and-take between Clinton and the teachers' union, Hillary Clinton maintained as low a profile as possible. Even so, she knew that everyone in the teaching profession knew that she, as chairperson of the commission, was the spearhead of the governor's project.

CHAPTER ELEVEN

From Israel With Love

On her visit to Israel in 1980, Hillary Clinton had been impressed by a preschool program developed by the National Council of Jewish Women to encourage parents to teach their own children the skills that would make them good students once they entered the public school system. The program was aimed at children four or five years of age, just prior to or about the age at which most started kindergarten. It was designed to help young mothers improve their parenting skills and also to help foster their children's educational development later on in school.

In 1985, Hillary Clinton became instrumental in establishing a similar program in Arkansas. In adapting the program to the United States, some changes had to be made, since the original Israeli program involved mothers who were not out of the home working but were rather in-house mothers. The program was called the Home Instruction Program for Preschool Youngsters, or as the acronym had it, HIPPY. Once it was under way Hillary spent a great deal of energy on bringing the program to the attention of the educators in Arkansas.

HIPPY was introduced in a statewide ground-breaking conference on preschool programs. Under the Arkansas program, tutors, teachers, and aides went into homes to show impoverished mothers how to teach their four- and five-year-old at home. Underprivileged children who would usually get little or no schooling at home were given a head start over their more affluent peers.

From the beginning HIPPY was an odds-on favorite of Hillary's. As she once said, "It became clear to me that we could have the most astonishing schools in the world and we would still not be reaching the needs of all of our children, because half of all learning occurs by the time a person is five. And the way that our children are treated in the first five years—the way their health is attended to, to say nothing of intellectual stimulation and family support—will have a very big influence on how well they can do for the rest of their lives.

"Most people who have the kind of impoverished, often neglectful backgrounds that we see so often among many of our children today just come into school with so many problems that it's very difficult to deal with. I do not believe that there are very many parents who are deliberately harmful to their children. There are some and there will always be some. . . .

"But there are countless numbers of adults who do not know what to do for their children and do not know how to be an effective parent. And they need help and they need support to be able to fulfill that most basic function. So a good preschool program, whether it's center-based or home-based, has to help the family understand how to fulfill its obligations to little children."

About the HIPPY program itself, she said, "I am just absolutely convinced that an investment in preschool is one of the smartest investments Arkansas can make. The single biggest determinant, based on the studies that I've seen, as to whether a child finished school and how well that child does, is the educational level of the mother. And a mother doesn't have to be, herself, well educated to see that her child succeeds, but she has to understand the value of education.

"A lot of other programs are well-meaning, but they basically put too much responsibility on the mother. I mean, if the mother knew what she was supposed to do, she would go do it. But to be told, on television, or to come to a community meeting or even to a school meeting where someone stands up and lectures and says here's what you should do for your child, is like speaking a foreign language to many of these people. They have to be shown how to do it. They have to be, in a sense, 're-parented' to be able to be a good parent. And HIPPY has a structure to try to do that, which is very simplistic in many ways, but within the grasp of even illiterate parents."

Hillary's interest in Arkansas's HIPPY was not misplaced. From its inception in the early 1980s, it became the largest HIPPY program in the United States, with over twenty-four hundred mothers participating.

"The HIPPY program builds in its own follow-up by changing the parent into the child's first teacher, which is what every parent should be," Bill Clinton said.

The results of the program went beyond the wildest hopes of those who founded it. Testing recently in one school district showed an average gain of thirty-three months during sixteen months of participation. Scores on the Metropolitan Achievement Test for HIPPY children came out much higher than expected.

While her activism with groups like HIPPY was considered outstanding and was at least noncontroversial, many of Hillary's statements and actions had the opposite effect. As she had always been during her college days, Hillary was an activist who could not resist a hands-on response to anything to do with education. In stating her thoughts on educational principles and practices she continually roused the ire of her husband's constituents. She had written a great deal about children's rights and had expressed other points of view in educational matters, taking positions that were not always in agreement with the majority.

Much of this talk had to do with the teaching of children. Because Arkansas was a state in which the electorate was at best conservative in its approach to life, many parents were not in favor of bureaucrats, government workers, and even teachers and social workers when they "interfered" with parental care of children. When Hillary spoke, she frequently stirred up those parents who did not believe in government involvement with their life-styles or those of their children.

One of Hillary's speeches belabored the "old boy network" in the Arkansas school system. "One thing which I think would improve the quality of education about 100 percent in five years is to increase by one-hundred-fold the number of women superintendents and principals. I think if you go into schools and talk with the people who understand children and are sensitive to their needs, many of them are women who have absolutely no chance of exerting leadership in the present system.

"What I find after going from school to school is that the good teachers, many of them are women, have adapted a strategy of defensiveness toward the outside administration. They basically close their doors and say, 'I'm not going to let those people get to me and my students; and I'm going to do the best I can this year.'

"The principal, who is often a fellow who took the night courses and wrote the thesis at the school of education about basketball theory and is working his way up to superintendent, doesn't have a clue about how to get the most out of his teachers, how to encourage that development, that spark, that enthusiasm. He's not a bad guy, he's a good guy. But he is not a leader in education."

Fortunately, most of Hillary Clinton's more progressive opinions did not surface to make trouble for her husband among his constituency. However, many involved educational matters, and they did cause the teaching community to rise against her several times. The governor was still in a day-to-day battle with two powerful teachers' unions, the AEA and the NEA. Hillary's remarks would frequently boomerang, taking a swipe at him as they passed.

In 1984, when the governor was preparing his campaign for reelection, his trouble did not stem from his policies of government or even from his policies with women. This time his difficulty involved his younger half brother, Roger Clinton Jr.

It was in May 1984 that Colonel Tommy Goodwin, the director of the Arkansas State Police, telephoned the governor. The call was about Roger. Clinton's younger brother, then twenty-eight, was under observation for the distribution of cocaine.

Clinton was dismayed. He had had his suspicions about Roger, and indeed it soon developed that Roger had been using drugs since he was fifteen years old. He was now up to four grams a day, deep into addiction.

And so it was up to the state police. "What do you want us to do?" Goodwin asked the governor.

Clinton sighed. "Do what you'd normally do."

Bill Clinton was in a quandary. Here was a police investigation going on involving his younger brother. Roger was bound to be caught in the act, since he was apparently dealing as well as using. Clinton turned to Hillary. She was the strongest one in his family. She was also the only one he could confide in. His mother could not be told; it would hurt her too much. One more blow might be too much for her. She had lived through so many crises in her life.

Roger's father had died in 1967 of cancer, after which Dorothy Clinton had married Jeff Dwire, who died of a heart ailment, complicated by diabetes, in 1974. In 1982 she had married Dick Kelley, a top executive with Kelley Brokerage Company in Little Rock.

It was not right, either, to expect Dick Kelley to come to his stepson's aid. Instead, it was all up to Bill Clinton. He knew what had to be done.

Hillary immediately reverted to form. She collected a box full of literature on drug addiction and read it with her husband. Unfortunately, understanding drug abuse did not give them any sort of handle on how to put a stop to it.

There was no getting close to Roger, either. Three months later he was arrested by the state police in Hot Springs and booked on five counts of distributing cocaine and one count of conspiracy to distribute.

Of course, the press knew immediately what had happened. The story made all the papers, radio, and television. Bill Clinton, who was deeply wounded both personally and politically by these charges against his younger brother, was unable to come up with anything but a typically boilerplate statement.

"This is a time of great pain and sadness for me and my family," he said. "My brother has apparently become involved with drugs, a curse which has reached epidemic proportions and has plagued the lives of millions of families in our nation, including many in our own state. I ask for the prayers of our people at this difficult time for my brother, for my family, and for me. I love my brother very much and will be of comfort to him, but I want his case to be handled exactly as any other similar case would be."

But inside, Clinton was having second thoughts about himself. He had spent frustrating and painful years with Roger Clinton Sr., his stepfather. Now Roger Jr. had become addicted to drugs as his father had become addicted to alcohol. Might not Bill Clinton be subject to an addiction of some kind himself?

He had always experienced such nagging doubts in those early years when he had observed Roger Sr. and tried to maintain his distance from him. His fears had caused him to maintain at all times an attitude of optimism and hope. Sometimes the facade appeared to be about to crack. But he had always been able to pull himself together and continue to radiate that in-control, very cool attitude of total self-confidence.

Roger persisted in his denials of addiction. It meant less to Bill Clinton that his brother was an addict than that Roger had been dealing drugs, feeding this poison to innocent people—some of them barely out of their teens. "You don't understand," he told Roger at one point. "You've been putting cocaine into the bodies of others for money. I want you to go to prison for ten years. You're my brother, and I love you, but I want you to go away for a long, long time."

If Roger had hoped that his brother, being the governor of the state, might be able to buy off the police or the courts, he eventually realized that he would not be given any breaks. In November, three months after he was arrested,

Roger was finally persuaded to change his plea from innocent to guilty on two drug-related charges. For the first charge, he got a suspended three-year sentence. On the second, he was sent to prison for two years.

"It was a nightmare," Clinton said later. "But it was the right thing to do. He had a four-gram-a-day habit. They said if he hadn't been in incredible physical shape, he would have died."

After his brother was sentenced to two years, the governor called a press conference. "I accept the judgment of the court with respect," he said. "Now all of us in my brother's family must do everything we can to help him free himself of his drug dependency. I hope the publicity this case received will discourage other young people from involvement with drugs and will increase public awareness of the staggering dimensions of the drug problem in our state and nation. I am more deeply committed than ever before to do all that I can do to fight against illegal drugs and to prevent other families from experiencing the personal tragedy and pain drug abuse has brought to us."

Roger went to jail thoroughly convinced that he had been betrayed by his brother, who, with his connections, should have been able to keep him from the humiliation of prison. Yet within the strictures of the prison system, as he was finally cured of his addiction, he realized that his brother had really saved his life.

As for the governor, his concern about his own motives and attitudes brought him around to a consideration that he had never dared admit before. Perhaps, he thought, he had ignored the needs of people close to him in order to realize his own ambitions. Perhaps his drive for supremacy was out of control.

Clinton said, "I finally realized how my compulsive and obsessive ambition got in the way. I think that dealing with [Roger's drug problem] helped me to achieve some better balance."

Roger recalled, "He [Bill] was my best friend . . . my brother . . . my father . . . my protector. It's always wonderful and never difficult to be the brother of Bill Clinton because he's a wonderful person. It's just his position that's sometimes awfully tough to handle."

After his release, Roger made a number of speeches about the dangers of drug abuse to children across the state of Arkansas. He was not required to do so as a condition of parole or probation, but simply spoke because he wanted to help young people avoid what he had gone through.

Two years later, at a Children's Defense Fund dinner, Hillary Clinton invited Bill to speak on drugs, and he commented: "Now 100,000 kids in my state know what can happen to them."

The story of Roger's problem did not end there. Although no names or details have been revealed, friends have noted that he was a cause for a second time of personal trouble between Hillary and Bill Clinton.

Roger's arrest had caused all of Bill's self-doubts to surface again, strongly enough to becloud his perception. His self-respect was in tatters. He felt himself a failure for not perceiving Roger's problem and helping him. His mood swings became more and more frequent.

Once again rumors of extramarital affairs began to waft through Arkansas newsrooms. Reporters who did not perceive themselves as attached to him watched carefully for any slip that might indicate the identity of the other woman—or women. But nothing came to light.

Hillary knew about the rumors. She knew more than her friends did. But she kept her silence. They had been married for nine years now. She was thirty-eight years old. They had weathered other personal storms.

Yet there were periods of tension and anger. Unsubstantiated stories spread about fights in the governor's mansion.

"Their rows used to get pretty loud," one informant was quoted as saying. "On one occasion Hillary and Bill got into a fight at his office—and when she came storming out, he stood at the top of the stairs yelling: 'I'm still the governor here, bitch, and don't you forget it!' "

When Roger was released from prison in 1985, a period of intense family therapy began. This exercise was presumably a good thing for Bill Clinton, who said later that it "forced him to wrestle with the dark forces inside him." It opened up a new field of interest for him. At that time he also began reading studies on children of alcoholics, in the search to understand himself better.

In 1986, the governor won the election for his third term. His inauguration address underlined his continued dedication to making education in Arkansas better and better.

"Our administration will pursue an ambitious agenda for Arkansas's future, an agenda based on our commitment to economic growth, our commitment to excellence in education, and our commitment to increased security and stability for our people."

He had more to say about the educational program. "Our education program has a simple goal: to retain the progress of the special session on education and build on it. . . . We must not weaken the standards or repeal the testing laws."

But the battle between the educational community and the Clintons continued even then. A determined Hillary Clinton spoke out: "I don't want to pick up another project and devote a lot of time to it until I feel like I have carried through on my responsibility to the people of Arkansas—as well as to my own daughter—to do what I can to make sure these education standards are in place and that they do what we hoped they would do when we passed them."

She added that part of the reason for those educational standards was to "provide a better-educated work force in Arkansas so we can be more competitive for jobs." She noted that Arkansas still had "a long way to go to convince ourselves, as well as people outside of Arkansas, that our citizens are educated to the point that will enable them to compete with workers from not just around the country but around the world."

Testing time for teachers, determined by the Arkansas government, was drawing nigh. The Arkansas Education Association was getting louder and louder in its denunciations of both Clintons. Hillary took as much abuse as her husband. She grew used to walking down school hallways facing the dirty looks of teachers.

At a meeting of education reporters in Atlanta, Georgia, Hillary said that she and her husband "sort of feel like combat veterans." She accused the AEA of not supporting many of the standards involving the school curriculum, standards they should have endorsed.

Finally, on March 23, 1985, 25,077 educators took the mandated test. That was over 90 percent of the Arkansas teachers and administrators. Nothing was easy when it came to the final action of administering these tests. First of all, rumblings spread about a threatened boycott, which did not materialize. More seriously, there were rumors everywhere that copies of the test had been leaked in advance to privileged people; the Department of Education had to release a statement denying the rumors and stating that the integrity of the test had not been compromised. A lawsuit challenging the constitutionality of the test was dismissed by a state court judge the day before the test was given.

When the results of the test were analyzed, black teachers had a higher rate of failure than white teachers. That produced more searing indictments of the Clintons. Teachers who failed the test were given a year's grace period in which they could retake it as many times as necessary to pass. About 10 percent failed each time the test was given. In the end, 1,315 teachers—3.5 percent of the state's total—were forced to leave teaching because they could not pass. Failure rates were higher in the areas of Arkansas that had large black populations. This brought about more criticism.

Despite all the criticism and dissension, Clinton told the *Arkansas Gazette* that, for him, improving the education system in the state was "more important . . . than anything I have ever done in politics."

Dr. Tommy Venters, director of the Arkansas Department of Education, considered the governor's role in educational reform second to Hillary Clinton's exemplary leadership as chair of the Standards Committee.

"She actually carried the ball, along with Dr. [Don] Roberts and me, when we were both directors of the Department of Education. I can remember periods of time where the governor's wife would be out on the road every night making meetings along with me and others. So I think that the credit for being the person that . . . works with the legislature and the people goes to Governor Clinton, but the actual groundwork goes to other people."

CHAPTER TWELVE

"*What a Windbag!*"

As far back as 1967, when Bill Clinton was in college at Georgetown and Hillary Rodham had not yet met him, he was a regular client of Danny Thomason's, an Arkansas optometrist who came from Hampton, population 838. Danny Thomason had a younger brother, Harry, an aspiring producer of low-grade motion pictures. Commuting between Little Rock and Hollywood meant making a living the hard way. He had a wife, a daughter, and a house to keep up in Arkansas, and the Hollywood life-style was expensive.

A graduate of Southern Arkansas University, Harry worked as a high school coach between commutes. He would hitch rides to Los Angeles on Federal Express planes, having befriended some of the pilots, and stay at a cheap Burbank motel. His peripatetic life-style did not sit well with his wife and daughter, and soon his marriage collapsed. His heart belonged to Hollywood.

Through Danny Thomason, Harry was introduced to Bill Clinton, who was interested in Hollywood for another reason. He wanted to entice the film industry into shooting films in Arkansas. Harry agreed to sell Arkansas to Hollywood.

In the early 1980s, Harry met Linda Bloodworth. They almost shared an

Arkansas birthright: She was born in Poplar Bluff, Missouri, near the Arkansas border. Linda had left Poplar Bluff and journeyed westward to California in the early 1970s. She tried journalism for a while, since she had always had a flair for writing, but tired of the work and became a high school teacher in Watts. Free-lancing at night, she wrote some television scripts and scored with an episode of "M*A*S*H" coauthored with an actress-friend. She wrote more sitcoms and tried to create her own series.

It was during these days of trial and error that she met Harry Thomason. His marriage had ended, and he was then working on "The Fall Guy," a series starring Lee Majors. They were married in 1983 in Linda's hometown. According to Linda, over six hundred guests attended. "It got out of hand," Harry admitted.

Linda Bloodworth did not see herself as Mrs. Harry Thomason. She became Linda Bloodworth-Thomason, thus keeping her own professional persona alive. Besides, the hyphenated name had a kind of show-biz air about it.

The couple struck it rich in 1986 when they produced a sitcom for CBS-TV, "Designing Women." That became the hit of the season. It was the story of a group of four women who owned an interior decorating business. The business operated in a suburban Atlanta home that served as office and showplace for their work.

Julia Sugarbaker, played by Dixie Carter, was the guiding force behind the company. Her baby sister, Suzanne, played by Delta Burke, was the charismatic, sexy woman who used her natural endowments to cover her ignorance of decorating. Charlene Winston, acted by Jean Smart, and Mary Jo Shively, played by Annie Potts, helped run the business, with Charlene the business manager. Hal Holbrook played the occasional role of Julia's boyfriend, Reese Watson.

It was an instant critical and popular success. The network began juggling its schedule in order to find a good slot for it. Meanwhile, the sitcom's fans complained so vociferously that CBS-TV finally anchored it on Monday, where it had originated. "Designing Women" even survived an initial cancellation in 1987 and was revived in 1988 after a feud between the producers and Delta Burke, who then left the show.

By now the team of Thomason and Bloodworth-Thomason had become an established success in Hollywood. Clinton renewed his friendship with Harry, and Hillary and Linda became inseparable friends. Harry and Linda finally brought several production units out to financially poor Arkansas.

Later on, the team created a show for Burt Reynolds. And it was to be set in Arkansas. Originally, they had planned to name the program after Harry's home state. However, Hillary advised them not to use the word "Arkansas"—which, she knew, had implications of Li'l Abner and the Beverly Hillbillies that did not add to its glamour—and suggested instead "Evening Shade," which, indeed, the show was named when it made its successful debut.

By that time Harry and Linda were producing for MTM, using the name Mozark for their production company—"M" for "MTM" and "Ozark" for "Arkansas-Ozark."

With the success of those two shows, Harry and Linda came up with "Hearts Afire," a more politically oriented sitcom featuring a group of men and women working for a Southern senator in Washington and starring John Ritter.

In the middle 1980s, however, "Evening Shade" and "Hearts Afire" had not yet been born. Nevertheless, the Hollywood connection had been established between the Clintons and the Bloodworth-Thomasons. It would turn out to be an important link once the Clintons became involved in a run for the presidency.

From the beginning of the friendship it was Hillary and Linda who struck the real sparks. Both women instinctively understood the close relationship between politics and show business, a connection that had been chided and giggled about during the eight years of Ronald Reagan's administration. The symbiosis of the two professions was obvious.

The 1986 governor's campaign went smoothly. The legislature had changed the law to extend the term from two to four years. In September, Clinton announced that when he had decided to run for reelection, he had effectively removed himself from contention as a candidate for President in the next national election.

"The person who's going to be nominated by the Democratic party in 1988, barring a total abandonment of the last twenty-five or twenty-six years of history, is somebody that's been out there [running] really for a year." However, during his inaugural address on January 14, 1987, he said that this might be his "last trip to the lectern under these circumstances." That meant he might not run for governor again.

Time magazine listed Bill Clinton that year as one of fifty top leaders in the United States. The article mentioned among his major achievements the passage of $47 million in new taxes and pointed out that he had wrested power from the legislature for his own office as governor. It speculated that he might run for Congress.

At a mock Democratic National Convention put on by students at Washington and Lee University in Lexington, Virginia, Clinton delivered an address and then mingled with some of the students. He danced with some of the coeds. Then he played the saxophone.

Speculation in Arkansas continued to mount that Clinton would run for the presidency. In April, he said that his mail was running three to one in favor of making a bid. He added he would not resign as governor if he did decide to run. The Democratic party's state committee adopted a resolution urging him to run. But the *Arkansas Gazette* said, "Bill Clinton is not ready to be president of the United States."

Hillary told reporters that she would support her husband's decision, whatever it was, and pointed out that he was a "very deliberative [man] when faced with a difficult decision." She also said, "I have no doubts that he would be an excellent President."

Gary Hart of Colorado dropped out of the race in May. The press had taken him to task for extramarital activities. Reporters immediately remembered the rumors that had surrounded Bill Clinton's activities in 1980, and the name of Gennifer Flowers was once again bandied about in the newsrooms across the state.

Speaking engagements consumed much of Clinton's time. He went to Tennessee, Indiana, Montana, and Wisconsin. By July, the *New York Times* reported that Clinton was going to run for President.

On July 15, 1987, Clinton himself said no. He had decided not to run because he did not think he could win. He added, "Our daughter is seven [years old]. In order to wage a winning campaign, both Hillary and I would have to leave her for long periods of time. That would not be good for her or for us."

The decision not to run, he admitted, had become a "tug-of-war" because he still thought that the year 1988 would be "tailor-made for my candidacy." However, he had made up his mind that 1988 simply was not his time.

Then he drew loud cheers from his associates and members of the press when he said: "For whatever it's worth, I'd still like to be President. I hope I will have another opportunity to seek the Presidency when I can do it and be faithful to my family, my state, and my sense of what is right."

Hillary was observed to brush tears from her cheek as her husband said he had promised himself "a long, long time ago" that "if I was ever lucky enough to have a kid, my child would never grow up wondering who her father was."

Although she "personally did not want to do another campaign at this time," Hillary said, it was "difficult to walk away from the encouragement that Bill received to run."

His daughter, Chelsea, the governor said, had told him that running for the presidency would be "a great honor" and that she could "handle it" if he decided to go for the job. He added, "But then I was gone for three or four nights in a row, and she said, 'You know, this is not such a good idea.' " Nevertheless, he said that he thought Chelsea "could probably handle it today. It may be me that can't handle it."

When asked if the fear of intense media scrutiny of his personal life in the past had anything to do with his decision not to run, he answered that it did not. "But I thought about it a lot, and we debated it a lot." "We" meant "Hillary and I."

Hillary told the press that she had never let her husband know what she thought he should do. "If he were to run and to win, he would be the one thinking about what to do in time of crisis, not me."

She said that there was a conflict between their own personal desires for their family life and their burning desire to promote a "new social contract" between the government and the public. "I don't think we have ever been through a more difficult time, even including the loss in 1980."

Even Bill's brother, Roger, said, "He'll be ready. I don't know if it's the next one [the 1992 race] or not, but he will be ready."

Of course, the Republicans came out with their own assessment of the governor's decision: "This bears out his indecisiveness by deluding his most ardent supporters into believing one thing and at the last moment doing another."

Soon all the furor died down, and life resumed its normal pace. In 1987, Hillary Clinton had been elected chairperson of the board of directors of the Children's Defense Fund. In Washington at one of the board's meetings, her old friend Susan Bucknell-Pogue met her one day just prior to Bill Clinton's announcement of his decision not to run for President.

Susan said, "I used to meet up with Hillary at Children's Defense Fund conferences in Washington. These conferences were extremely busy times for Hillary. But she always made the time to snatch a lunch with me and renew our friendship.

"I remember those lunches with pleasure. The conversations were a delightfully intense mixture of children's social policy issues, a catch-up on our careers, and very personal exchanges on how many children he hoped to have and the tensions of balancing family and work and especially politics. Was Bill going to fun for President? I asked [her] on one occasion."

Hillary told her, "Not this year. We both decided it would take too great a toll on our daughter, Chelsea."

"At one of these lunches," Susan recalled, "I heard Hillary speak. I was impressed by how 'grown up' she looked and how accomplished a speaker she was. I was struck by the strength of her passion for changing children's lives for the better and by how much she had matured and developed from our early student days."

That same year, Hillary was also elected to the board of the New World Foundation, one of the philanthropies that had helped launch the Children's Defense Fund. She was voted chairperson of the organization. Its meetings took place in New York City, where the foundation maintained its headquarters.

Hillary held the position of chair for two years, opening up the board and the award process to greater participation of women and minorities. During that time the foundation gave grants to Norman Lear's People for the American Way, Randall Robinson's Trans-Africa Forum, and the NAACP Legal Defense and Education Fund.

Hillary and Bill Clinton were awarded the National Humanitarian Award by the National Conference of Christians and Jews. During the national meeting of the conference in Little Rock, Mayor Andrew Young of Atlanta said that the Clintons symbolized the best of the South. They were contributing to society as full participants of democracy, yet were still devoted to each other. He said this showed what families would have to be like in the future to survive.

Although there was a great deal of skirmishing during the first weeks of the 1988 Democratic primaries, by late spring there was no question that Governor Michael Dukakis of Massachusetts would be the nominee. Clinton had picked Dukakis as the most likely candidate and had aligned himself with him. They traveled extensively together, with Clinton acting as Dukakis's adviser and promoter. In July, Dukakis asked Clinton to deliver his nominating speech.

Both Hillary and Bill were excited when this plum dropped into his lap. His appearance would give Clinton the chance to shine on national television. Appearing in the keynote spot at the Democratic Convention was the next best thing to being the nominee himself. It might lead to a chance to run later.

Through his years on the podium in Arkansas, Clinton had polished his speaking style and had become adept at using television cameras and microphones for maximum effect. He had learned exactly how to dominate a camera lens one-on-one so that it would seem as if he were in the living room with the person viewing him. He was also very good at speaking extemporaneously. He had long ago developed a mode of articulation that made him seem completely in command.

In addition to his own talents and abilities, he had one special asset. He had Hillary Clinton, who was more the pragmatist and logician. She had worked with him in campaign after campaign, getting him to explain his ideas more clearly. She was basically a creator, a writer, a theoretician whose essays brought light and heat with them.

They worked all day on the Dukakis nominating speech. Together they polished it until it seemed to glow. They sent a copy to Dukakis. Back came the copy with emendations, additions, and deletions. They incorporated the changes, polished again, and sent it back. More corrections. More incorporations. That night, when Bill Clinton took center stage in the Atlanta Omni, every word of the speech that he carried with him had been not only polished by Hillary but approved by Dukakis himself.

Once on the podium, Clinton sensed he was in trouble. The delegates were in no mood to listen to someone talk. They were yelling and stamping their feet. "We want Mike! We want Mike!"

Clinton tried to override the noise and the clamor. He had to stop once to ask the crowd to quiet down so he could tell the rest of the country "why they should want Mike." The longer he spoke, the louder the commotion. Those who weren't yelling at him to get off the stage were milling around and talking to friends, ignoring the podium.

Hillary, watching, was appalled. As they had approached the podium, Hillary had asked the woman who was escorting them there to make sure that the houselights would be lowered when Bill started to speak. If they were, the emphasis would be on the stage, which was brightly lit. The woman promised Hillary that she would check on it.

"The lights did *not* go out," Hillary reported later. "The Dukakis campaign whips—the people who keep the delegations in line—were not telling their delegates to listen. In several instances, they were telling their delegates to yell every time Bill mentioned Dukakis's name—which was a lot, since it was a speech about Dukakis. "The platform, the Democratic National Committee people, who actually run the platform, had not been told that Bill was going to talk for [fifteen] minutes. Something was wrong in the signals that were given."

And so Clinton had to fight his way through shouts, yells, and inattention.

"And I sat there knowing that there was something really, really wrong," Hillary said, "because if the lights had gone down, if the crowd had been quiet, if the speech had been given the way we had been told that it was supposed to be given, it would have done exactly what Bill had prepared for it to do.

"Bill had told Dukakis he'd give the speech, so he gave the speech."

That night, John Chancellor, the NBC analyst, commented, "I am afraid Bill Clinton, one of the most attractive governors, just put a blot on his record."

The only applause came when the speaker said, "In conclusion . . ."

The Associated Press quoted Clinton: "I just fell on my sword. It was a comedy of errors, one of those fluky things."

The *Washington Post* headlined the keynote speech "The Numb and the Restless." Tom Shales wrote that while Jesse Jackson's speech had electrified the audience, Clinton's had calcified it. But that comment was mild compared to what Johnny Carson said on "The Tonight Show" about the incident. He joked that the Surgeon General had just approved Governor Bill Clinton as an over-the-counter sleep aid.

"What a windbag!" Carson said.

Clinton had not been far off in his assessment to the Associated Press. He had indeed fallen on his sword in the fashion of a suicidal Roman emperor. But the wounded warrior was still in the political arena, and somehow he had to arise and continue the fight.

The Hollywood connection came to the rescue. Linda Bloodworth-Thomason and Harry Thomason put their heads together after a frantic telephone call from Hillary. They had seen the fiasco and didn't want to believe it. Bill Clinton was a show-biz bomb.

Harry and Linda came up with the antidote. The reasoning went like this: It was Johnny Carson who had really alerted the country to Bill Clinton's blabbermouth. Why not get Clinton on "The Tonight Show"?

Clinton was horrified at the idea. The man had made him a laughingstock. If Clinton got on the show, Carson would kill him.

Harry and Linda went after the show's producers. The idea amused

Carson's handlers, but a full-fledged politician, even if he happened to be the governor of a very small Southern state, was not really within the Carson show's parameters. Suddenly it popped into Harry's mind: Here was a politician who played the saxophone. Now Carson's people showed interest. A saxophone-playing governor, not bad! Harry and Linda looked at each other. Neither had consulted Bill Clinton.

When the deal was set, they told Bill he would have to play the sax for Carson. Clinton was dead-set against the idea. He would make a worse fool out of himself. Too late. Carson was already on the air promoting the governor's appearance. Clinton was committed to play in front of millions of people.

So a few nights later a somewhat benumbed, but game, Bill Clinton flew to the West Coast to appear on "The Tonight Show." Carson's writers whipped up a parody of the Clinton speech for Carson to deliver that included a rambling biography, along with a bunch of trivia about Arkansas. It was funny, and it was enough to drive a knife through the heart of any politician.

The curtains parted, and Bill Clinton appeared. But this was a different Bill Clinton, a rehearsed, all-in-control Bill Clinton. He had studied with the experts, Harry and Linda, and he knew exactly how to play the game. He entered laughing, not an easy thing to do under the circumstances.

He told Carson that Dukakis had read the speech and begged Clinton to save it and deliver it for George Bush instead. Clinton then said that his ultimate strategy in writing the speech the way he had was to make Dukakis look good when he delivered his acceptance speech the following night. He then said he appreciated all the support the people in Arkansas had given him, even though his speech had not been well received by the country.

Carson said, "Your saving grace is that you have a good sense of humor."

Then Clinton got out his saxophone and played the melody of the Gershwin brothers' "Summertime." After the solo, he sat in with Doc Severinsen and the studio orchestra for an ad-lib session.

The audience applauded loudly and warmly as Bill Clinton left the stage. Carson noted that he would probably have to find a couple of new targets for his monologues.

Clinton had blown life back into his own punctured image. The "windbag" had proved himself to be a real live person with the ability to laugh at himself. And he could actually play the saxophone.

The Hollywood connection had put Bill Clinton's future back on track. At a party later that night at the Thomasons' new house outside Los Angeles, there was a sign on a well in the garden that said: On the Road Again . . . Clinton '96.

There was more to come. The next morning, when the governor went to the state capitol, the owner of the souvenir stand next to the door stood up and applauded.

"The Tonight Show" received hundreds of letters from Arkansans who supported Clinton. Carson read one of them, from Sharon Rector of Little Rock, on the air.

Clinton said he was happy that Carson's parody of his speech had gotten in "a lot of good information about Arkansas." He also remarked, "I've wanted to play with Doc Severinsen longer than I've wanted to be on 'The Tonight Show.'" Clinton was paid $475 for playing the saxophone, in addition to the $200 for his appearance. The earnings went to Hillary's Children's Defense Fund.

Not all Arkansans were so enthusiastic about Clinton's appearance. Some asserted that the Atlanta speech had shown the world the real Bill Clinton. Others pointed out that it had turned off the "big-money people" in the Democratic party.

"His Arkansas-reinforced arrogance deluded him," political columnist John Brummett wrote in the *Arkansas Gazette.*

No matter. The Hollywood connection had been established. And it worked. Perfectly.

CHAPTER THIRTEEN

A Dry Run

In 1988, Democrats and Republicans were embattled over Nicaragua. Marxist Sandinista guerrillas had forced General Anastasio Somoza Debayle, elected president in 1967, to resign in 1972. Somoza was reelected in 1974. The guerrillas seized various officials in December 1974, after which martial law was imposed.

The country's Roman Catholic bishops charged that government troops had mistreated civilians in their extensive antiguerrilla activities. By 1978, the entire country was in ferment, and a nationwide strike in August soon escalated into a true civil war.

Thus weakened, the country was a prime target for the Sandinista guerrillas, who seized the government after a seven-week offensive and forced Somoza's resignation and exile. The Sandinista government then began supplying arms to Marxist guerrillas in El Salvador. Meanwhile, the United States began supplying arms to an opposition army rising in the Nicaragua wilderness composed of "contra-Sandinistas," or "anti-Sandinistas," who became known simply as "contras."

In the United States the administration turned sympathetic to the contras. Many others sympathized with the Sandinistas. This division seemed to align the U.S. political parties into separate camps: Democrats for the Sandinistas; Republicans for the contras.

A man named Larry Nichols was interested in overthrowing the Sandinistas in Nicaragua. He worked for the Arkansas Development Finance Agency, which issued bonds that helped finance low-interest mortgages for the state. Because of his interest in the Sandinistas, Nichols was a member of the Freedom Feet Project, a part of the Caribbean Commission, a New Orleans group that was afraid the Sandinistas in Nicaragua would spread the Marxist doctrine to nearby countries, as they were obviously trying to do in El Salvador. Nichols's big fear was that communism would become a dominant political force in Mexico.

Adolfo and Mario Calero, two contra leaders, were operating in the United States, raising funds and running a publicity shop just outside New Orleans. In January 1988, the Associated Press reported that Nichols had made more than 142 phone calls to contra leaders in the United States, including the Calero brothers. He had also made 330 phone calls to Bill Simmons, an AP reporter. The total bill, charged to the Arkansas Development Finance Agency, amounted to over eight hundred dollars.

When questioned by the press, Nichols said that the calls were legitimate. The contra leaders were referring him to congressmen sympathetic to their cause so Nichols could talk to them about mortgage revenue bonds. He claimed that his boss, Wooten Epes, had authorized the calls. Epes said he had not. At this point the governor got into the act. He issued a statement that he doubted Nichols's calls had been about bonds.

The publicity resulted in Nichols's resignation under pressure from the Arkansas Development Finance Agency. But when he quit his state job he said that both Epes and the governor had forced him out. He claimed that he had never used the Arkansas taxpayers' money to help the Nicaraguan contras. He also complained about "the knee-jerk liberal reaction from the governor's office."

In September 1989, in the midst of the Nichols affair, Hillary and Bill Clinton went to Charlottesville, Virginia, to take part in President George Bush's national education summit. Hillary took the opportunity there to express her views on urgent childhood issues.

At one luncheon she sat next to President Bush and managed to speak to him about the issue of children's health care, which she thought to be inadequate in the United States. "You know, Mr. President," she said, "depending upon what statistic you look at, we're at seventeenth or nineteenth in the whole world in infant mortality."

"Whatever are you talking about?" Bush asked. "Our health care system is the envy of the world."

"Not if you want to keep you child alive to the year of his first birthday," she told him. She took that moment to say that she did not think the United States had been aggressive enough in providing for children's health. Feeling that the President did not really know much about the issue, she offered to have her husband provide him with statistics at the next day's working sessions.

"Well," Bush said, "I'll get my own statistics."

"Fine. I wish you would," Hillary replied.

The next day, the President handed a note to Bill Clinton. It read simply, "Tell Hillary she was right."

In spite of their traveling about together, this was not the happiest year for the Clintons. Bill Clinton's fiasco at the Democratic Convention in Atlanta still rankled in his mind. Even though he had resurrected himself, thanks to the help of Johnny Carson and the Clintons' Hollywood connection, he was disturbed about the gaffe he had committed in front of the entire nation. He had also appeared to be wishy-washy and ineffectual at making up his mind in his on-again-off-again presidential bid.

The rumors that had reverberated throughout the state about Clinton's affairs with women in 1980 had subsided. Now gossip reappeared like some phantom apparition. An unnamed "longtime friend of Hillary" was quoted by the *National Enquirer* as saying, "By 1989 the Little Rock rumor mill was on fire, spitting out allegations of Clinton's affairs with Gennifer Flowers and other women."

The tension even spread to Chelsea, who was now nine years old. One story contended in December 1989 that the Clinton marriage was about to fall apart. The story went that one night Hillary and her daughter were in their third-floor living quarters in the governor's mansion talking about what Christmas presents to buy for Bill. Quite suddenly, Chelsea started to weep. "Mommy, why doesn't Daddy love you anymore?"

Hillary had become hardened to all the negative rumors during her marriage, but she felt unable to discuss them with her daughter. Instead, she told her, "Daddy is so busy these days that sometimes he doesn't have enough time to spend with us."

Hillary realized that she would have to do something immediately in order to save her family. She had always been able to rely on her strong faith in religion to get the proper bearings in any situation, and she knew that her church would not let her down now.

She called Dr. Ed Matthews, the senior minister at her church, the First United Methodist Church in Little Rock. The pastor immediately agreed to meet with the Clintons for counseling. Now it was up to Hillary to convince her husband that the meeting was necessary.

When he came home that night she led him into their family quarters and told him she had to talk to him. He was annoyed at first. He pointed out that those were only rumors, that they were not true.

Hillary told her husband that she loved him but that she could not allow him to continue to make a fool of her. And the rumors about his womanizing made her look even worse than a fool. Then she told him about Dr. Matthews and his promise to help them.

Bill Clinton argued that she was overreacting, that he was the victim of a bad press, and that there was nothing to the gossip about him. At that point Hillary burst into tears. "I can't take any more," she told him. "Unless you're ready to change, we're getting a divorce!"

Clinton finally agreed to meet with Dr. Matthews and Hillary. It was just a few days before Christmas when they assembled in the pastor's study at the church. "The meeting was charged with emotion," said one unnamed source. "Hillary said that if Bill would change, she'd try to make the marriage work."

Dr. Matthews asked Clinton, "And what about you, Bill? Are you ready to save this marraige?"

He said that he would do anything to save the marriage. "I love Hillary and Chelsea more than anything in the world."

A close friend of the family recalled, "Hillary and Bill wept as they held hands, knelt, and prayed together. Bill gave Hillary a solemn promise to change his ways, and they renewed their pledge of love for each other."

There were several more sessions in Dr. Matthews's study, and in the end the two seemed closer than they had been before. Remembering the effectiveness of her fashion makeover in 1980, after Bill Clinton lost his first campaign for reelection, Hillary decided it was time to resort to cosmetics once again to improve her image.

Accordingly, she went to a number of fashionable stores in Little Rock and got herself an entirely new wardrobe. She purportedly paid $2,400 for one red cashmere jacket and bought some St. John knit dresses at $850 apiece. By the time she was through with her shopping spree, she had spent ten thousand dollars.

She also restyled her hair. For years she had streaked it with lighter tints. Now she went completely blond. She had just read the autobiography of Margaret Thatcher, the prime minister of Great Britain, and had taken her words about tinting her hair blond at face value.

Her new makeup, with her eyes as the focal point, made her wide face look longer. She also lost twenty pounds to trim down her figure.

The marriage was rejuvenated by the counseling sessions. Even their close friends realized that something new had been kindled between them. Patty Criner, a friend of Hillary's, said, "It's no secret that Bill and Hillary have battled through some very troubled times in their marriage. The allegations about Bill and other women made life very difficult for Hillary."

She went on to say Hillary had confided in her: "I am determined that nothing will destroy our marriage." And of course she had to do something about it.

"To see Bill and Hillary together now is a joy," Patty said. "They have a very close romantic relationship and adore each other."

Early in 1990, in position as board chair for the Children's Defense Fund, Hillary joined a study team of child-care professionals for a two-week visit to France. The trip was made under the auspices of the French American Foundation, which promoted various ties between the two nations. She was in the company of a pediatrician, a Senate aide, and a state government official, along with groups of academics, day-care administrators, and representatives from organized labor and business. They visited schools and spoke with ministry officials, other officeholders, educators, health professionals, and business and labor representatives.

Hillary wrote in the *New York Times:* "What we saw was a coordinated, comprehensive system, supported across the political spectrum, that links day care, early education and health care—and is accessible to virtually every child."

France, Hillary pointed out, thought of its children as "a precious national resources for which society has collective responsibility." She went on to say that "mandated paid parental leave for child birth and adoption acknowledges society's obligation to nurture strong parent-child ties." Statistically, she pointed out, France ranked fourth lowest in infant mortality. The United States was eighteenth, almost exactly what Hillary had told President Bush.

"Child care is not just a family matter," she wrote. "To do our children and our country justice, we need to develop a nationwide consensus on how to best nurture our children, and, through that nurturing, prevent the personal and social costs we all pay when children's needs are not met.

"Before we lock ourselves into a makeshift, inadequate child care policy, we ought to consider valuing children, French-style."

In the meantime, Bill Clinton was still the subject of whispering voices. On September 2, 1990, Larry Nichols filed a suit that sought over three million dollars in damages for what he termed "unjust firing." Among its allegations was that Governor Bill Clinton had engaged in extramarital affairs with five different women. Nichols claimed that he had been fired as a part of a cover-up of a slush fund used to finance the governor's affairs with beauty queens, a Clinton aide, and Gennifer Flowers.

The suit had obviously been timed for the coming election, in which Clinton was running against Sheffield Nelson, a strong candidate. Two days before the election, Mike Gauldin, Clinton's press secretary, was called by Nichols to meet at a truck stop. According to Gauldin, Nichols offered to drop his suit in exchange for a house and $150,000 in cash. Gauldin refused.

Few newspaper stories about the lawsuit appeared, and those that did were relegated to the back pages. The Little Rock press had decided that the charges of sexual and financial misconduct brought by Nichols were slanderous and held back on publishing them. Both Little Rock newspapers started to investigate the charges. Teams of journalists fanned out to take a closer look at Bill Clinton's private life. None of them uncovered any new information, so nothing reached print.

However, a tiny Little Rock radio station, KBIS-AM, listed the five women's names as given in the lawsuit. One of them was Gennifer Flowers. Flowers's attorney immediately wrote to KBIS maintaining that the station had "wrongfully and untruthfully alleged an affair between my client, Gennifer Flowers, and Bill Clinton." Even though the letter implied a lawsuit might be forthcoming, none was ever filed. So the rumor mills slowed down for a while after Clinton beat Nelson in 1990.

By 1991, there was no question: Bill Clinton would make a run for the presidency. After all, he had become a national figure—even if the reason was a negative one, his long-winded introduction of Dukakis in 1988.

Hillary, too, had attained national prominence. In 1988 and 1991, she was cited by the *National Law Journal* as one of the "One Hundred Most Influential Lawyers in America." Her talents at academics and her ability to research law were probably superior to Bill's. However, he, too, was brilliant. Both were voracious readers.

Patty Criner said, "I've helped them move three times, and I'll never do it again, just because of the books." Bill had them arranged in alphabetical

Hillary listens as Bill speaks during his first term as governor of Arkansas. (AP/Wide World Photos)

Campaigning with former Governor Bill Clinton in his race against the incumbent Frank White in 1982 after his defeat following his first term. (AP/Wide World Photos)

A year later, with her husband victorious, Hillary, thirty-six, moves back into the Governor's Mansion as Arkansas' First Lady. (Arkansas Democrat Gazette)

Hillary, forty, and seven-year-old Chelsea at one of Chelsea's soccer games in March 1987 in Little Rock. (Arkansas Democrat Gazette)

The Clintons take time off from their hectic schedules in 1984 to visit Disney World in Orlando, Florida. Here they pose with Donald Duck. (Arkansas Democrat Gazette)

In 1979, during Bill Clinton's first term as governor of Arkansas, Hillary and her husband attend a Governors' Conference held by President Jimmy Carter at the White House. (AP/Wide World Photos)

Seven years later, Governor Clinton and his wife arrive for a dinner given by President Ronald Reagan and his wife Nancy at the White House. (AP/Wide World Photos)

Arkansas' First Lady, in her inaugural gown, 1985.   (AP/Wide World Photos)

During a respite in the presidential campaign, Hillary and Bill take time off to jog near the Governor's Mansion in Little Rock. (AP/Wide World Photos)

Hillary Rodham Clinton waves to the crowd at the Lincoln Memorial after she and her husband, President-elect Bill Clinton, arrived in Washington following a bus trip from Thomas Jefferson's home in Monticello, en route to their final destination, the White House. (AP/Wide World Photos/Greg Gibson)

Hillary and Bill dancing at the Western Inauguration Ball held at the Kennedy Center (AP/Wide World Photos/Lynn Sladky)

The First Lady puts her arm around Chelsea at the MTV Inauguration Ball at the Washington Convention Center (AP/Wide World Photos/Greg Gibson)

order at one time. "Then he had them by subject matter," Criner recalled. "Every time they've moved, that's been the biggest thing, because he reads nonstop. He reads nonfiction. He reads fiction. He reads historical things. He reads political publications. He's always been that way. Since he was a kid, he always had another book under his arm."

Hillary agreed with Criner. "If he could get away with it, he'd read when he drove. He is insatiably curious about everything. He reads constantly."

Carolyn Staley, a next-door neighbor in Hot Springs and a close friend, said he would read at least four or five books a week. Carol Allin, who at one time ran the Capitol Book Store in Little Rock, said he used "to browse in her shop about once a month and never left without an armful of books."

Clinton was also an avid fan of working crossword puzzles. He worked at them with a pen rather than a pencil and completed them in record time. Ali Segal, a chief financial adviser, said that he once took Clinton to the New York office of *Games* magazine and had the editor clock him in working out one of the toughest crosswords. "He completed it in seven minutes," Segal recalled. "That's championship time."

Hillary said that Bill could perform multiple tasks and still concentrate. "He'll be watching some obscure basketball game, and he'll be reading and talking on the phone all at the same time and knowing exactly what is going on in each situation. If you stopped him and said, 'What's the score?' he'd tell you. If you stopped him and said, 'What did the person you were talking to just say?' he'd repeat it verbatim, and if you stopped him and said, 'What did you just read?' he'd say what he read."

She said that he also had an incredible ability to catnap and yet at the same time not miss a word of what had been going on around him. "Bill often falls asleep if he gets a minute to rest and he's been on the road; if he sits down in a car; if he has a minute off." She believed this ability was "part of what keeps him fueled up."

Hillary and Bill once attended a legal seminar. Hillary recalled, "The fellow was showing us a problem on the screen, and it was a pretty hard problem and Bill was asleep. Well, I wasn't going to wake him up. It was a little embarrassing, but the lights were off, so I didn't think anybody would know he was sleeping. And the fellow was asking about the answer to this problem. None of us were really catching on. Bill woke up, answered the problem, and fell back asleep."

Hillary said her husband's favorite work was the *Meditations of Marcus Aurelius*. He usually read it once a year. Marcus Aurelius Antoninus was a second-century Roman emperor, a stoic by disposition, whose victories in battle tended to be Pyrrhic ones at best. For one horrible example, his conquering troops once brought home victory—and a plague.

Aurelius consoled himself with a mind-over-matter impassivity exemplified by statements like "All is ephemeral—fame and the famous as well." Or, "Look beneath the surface; let not the several quality of a thing nor its worth escape thee." And, for the politician to ponder: "It is man's peculiar duty to love even those who wrong him."

Given Hillary and Bill Clinton's ability to absorb information, their powers of concentration, and their devotion to public life, it was no surprise that Bill, with Hillary helping run the campaign, would enter the race for the presidency in 1992. It would be a dry run, of course, because it seemed a foregone conclusion that Governor Mario Cuomo, the New York political heavyweight, would be the Democratic nominee.

Hillary's polished look and the governor's self-confident image would make the two of them formidable competition. So Hillary Clinton and the governor went lightheartedly into the primary campaign in late 1991 assuming that Bill Clinton would be there again in four years for the big one. Since this one would not count, Hillary figured that she could talk freely about the concerns of women and their children. And that was exactly what she did.

Along about this time Mario Cuomo began to play his "I'm not going to run" game with the press. Cuomo had played that record before, and nobody in the media would believe him now. When Cuomo said no, he meant yes: that was the general impression passed on to the public. But the Cuomo no thrust Bill Clinton into a light much brighter than usual for him.

With the Arkansas governor looking more and more like a bona fide candidate, the members of the media began searching out strengths and weaknesses to work on. It did not take long for the more alert journalists—especially those with huge morgues in their employers' libraries—to winnow out the many rumors of Clinton's extramarital relationships in the past. He looked just like another Gary Hart.

As early as the middle of September 1991, the issue of Clinton's sexual activities outside his marriage became the primary concern of an interviewer from the *Boston Globe*. The governor, with Hillary at his side, listened quietly while being questioned about his alleged affairs with other women. Then he responded that it was his view that presidential candidates, as they had in 1988, should refuse to divulge detailed personal information at the request of reporters. However, he did go so far as to say, "Those things were false and I said so at the time."

The reporter, Michael K. Frisby, was not to be dismissed so quickly. If Clinton were to declare his candidacy for President officially, how would he confront that issue?

While Hillary looked on unabashed and aloof from the give-and-take, Clinton said that he and his wife had been married for sixteen years and that they loved one another very much. He went on, "Like nearly anybody who has been together twenty years, our relationship has not been perfect or free of difficulties, but we feel good about where we are and we believe in our obligation to each other and we intend to be together thirty or forty years from now, whether I run for President or not."

Clinton closed the interview. "And I think that ought to be enough."

Frisby wrote: "Clinton's discussion of the issue was more direct than most candidates, reflecting the degree to which it has already dogged his precampaign activities. The presence of his wife, a Little Rock attorney, at the Washington breakfast meeting was also unusual."

On December 20, Governor Mario Cuomo announced that he had not been kidding, although it seemed that he had been trying to fool everyone when he said he would not run. He blamed the state budget for his final decision. "It's my responsibility as governor to deal with this extraordinarily severe problem," he said in a politician's ringingly sincere tones.

Hillary's reaction was to scream, "Oh, my God!" This meant that the Clinton campaign in 1992 might have a real chance. Every word she uttered would be analyzed by the media, and she could say absolutely nothing wrong. "I realized people were drawing impressions of me based on little snippets because that's all they had," she confided to a friend.

Once Cuomo declared he was not a candidate, critics began to attack Bill Clinton, and Hillary as well. The attacks on her were particularly vicious. She was a mother who valued her successful law career too much. What kind of selfish woman was she?

"Something is not coming across here," Hillary told herself with a nervous laugh. "I had to think hard about why people could have an impression of me so at variance with what my friends and I believed to be the case."

Bill Clinton exulted at the turn of events. He had already managed to raise nearly three million dollars for a dry run. A New Hampshire poll on December 23, 1991, showed him second after Paul Tsongas, with a quarter of the vote. Another poll, taken after Christmas, reported Clinton and Tsongas were even.

But there was trouble ahead. It surfaced at so-called dial groups. Participants viewed candidates' appearances on TV and charted their reactions by moving an electronic needle along a calibrated scale. During a video of the Clintons' appearances, whenever Hillary Clinton appeared, the needle dropped. The viewers were not in favor of her.

Clinton joked that maybe she just had a bad hair day. Nevertheless, although it was difficult to communicate the idea, Bill Clinton's advisers told him to get her out of sight and let her reappear after some kind of preparation had been made for the public to accept her.

Hillary was not happy. But she agreed and withdrew for the time being—until January 1992.

CHAPTER FOURTEEN

The Family Circle

Chelsea Clinton was not quite twelve years old when her father became a viable candidate for President of the United States. Overnight, quite like Hillary, Chelsea was catapulted into the never-never land of instant celebrity. Unlike Hillary's, her fame was simply a matter of blood relationship. Yet her prominence was every bit as real as her mother's and in a way even more upsetting and daunting.

Even as the rumors about Clinton's affairs were reverberating throughout the media, Chelsea became the most watched and talked-about adolescent in America. There was nothing Hillary could do to prevent the media from descending upon her daughter.

Instantly, Chelsea became the butt of rude political humor—exactly the way her parents had. One of many jokes about her looks said she could win a Queen of England look-alike contest.

Curtis Sliwa, leader of New York's Guardian Angels—a soi-disant group of volunteer police who tried to keep law and order on the city's streets—joked on his WABC show that Chelsea was "Southern-fried Carter." He went on, referring to her braces, "She looks like she got hit in the face with a bag full of nickels."

Listeners called in and protested his insults. Even his own mother raked him over the coals.

Political comedian Will Durst pretended to sympathize with the adolescent. "Imagine going through puberty, with hormones pouring out of your skin like hyperactive geysers, in front of the whole world, especially Sam Donaldson." But Durst showed no mercy for Chelsea. "She makes Amy Carter look like a babe. What? You expected me to cut the [Clintons] some slack?"

Joy Behar, a talk-show host and comedienne, commented, "People are vicious, they're on her case already. It reminds me of when Lyndon Johnson was unpopular. There was a bumper sticker that said, 'Impeach LBJ: No More Ugly Children.' " She herself would lay off Chelsea because she was just a kid. "You can talk about Hillary's legs. Bill's fat roll. But kids shouldn't be trashed."

The target of all those rotten jokes was a gangly teenager with long, curly hair and trademark braces. If Clinton won the election and became President, she would be the first presidential child in this century to suffer through puberty in the White House. Its other recent adolescent occupants had been either younger, like Amy Carter, who was only nine when her father became President, or older, like Luci Baines and Lynda Bird Johnson, who were sixteen and eighteen, respectively.

Chelsea Clinton's coming of age would be scrutinized by the media as closely as they analyzed a Hollywood movie queen. They were already circling the campaign trail like sharks waiting for lunch so they could rip into her and tell the whole world about it. So far their reports themselves were harmless. She liked ballet and played on a dentist's softball team, the Molar Rollers. Her batting average, however, remained a secret. Her favorite vegetable was broccoli.

Hillary Clinton, not surprisingly, was visibly upset over the sudden intrusion of the media. Hillary knew that fighting them was a losing battle. She tried to force herself to keep away from the reporters when they were onto her daughter, but she did fend off some of their questions herself. For instance, she informed the media that her daughter didn't really care about a person's appearance, so it didn't matter if she was not Hollywood beautiful. Chelsea did, though, soon start to wear shorter skirts to make herself look older.

One magazine story revealed that Chelsea was a cardsharp and liked to frequent malls, where she and her father could dine on Mexican and Greek cuisines, their favorites. When not scarfing down tamales and enchiladas, she liked to browse through bookshops.

When Chelsea first hit the media scene, her parents allowed her to watch "Murphy Brown" on television, along with a few other shows, including "Designing Women" and "Evening Shade," the two popular sitcoms whose producers were good friends of the Clintons. Once she went to see an R-rated movie, the cop-buddy picture *Lethal Weapon 3.*

The big story of the first week of Chelsea Clinton in media land was that she wanted to get her ears pierced but her parents wouldn't let her. Hillary had definitely put her foot down on that one. She herself wore clip-ons and could not get excited about pierced ears—except to forbid Chelsea from having them.

Chelsea had said when she was nine that she didn't like politicians. As she put it, "Both of my parents are politicians and they talk at the dinner table, politics-this and politics-that, and I'm just kind of getting sick and tired of it. I just don't think I want to be a politician when I grow up." Nor did she want to be an attorney like Hillary and Bill. She hoped to become an aeronautical engineer.

Despite the inevitability of media attention, the Clintons wanted to protect their daughter. Their spokeswoman, Lisa Caputo, said, "The Clintons will do whatever they can within their means to make sure Chelsea has as normal a childhood as she possibly can."

Oddly enough, considering all the publicity that Chelsea was receiving, most Americans thought the Clintons were childless at the time Bill Clinton began his run for the presidency, at least according to one poll cited in *Newsday.* The Clintons turned to *People* magazine, which published a spread about the whole family.

The only child of the Clintons was named at birth for the song "Chelsea Morning," a tune not familiar to many people outside the Baby Boomer generation. Joni Mitchell wrote the song, but the Clintons preferred Judy Collins's rendition of it.

Chelsea was brought up in Little Rock under the tutelage of live-in baby-sitters and grandparents who resided nearby. Her baby-sitters were usually students who attended a nearby college. Hillary's mother and father, Dorothy and Hugh Rodham, had moved to Little Rock in 1987. Virginia Kelley, Bill Clinton's mother, lived an hour away from Little Rock in Hot Springs with Dick, her fourth husband. On her eighth birthday, Chelsea persuaded Virginia to forswear smoking. Virginia complied but resumed the habit later on.

At the time her father started his run for the Oval Office, Chelsea attended Mann Magnet Junior High in Little Rock, an Arkansas public school. She was smart and had skipped a grade.

Chelsea was on the school volleyball team. This caused Bill Clinton to become a fan of the school's sports schedule. The only thing that bothered Chelsea about her father's interest in sports was that he yelled and cheered much too loudly whenever she did anything right on the volleyball court. After all, it was a *team* sport.

At the end of the school year Chelsea usually went to a summer camp called the Concordia German Language Village, which gave children from the ages of seven to eighteen the chance to study a foreign culture. It was located on Turtle Lake, some ten miles northeast of Bemidji, in northern Minnesota. As of 1992, Chelsea had attended for five years. Clinton's visit to the camp that summer to pick up Chelsea was kept secret from the press so that huge crowds would not congregate there and pose a security risk. The media believed Clinton was trying to decide on his running mate when in reality he was picking up Chelsea at the summer camp to take her home.

Chelsea's favorite hobby was ballet. A skilled ballerina, she once won a lead role in a Little Rock production of *The Nutcracker.* She loved to dance and once wound up in the hospital with a stress fracture as a result of her constant practicing. Undaunted, she hobbled out of the hospital on crutches.

Chelsea was always Daddy's girl. Bill would go out of his way to help her with her homework. When Chelsea was eleven, she had trouble one day solving a school math problem in Little Rock. Hillary was in Washington campaigning for Bill. Chelsea picked up her phone and called her mother, who tried to solve the problem but couldn't. She told Chelsea to fax the math problem to Daddy, who was campaigning between Boston and Florida. The next morning, Bill called Chelsea. They put their heads together and came up with the solution.

Hillary made sure the Clintons spent time with their only daughter. Family life was always a primary concern for all three of them. As Hillary put it, "I'm a believer in quantity as well as quality time, and we need to make sure our daughter's life is stable."

When Chelsea was younger, her father used to drive her to school every morning. Even celebrity Burt Reynolds came second to Chelsea. Clinton passed up an engagement with Reynolds once in order to attend a ballet recital in which Chelsea was a featured dancer.

Hillary Clinton always knew how rough it was for a child to have a politician for a parent—let alone *both* parents. She once told Chelsea that she would have to get used to negative campaign barbs aimed at her father. "We've told her to be ready for it. We try to take criticism—fair or unfair— seriously, but not personally."

Sounding like a candidate herself, Hillary then said that Chelsea must remain positive in spite of hostile criticism. "There is enough positive energy out there to solve problems if it's harnessed and led," Hillary said. "We need to group and deal with problems on the front end so we don't have to pay more later—and I think the federal government could play a bigger role."

Mayim Bialik, a teenage actress from TV's "Blossom," commiserated with Chelsea on the perils of being a celebrity. "It's difficult for me, and, in a way, I have it better—I don't have to go to school with kids. I did try, I went back, but it was a combination of harassment and autographs."

Bialik's advice to Chelsea was to consort with old friends "by way of keeping grounded. It's hard, and it's hard to meet new people—she's part of one of the strongest and most influential families in the world. But, for what it's worth, it won't do any good to sulk. She has to deal with it as it comes."

Another TV actress, Melissa Joan Hart, the sixteen-year-old in "Clarissa Explains It All," said that Chelsea would find it easy to make friends because she was a celebrity. Melissa said, "I find it's easier to have something to talk about when you have an interesting or different life. You have more to talk about."

The last presidential child to go to a public school in Washington, D.C., was Amy Carter. Every day in 1977 she attended her fifth-grade class at Stevens Elementary School near Washington Circle, surrounded by Secret Service agents. The next year she transferred to Hardy Middle School on Foxhall Road, another public school. Before her, no presidential child had attended a public school since 1906.

Speculation about Chelsea's choice of school ended on January 5, 1993, when President-elect Bill Clinton announced in a carefully prepared statement, "After many family discussions and careful consideration, we have decided that our daughter, Chelsea, will attend the Sidwell Friends School in Washington, D.C. As parents, we believe this decision is best for our daughter at this time in her life, based on our changing circumstances."

Sidwell, a Quaker school founded in 1883, won out over the public school system, as private schools so often do among Washington politicians. Though not as tony as the National Cathedral School attended by the Albert Gore children, Sidwell is still one of the more costly schools in the country; its annual tuition is over ten thousand dollars.

People everywhere gave advice to Chelsea, including the popular teen magazine *Sassy*, which told her before the Sidwell decision to "stay in public school because elite private schools are filled with politicians' snotty kids who'll rip you limb from limb because you're from Arkansas.

"Don't let the Gore sisters bully you around. They look like they know their way around. But don't lose your Amy Carter freshness.

"Play up the hippie side of your personality—keep those Birkenstocks but lose the prissy dresses. In other words, don't let your mom dress you.

"Don't let some magazine make you over and create some Hillary-do—like chopping off your hair. Keep the rougher edges. The polished stuff, the Gap look, is so *coordinated*, so *boring*.

"Update your dad's musical tastes and invite the Beastie Boys to perform in the Rose Garden."

Another member of the Clinton household that suddenly came under the harsh glare of the media's spotlight was Chelsea's pet, Socks the Cat. Chelsea used to own a cocker spaniel named Zeke, but after he got run over by a car, Chelsea was so upset that Hillary and Bill decided not to buy her another dog.

Susie Whitacre, a spokeswoman for Clinton, pointed out, "After Zeke died, the Clintons were besieged with offers of a new dog, and they didn't accept them because Chelsea was just too upset about Zeke. Once Socks came along, they let her keep him even though both the governor and Mrs. Clinton are allergic to him. Socks is pretty much Chelsea's cat, and I don't expect them to get another dog."

In November 1992, when the campaign was over and Bill Clinton had been elected President, Socks the Cat made his initial appearance in the national media. His fame already rivaled Morris the Cat's. Directly after his first TV appearance, his name appeared in all the Washington "in" columns. Not to be outdone, the Humane Society requested an official bio on the incoming First Cat.

Socks was believed to be two and a half years old. The Clintons found him as a stray and adopted him for Chelsea. The black-and-white cat's face has green eyes and a white nose with a patch of black on its nostrils.

Speaking for the Humane Society in Washington, D.C., Rachel Lamb said, "They say Clinton [will be] the president for a new generation of Americans, and he's already reflecting that. Cats have, indeed, surpassed dogs as the most popular pet in the country, and the Clinton household reflects the trend." Cat lovers were delighted. Allene Sergi, associate director of the Cat Fanciers Association, commented, "I wouldn't say I'm gloating over the prospect that a White House cat has replaced Millie. But we are very pleased to see that cats are finally going to get some positive attention."

After Socks hit the headlines, dog lovers became irate with Bill Clinton. The American Kennel Club's director of communications, Wayne Cavanaugh, quipped, "I voted for Clinton. I studied every aspect of his plan, and I can't believe I didn't think to ask about his pets. If I'd known he wasn't a dog person, I might have reconsidered."

Pet politics has always been as American as apple pie.

In recent history—ever since LBJ aroused the wrath of animal lovers when he lifted his beagles by their ears—Republicans tend to prefer dogs, while Democrats go for cats.

The Carters had both a dog and a cat in the White House at the same time, but the dog refused to obey White House protocol and was impeached. The Carters kept daughter Amy's cat, Misty Malarky Ying Yan, as First Pet.

Dogs have been politically active in the White House. The author of *Presidential Pets,* Niall Kelly, claimed Republicans favor dogs because they make for better photo opportunities. It was official White House photographer David Kennerly who presented the golden retriever Liberty to President Ford as Ford began his term.

The Reagans entered the White House without a dog. That did not last long. After dining with William F. Buckley and meeting his dog, a Cavalier King Charles spaniel, the Reagans obtained their own Cavalier and named him Rex. Political insiders claim Rex was trained to yank the President away from reporters when controversial questions were posed.

Kelly noted, "I'd be very surprised if Clinton didn't get a dog once he was in the White House. But you never know. Socks could be a very photogenic cat."

If Clinton doesn't buy a dog in the future, he will go down in the history books as the first dogless President since another Democrat, Woodrow Wilson, left office.

Khrushchev once gave John Kennedy a puppy; fearing the dog might be a spy, the Kennedy administration had him dispatched to Walter Reed Hospital and searched for surgically implanted mikes. And of course Checkers, the black-and-white spaniel, figured prominently in Nixon's defense of his accepting gifts from backers. Checkers himself was one such gift.

Millie, a springer spaniel, assumed office as First Dog during George

Bush's administration after C. Fred, a cocker spaniel, died. She earned her place in history by writing *Millie's Book* for President Bush's wife, Barbara. As testimony to her authorial skills, $889,176 in royalties poured into Millie's doghouse coffers in 1991. When not writing best-sellers, Millie spent her time chasing squirrels, frolicking on the White House lawn, or rooting up flowers.

Dr. Michael W. Fox, vice president of the Humane Society of the USA, was worried that Socks would be unable to take the pressure of living in the White House. "The Clintons' cat, used to a peaceful life in Arkansas, has suddenly become the center of media attention—and this sudden change can have dire effects on the little fellow. He will become nervous, irritable, and reclusive unless the Clintons give him privacy and tender loving care."

He pointed out that news reporters might again subject the cat to dirty tricks as they once did outside the Arkansas governor's mansion. Clever photographers in search of a story laid a trail of catnip to lure Socks outside the gates of the mansion. As Socks emerged onto the sidewalk a pack of fanatical paparazzi besieged the helpless animal. According to Fox, Socks could not take the pressure of the media assault. After seeing photos of the encounter Fox said, "The little cat's body language said it all. He turned away from the newsmen and tried to get away."

Fox went on to say that Socks might become stressed out at the White House and take off for Arkansas, where he grew up. "A cat has a natural sense of home, and to uproot Socks from his Arkansas home and thrust him into the White House will cause him several weeks of anguish.

"Many people lose their cats when they move to new houses—cats have been known to travel hundreds of miles to get back to their original homes." Fox advised the Clintons to keep Socks inside.

Michael J. Rosen, who wrote *The Company of Cats,* was all in favor of a presidential cat. "With no barking, no sudden interruptions, fewer demands on the President's time, a cat should create a more reflective atmosphere in the Oval Office so that the presidential art of complete thoughts and whole sentences will be restored," Rosen said in an obvious dig at dog-owner President Bush.

Writer Peter Tethers concurred that Socks would be better than a dog in the White House. "My guess is Millie would have bounded over to lick the hand of Saddam Hussein. Socks would have seen him for what he was."

CHAPTER FIFTEEN

Zone of Privacy

In spite of the negative vibes that had been generated by Hillary's campaign appearances, Bill Clinton's star was rising. By January 8, 1992, L. Douglas Wilder, the Virginia governor, had dropped out of the race entirely, citing lack of funds. Paul Tsongas was gamely fighting along, still the odds-on favorite to win the primary in New Hampshire.

Hillary had called on Linda Bloodworth-Thomason and Harry Thomason for help in selecting the correct background for Clinton's first preprimary town meeting. News and pictures of it would go out all over the country and would be some people's first impression of Bill Clinton.

All Clinton's handlers were there, too. Frank Greer, the media adviser, was learning a few things from the sitcom producers, and even from Hillary. Greer recalled walking into one studio with Harry Thomason. The two of them glanced around and then looked at one another. The place was about the size of a small closet.

"It's certainly not Hollywood, is it, Harry?" Greer asked.

It was New Hampshire.

A place was soon found, and once everyone had looked it over, it was decided that a blue carpet was needed to give the proper tone. Harry

Thomason bought the carpet and helped to lay it. "I kept thinking, he's the guy who's the producer of *Designing Women,* and he's on his hands and knees with me," Greer said.

Once the setting had been approved by Hillary and Linda, the press conference was scheduled, and the first day's interviews were conducted. The sound bites looked good, and everything seemed promising.

Then, on January 13, the *Star,* a supermarket tabloid owned and operated by Rupert Murdoch, appeared with a lead story claiming that candidate Bill Clinton had carried on extramarital affairs with at least five women. The story had obviously been generated from the lawsuit that Larry Nichols had instigated against Clinton in 1990.

The Democratic party had friends in the New England print fraternity. The New Hampshire papers all but ignored the story, burying it on inside pages. It was only a compendium of "rehashed lies," anyway, according to Clinton. One who wasn't surprised at all was Hillary, who had suspected the Republicans would soon begin hitting them with everything they had.

The attack, when it came, was a frontal assault on the most vulnerable spot: Hillary Clinton.

In a story from Bedford, New Hampshire, datelined January 19 and written by Cathleen Decker of the *Los Angeles Times,* Hillary Clinton was asked the general question of whether she thought that marital fidelity was an appropriate concern for voters. The question, of course, was a trap. But no one was kidding Hillary; she knew all about where it had come from.

Her immediate response was to assure the reporter that she and her husband had expected the matter of Bill's alleged extramarital relationships to surface sometime during the campaign. "From my perspective," she went on, looking right at the reporter, "our marriage is a strong marriage. We love each other." Her voice broke just a bit.

"We support each other, and we have had a lot of strong and important experiences together that have meant a lot to us. In any marriage, there are issues that come up between two people who are married—" she paused and stared into the reporter's eyes again—"issues that I think are *their* business."

Hillary went on to say that both she and her husband, as well as their eleven-year-old daughter, had the right to a measure of privacy even in a presidential campaign. "It is very important to me that what I care about most in this world—which is my family, what we mean to each other, and what we've done together—have some realm of protection from public life."

Her marriage, she noted, had survived sixteen years, eleven of them spent in what she termed the "fishbowl" of the governor's office in Arkansas.

At the end of Hillary's interview, her husband embraced her, took the microphone, and spoke of the man who had first made the charges in the 1990 lawsuit and was now apparently trying to use those same charges to damage the Clinton campaign. He cited Larry Nichols by name.

On Saturday, the next day, Hillary addressed a group of voters at a rally in Bedford. Someone in the crowd called for a statement on the report in the *Star* about the allegations of infidelity against her husband.

Hillary denounced the tabloid immediately, and, by implication, its charge. Then she turned back to the crowd of New Hampshire citizens, who were in the midst of a deep recession without much hope of moving out of it quickly. "Is anything about our marriage as important to the people of New Hampshire as the question of whether they will be able to keep their own families together?" she asked.

Meanwhile, at a television station, Bill Clinton was asked by his interviewer whether he had ever had an extramarital affair. "If I had," a testy Clinton snapped, "I wouldn't tell you."

Later on, at a joint appearance, Hillary gave a short pep talk for her husband, and then he spoke. During the question-and-answer session afterward, one voter asked her if she thought questions about a candidate's personal life were fair game during a campaign.

"We've been hit with all kinds of accusations," Hillary answered quickly. "The kinds of accusations that are in the tabloids next to the people with cow heads and the like!" She drew a laugh from the crowd.

An interview appeared the following Monday in *Women's Wear Daily* headlined "Hillary Clinton Stands by Her Man, Bill Clinton." In it, Hillary was able to discuss quite reasonably what to her seemed the obvious ramifications of the ongoing campaign. She said that from the beginning she had expected a dirty campaign. She added that she had no intention of talking about the Clintons' sex life.

As if to settle that issue once and for all, the interviewer asked: "Do your marital obligations include fidelity?"

"Yes," she said.

"Has that been a problem in your marriage?"

"I don't talk about it," Hillary answered. "I think my marriage is my marriage and my relationship with my husband is solely between us."

But Hillary was just beginning. "I have watched my husband for seventeen years in Arkansas handle every imaginable situation. I have always been impressed and extraordinarily respectful of the ways in which he deals with problems that I think are extremely taxing."

She was far from through. "We demand much too much of our political people in terms of the way we expect them to live, the kinds of external, reactive life-styles we expect them to have. We have really collapsed the space in which public people can live, to the detriment of our overall politics. That's the way it is in this country. You lose not just privacy—you lose the opportunity to be a real person."

And an ordinary marriage could be a problem for certain candidates. "It depends on the candidate and the marriage. Any stressful undertaking can be made either better or worse by the relationship between the spouses. But if it's a supportive one, if people believe in each other, if they love each other, if they have a commitment to what each is trying to do, it makes life a lot easier than it is alone."

"What about your concern that the upcoming election is expected to be one of the dirtiest in recent memory?" the interviewer asked.

"At a certain point," Hillary said slowly, "every campaign gets that way. People get desperate. I hope that doesn't happen in this one, but I expect there will be desperation afoot. My attitude is if you're doing what you believe in and you think it's important, you have to be ready to take the offensive when necessary."

In the five terms she served as Arkansas's first lady, she said, "we've had to deal with a lot of dirt and negative advertising. We've learned our lesson about how you stand up, answer your critics, and then just counterpunch as hard as you can. That's what we'll do in this campaign."

Although Hillary stood up well to the onslaught of the media, her role of faithful wife who believed in her husband and her marriage did not sit well with all the Clinton handlers. They felt that the problem was really Bill's, and therefore it was up to him to clean it up. If Hillary solved the problem, it would make Bill look as if he relied on his wife to mop up his messes after him.

Besides, Hillary was too good on her feet. Her lawyerly instincts were always on tap. She was a born litigator. And as an in-house Clinton attorney, she seemed to have intellectualized the entire personal situation of her husband's rumored affairs.

On January 23, while the Clinton group tried to figure a way out of the dilemma, the *Star* forwarded advance copies of its February 4 issue. In this one, there was real dynamite. Gennifer Flowers stated that she had carried on a twelve-year affair with Bill Clinton.

But, far more dangerous than her printed assertion, she said that she had taped phone conversations with Clinton—tapes that were being held by the *Star* management. A statement from Clinton headquarters asserted that the allegations in the *Star* tabloid were "false."

Hillary was campaigning in Atlanta at the time. "It's not true," she said. "I just don't believe any of that." It was her husband's political enemies who were causing the trouble, she said. "All of these people, including that woman, have denied this many, many times. I'm not going to speculate on her motive." Then immediately she went back on her word and did speculate: "We know she was paid."

The Clinton camp had friends in the media. After a great deal of checking and rechecking the facts in the tabloid story, a number of discrepancies were noted.

The copyrighted story said that Gennifer Flowers had received a nursing degree from the University of Arkansas School of Nursing in Little Rock. It said that she had attended both the University of Arkansas at Little Rock and the University of Arkansas at Fayetteville. No record could be found of her name at the nursing school or the two campuses of the university.

Gennifer Flowers claimed that she was Miss Teenage America in 1967. Linda Bernson, a promotion and marketing assistant for *Teen* magazine, which runs the pageant, said that the records showed she was not. "I can tell you for sure she did not win the title in 1967—or in the 1960s," Bernson said. "I went through everything we have here, and I am not coming across her name at all."

The story mentioned that Flowers had performed on the "Hee Haw" television show, a country-music revue involving running gags, blackouts, cameos of guest stars, and corny one-liners all delivered in appropriate hillbilly dialect. It played on ABC-TV from 1969 to 1971. Sandy Liles, an official at the show's production office, said that she had never heard of her. "I've been around here a long time. If she was on the show, I feel sure I would remember the name."

The *Star* article also said that Flowers had been an opening act for Roy Clark, the country-music great who was the star of "Hee Haw." Clark's personal secretary, Julia Staires, and his publicist, Carol Anderson, denied that Flowers had ever sung with him. "I never heard of her," Staires said flatly. "I've been getting calls on this, and I've checked around, and no one's heard of her."

"I've been with this organization for twelve years, and I've never met anyone named Gennifer Flowers," Anderson said. She herself had been a backup singer for Roy Clark for many years. "Gennifer Flowers was not one of them."

Unfortunately, the fact that the Flowers story was punctuated with half-truths and outright lies was not enough to get Bill Clinton off the hook. It was the affair that was the gist of the story, not who the woman was.

Someone finally reached Larry Nichols, whose lawsuit had been the source of many of the rumors about Clinton's love life. Nichols, it turned out, had undergone a change of heart. He had never intended for things to go this far. In a low-comedy episode Nichols related that he had just finished taking a shower and was trying to towel off in his bathroom when he looked out to see a television crew in his living room waiting to tape a live interview.

Nichols issued a statement. "It is time to call the fight I have with Bill Clinton over," Nichols wrote. "I want to tell everybody what I did to try to destroy Governor Clinton. I set out to destroy him for what I believed happened to me. I believed I was wrongfully fired from my job. Nobody has wanted to listen to me. All I wanted was a fair and honest hearing about what really happened. I want my family to know that I didn't do the things I've been accused of.

"This has gone far enough. I never intended it to go this far. I hoped all along that the governor and I could sit down and talk it out. But it just kept getting bigger and bigger.

"My family was hurt. And unfortunately no one can make an ass out of myself better than I can, so I've got to be the one that corrects it and stops it. There's a big difference between what I set out to do and what happened.

"The media has made a circus out of this thing and now it's gone way too far. When the *Star* article first came out, several women called asking if I was willing to pay them to say they had an affair with Bill Clinton.

"This is crazy. One London newspaper is offering a half-million dollars for a story. There are people out there now who are going to try to cash in.

"I apologize to the women who I named in the suit. I brought them into the public's eye and I shouldn't have done that. The least significant parts of my case were those concerning the rumors. I have allowed the media to use me and my case to attack Clinton's personal life.

"There were rumors when I started this suit and I guess there will be rumors now that it is over. But it is over. I am dropping the suit.

"In trying to destroy Clinton, I was only hurting myself. If the American people understand why I did this, that I went for the jugular in my lawsuit, and that was wrong, then they'll see that there's not a whole lot of difference between me and what the reporters are doing today."

The Nichols statement did little good in New Hampshire. Bill Clinton had been surging in the polls against Paul Tsongas, scoring his best numbers yet. Now, with the release of the *Star* story, he plummeted twelve points, down to 27 percent, where he was now tied again with Tsongas. His hard-won top spot was a thing of the past.

Bill and Hillary knew that they had to do something hard and realistic to convince the American people that whether Clinton's womanizing was a fact or a figment of the imagination, its impact on his marriage had been resolved successfully.

They needed a huge, national forum, something as compelling as the Super Bowl. Of course, a sports event could not serve as a political platform. But the 1992 Super Bowl was broadcast by CBS-TV, and it would air just before the most durable and believable show on television, "60 Minutes."

Clinton wanted to wind up a triple-threat response before the public with an appearance on "60 Minutes." His team had already scheduled him on Cable News Network's "Newsmaker Saturday" and on the ABC-TV news program "This Week with David Brinkley." He would appear with Hillary on CNN and alone on the Brinkley show.

Don Hewitt would have none of that. The Clintons had to be exclusive with "60 Minutes" or not at all. After some squabbling, the Clinton camp agreed, since the biggest audience, an estimated twenty-four million households, would be watching CBS.

David Glodt, the executive producer of the Brinkley show, muttered, "It disturbs me that a guy who is running for President is deciding back and forth" between a number of programs. CNN was also piqued.

"We felt bad canceling CNN and the Brinkley program," said Dee Dee Myers, a spokesperson for Clinton. "But, in the course of our negotiations with CBS, they wanted exclusivity. The combined audience for 'Newsmaker' and 'Brinkley' is a fraction of what we'd reach on CBS, and their audience is more of a political-insider audience than the national audience of '60 Minutes.' We felt it was in the best interest of the campaign [to choose the CBS program]."

The schedule called for CBS correspondent Steve Kroft to interview the Clintons on Sunday morning, January 6. The tape would then be edited by CBS and broadcast that evening.

Two calculated risks were taken by the Clinton camp.

One concerned the polls that showed some 39 percent of the respondents would have reservations about voting for a candidate who was unfaithful to his wife. However, the number would go down if the wife happened to find out about it and accepted the fact. But—and this was the risk involved—would the number go down far enough to clear the candidate?

Another concerned an attempt to use Hillary's image to enhance Clinton's. The idea was to compare photographs of Gennifer Flowers and Hillary Clinton. Except for the dark roots of the blond hair, the hanging earrings, and the light-colored see-through eyes of Gennifer Flowers, the two were look-alikes. Both had thin blond bangs hanging down over the forehead. Both were fair-skinned. Both were blue-eyed. The plan was to make Hillary out to be a quality version of Flowers. But—and this was the second risk—what would happen if the comparison backfired and Gennifer Flowers became the preferred one?

To make absolutely certain that "60 Minutes" would do right by the Clintons, Hillary and Bill met in Boston with the television crew and Steve Kroft. She talked about camera angles, colors, and the set itself with the crews. In Gail Sheehy's *Vanity Fair* story, Steve Kroft notes: "You can quote me as saying that my sense of it was that she [Hillary] was in control. . . . We fiddled around with who should sit on which side, and they fiddled around with chair heights and things like that. You didn't know she was his wife, you'd have thought she was a media consultant. She didn't do it in a dictatorial sort of way. . . . She was very delightful and charming."

An hour and a half's worth of tape was shot, but only eleven minutes were broadcast. Hillary's hand was in everything that was used—whether she was on camera or off—and much of the material that was edited out was hers. Kroft said, "We found ourselves rationing her sound bites to keep her from becoming the dominant force in the interview."

The broadcast version opened with a "teaser" from the interview, Kroft asking Bill Clinton, "Are you prepared tonight to say that you've never had an extramarital affair?"

Clinton replied, "I'm not prepared tonight to say that any married couple should ever discuss that with anyone but themselves." That was definitely a lawyerly response to a loaded question. Either Hillary or Bill might have composed it.

Kroft then introduced the Clintons, pointing out that they were going to talk about their life, their marriage, and allegations that had been made against him, allegations that were stalling his campaign for the presidency.

He sketched Bill Clinton's recent successes—his picture on the cover of *Time,* his position in the polls as leader in the Democratic race for nomination. He mentioned his problems—the sudden resurrection of rumors of marital infidelity against him in a tabloid and their widespread circulation in the press.

Overnight, the governor had become a target for unsubstantiated smears and vilification. His private life was now the main issue of the campaign.

The charges of infidelity had been leveled by a TV reporter and singer named Gennifer Flowers, who, in a paid interview, wrote that she had carried on an extramarital affair with Bill Clinton from the late 1970s to the end of 1989.

Kroft asked Clinton, "Who is Gennifer Flowers? You know her?"

"Oh, yes."

"Was she a friend, an acquaintance? Did your wife know her?"

"Yes."

"Oh, sure," Hillary confirmed.

"She was an acquaintance," Clinton added. "I would say a friendly acquaintance."

"Mm-hmm," Hillary agreed.

"She's alleging and has described in some detail in the supermarket tabloid what she calls a twelve-year affair with you," Kroft said.

"That allegation is false," Clinton said.

Hillary spoke up. "When this woman first got caught up in these charges, I felt as I felt about all of these women, that, you know, they've just been minding their own business, and they got hit by a meteor. I mean, it was no fault of their own."

"It was only when money came out," the candidate said, "when the tabloid went down there offering people money to say that they had been involved with me that she changed her story. There is a recession on. Times are tough, and I think you can expect more and more of these stories as long as they're down there handing out money."

"I'm assuming from your answer that you're categorically denying that you ever had an affair with Gennifer Flowers," Kroft cut in quickly.

"I've said that before and so has she," Clinton rejoined.

It was at this point, according to Sheehy, that Hillary cut in on the conversation. "I don't want to be any more specific," she said quickly. "I don't think being any more specific about what's happened in the privacy of our life together is relevant to anybody besides us."

This was one of the many statements by Hillary that the editors cut when they put together the final tape. She saw more clearly than Bill where Kroft was going. He was slowly loosening up the candidate. Clinton had already said that he was not going to talk about any specific case, and yet because he was a talker, always up front, he was about to go public on Gennifer Flowers.

Her reminder got through to him. Later, he said: "I'm not prepared tonight to say that any married couple should ever discuss [extramarital affairs] with anyone but themselves. I'm not prepared to say that about anybody." This was the interview segment the editors chose as the lead-in to the broadcast.

Hillary later cut into the dialogue to underline what Clinton was saying. "There isn't a person watching this who would feel comfortable sitting on this couch detailing everything that ever went on in their life or their marriage. And I think it's real dangerous in this country if we don't have some zone of privacy for everybody. I mean, I think that is absolutely critical."

Kroft was agreeable. "Everyone wants to put this behind you. And the reason it hasn't gone away is that your answer is not a denial, is it?"

"Of course it's not."

Later, Kroft said, "Fourteen percent of the registered voters in America say they wouldn't vote for a candidate who's had an affair."

Clinton took that one on with a grin. "That means 86 percent of the American people either don't think it's relevant to Presidential performance or look at whether a person looking at all the facts is the best person to serve."

And Hillary agreed. "We've gone further than anybody we know of, and that's all we're going to say."

Kroft nodded. "I think most Americans would agree that it's very admirable that you have stayed together, that you've worked your problems out, that you seem to have reached some sort of an understanding and an arrangement."

Hillary burst in. "Wait a minute, wait a minute! This is not an arrangement or an understanding. This is a marriage. That's a very different thing."

She went on, "You know, I'm not sitting here some little woman standing by her man like Tammy Wynette. I'm sitting here because I love him and I respect him and I honor what he's been through and what we've been through together. And, you know, if that's not enough for people, then, heck, don't vote for him."

A moment later she was saying, "I think if the American people get a chance and if they're trusted to exercise their vote right because people talk to them about real issues, this country will be okay. That's what we're betting on, and we're just going to roll the dice and see what happens."

CHAPTER SIXTEEN

The Other Woman

Immediately after the "60 Minutes" interview, Hillary and Bill Clinton returned to New Hampshire, where they continued carrying out their campaign schedules. In general, the consensus seemed to be that they had both done the best they could do under the worst of circumstances: Bill Clinton had played down the alleged affair as much as he could without blatantly denying it; Hillary Clinton had played the faithful wife who believed in her marriage and her husband.

Still, the Gennifer Flowers thing would not go away. Richard Kaplan, the editor of the *Star,* was holding Gennifer Flowers in an undisclosed location until she could meet the press to answer questions about the allegations she had made in her *Star* story and to respond to what the Clintons had said on "60 Minutes."

The day after that broadcast, representatives of the media were crowded into a conference room in New York's Waldorf-Astoria Hotel to hear what story Flowers would be telling today, inasmuch as she had in 1990 denied that she had ever had an affair with Bill Clinton and now in 1992 declared that she had been having an affair with him ever since 1980. When she appeared, she was accompanied by Blake Hendrix, a Little Rock lawyer introduced as her attorney, and a number of *Star* employees.

She began her statement by indicating how "angry" she became with the candidate's denial that the two of them had had an affair. She was being forced, she intimated, to go public for that reason. "When I heard the *Star* was going to run a story about Larry Nichols's lawsuit, when I heard Bill describe our relationship as an absolute, total lie, I knew what my decision should be—to tell my side of the story truthfully and as quickly as possible."

After a short, dramatic pause, she went on. "Yes. I was Bill Clinton's lover for twelve years, and for the past two years I have lied about the relationship. The truth is, I loved him. Now he tells me to deny it. Well, I'm sick of all the deceit and I'm sick of all the lies."

She said that watching "60 Minutes" the night before had left her feeling disgusted at the man she thought she had known so well. This was not, she went on, the man she had fallen in love with. It was a one-dimensional side of Bill Clinton that she had never seen before.

The audiotapes were made in 1990–91, she explained, when Flowers had telephoned Clinton about Larry Nichols's lawsuit—the lawsuit that implicated five women, including Gennifer Flowers, as Clinton's lovers. There were, in fact, several calls, all made between September 1990 and January 1991.

The tapes were typically amateur. They were garbled in spots and replete with unexplained pauses. But in some instances it was obvious what the two people were talking about.

Near the beginning of the ten minutes of recorded conversation, the following exchange occurred:

"My parents are here," Flowers said, "and I'll tell you what. That last thing I needed was to—"

A male voice, identified by Flowers as Clinton, broke in, "—have that happen."

"Have that happen, because my mother would get very concerned and worried, and so far, you know—"

Some garbled talk followed, then the male voice said, "If they ever hit you with it, just say 'no' and go on. There's nothing they can do."

A little later, the talk turned to specifics about Larry Nichols and the possibility that he might be doing interviews on television shows like "Hard Copy" and "Inside Edition." "Right," Flowers said. "Well, he better not get on there and start naming names."

"Well, that's what I mean. You know, if all the people are named, deny it. That's all. I mean, I expect them to come look into it and interview you and everything, but I just think that if everybody's on record denying it, you've got no problem."

"Why would they waste their money and time coming down here unless someone showed them some interest?"

"That's it. I mean, they're going to run this Larry Nichols thing down, they're going to try to goad people up, you know. But if everybody kind of hangs tough, they're just not going to do anything. They can't."

"No. They can't."

"They can't run a story like this unless somebody said, 'Yeah, I did it with him.' "

Later on, Flowers asked him: "Are you going to run?"

"I want to. I wonder if I'm going to be blown out of the water with this. I don't see how they can [garbled word or words] so far."

"I don't think they can."

"If they don't have pictures . . . and no one says anything, then they don't have anything, and arguably, if someone says something, they don't have much."

"If they could blow you out of the water, they would have already blown you."

Flowers soon became chatty. "Oh, I'd love to see you be President. I think that would be wonderful. I think you'd make a damned good one. I don't like Bush. I think he's a sneaky bastard. [garbled word or words] He's two-faced. . . . Whatever you need me to do, just let me know."

"I will."

Later, they began talking about the campaign. "I might lose the nomination to Bob Kerry because he's got all the Gary Hart–Hollywood money and because he's single, looks like a movie star, won the Medal of Honor, and since he's single, nobody cares if he's screwing."

Talk eventually wandered to Governor Mario Cuomo. "Cuomo's at 87 percent name recognition," Clinton said, "and I have 54 percent. . . . I'm at a terrible disadvantage in name recognition still, but we're coming up. . . . We're moving pretty well. I'm really pleased about it."

"I don't particularly care for Cuomo's demeanor."

"Boy, he is so aggressive!"

"He seemed like he could get real mean. . . . I wouldn't be surprised if he didn't have some mafioso major connections."

"Well, he acts like one."

Flowers eventually told him to "hang in there." "I don't mean to worry you, I just—"

"If I can help you, you let me know."

"I don't know where to turn. . . . I mean, my contacts have just sort of fizzled in Nashville, it's been a long time, and, I don't know, I don't know anybody. . . . You let me know if you know anything I need to know about."

"I will."

The tapes actually proved nothing conclusive beyond what Hillary and Bill Clinton had said on "60 Minutes," but there were other questions the media wanted to ask Flowers in the crowded room. Hendrix tried to keep the press conference in order, but soon enough it turned into a shouting and shoving match.

One revelation that Flowers made was that she had been in conversation with what she termed a "local Republican candidate"—"local" meaning oriented to Little Rock—who had suggested that she go public with her claims. She would not identify the candidate. When the shouting and battling for position among the television and print photographers turned too boisterous, Hendrix threatened to end the session. As the questions got more and more out of line, he said again that he would close it down.

"Did the governor use a condom?" some journalist shouted across the room.

That was the end.

Exactly how much money the *Star* paid Gennifer Flowers for her story and for the use of the tapes at the press conference was never made public. The *Wall Street Journal* wrote that she received between $130,000 and $175,000. The Clinton camp thought the total might have been around $50,000.

Hillary was about to fly out to Colorado on her campaign schedule. Before she left, she and Clinton analyzed the tapes and the transcript of the press conference in minute detail, Hillary acting as if she were working on a case in litigation. "We now know," she told a Colorado audience, using her homework to good effect, "that when Republicans had first offered money to this woman to change her story she held out, apparently negotiating with the media, *Star* magazine, to change a story she had denied repeatedly."

It was, in fact, Hillary who got the most mileage out of the story in the *Star* and the release of the tapes. The Thursday after Flowers met the press, Hillary was invited to participate on the ABC-TV show "PrimeTime Live," to be interviewed by Sam Donaldson.

The program featuring Hillary was broadcast on January 30, 1992, at ten

P.M. EST. Her segment was titled "The Other Woman"—meaning Gennifer Flowers. Of course the main subject of the interview was the absentee candidate, Bill Clinton.

It was a tough, rock-'em-sock-'em interview, and one that Hillary was peculiarly suited for. Donaldson wanted to set up Hillary as Clinton's helpmeet, then the wronged woman, then ask questions that were actually directed at the candidate, though posed to her as his loyal supporter and defender. His opening set the tone:

First of all, he pointed out how Governor Bill Clinton had become mired in an extramarital scandal that might compromise his chances of running for President. His wife, nevertheless, had stood by him and in fact fought against those who were trying to bring him down.

The crux of the matter was really Hillary, Donaldson intimated, not her husband. It had developed into a fight between two women for public support. There was Gennifer Flowers, who claimed to have carried on an affair with the governor. And there was Hillary Clinton, his wife.

Donaldson characterized Hillary as her husband's "primary defensive shield" in confronting the charges of infidelity that had been raised against him. Without further comment, he turned to her and asked her point-blank if she had heard the excerpts from those "alleged" tapes.

"Yes. And read the transcripts. Sure."

"When you hear someone whose voice—is it your husband on those tapes?"

The temptation at this point was to deny that Clinton was on the amateurish, scratchy, garbled tapes. But Hillary was a skillful lawyer. She knew that there could be as much danger, if not more, of raising doubts about a witness's integrity in an outright denial as in an admission.

She took the trained litigator's way out. "Who can tell?" she asked rhetorically with a wave of the hand. "I—" She paused, letting puzzlement show. "I don't have any idea." At this point it was obvious that even though she had been married to Bill Clinton for sixteen years, she was not sure whether the man on the tapes was her husband or some actor talking like him.

With that idea planted firmly in the minds of every viewer, she played it cool. "But I—" Change of pace. "But he's talked to her," she admitted. "We know that." She meant, "I know that." "I sat there in the kitchen one night when he returned a call to her."

Donaldson pounced on that point. "Well, when you hear something like—if the transcript is correct, she signs off a conversation saying, 'Goodbye, darling,' and he says, 'Good-bye, baby.' "

Hillary shook her head. "Oh, that's not true," she said. "That's just not true."

"That didn't happen?" Donaldson quizzed her.

"No, of course not."

Donaldson went right on. "Or he says, you know, 'They don't have the pictures.' "

"Well, I'll tell you what," Hillary said. "This was a woman who at least pretended that her life was ruined because somebody had alleged that she had a relationship at some point with Bill Clinton." While ignoring the point about pictures, she was underlining the idea that there might never have been an affair.

She went on, "Anybody who knows my husband knows that he bends over backwards to help people who are in trouble and is always willing to listen to their problems."

"You mean," Donaldson said, "in those telephone conversations he was just trying to help her out?" His expression showed his astonishment at her suggestion.

"Well, he—he—" Then Hillary had it. "The first time he called her, I mean, we were in the kitchen together and he said, you know, 'This woman thinks her life is over,' and he felt very sorry for her."

Excerpts of tape from Flowers's press conference showed her telling about her love affair with Clinton.

"Sam," Hillary said, "if somebody's willing to pay you $130,000 or $170,-000, to say something and you get your fifteen minutes of fame and you get your picture on the front page of every newspaper and you're some failed cabaret singer who doesn't even have much of a résumé to fall back on, and what's [more], she's lied about—you know, that's the daughter of Willie Horton, as far as I'm concerned. It's the same kind of attempt to keep the real issues of this country out of the mainstream debate where they need to be."

That is, the real villains were the Republicans, although she did not name them. Whether or not the "Willie Horton ploy" lost the 1988 election for Michael Dukakis, it was a bugaboo that could be conjured up again and again to illustrate the campaign mind-set of the GOP. Here the implication was that the dirty-tricks squad invented, or manipulated, Gennifer Flowers so she could destroy Bill Clinton.

Hillary Clinton's defense strategy was clear. She had managed to cast doubt on Bill Clinton's extramarital affair or affairs. Donaldson knew it.

"Tough words," he commented. "But unlike her husband, whose speech tends to round off the sharp edges, Hillary Clinton, campaigning this week in Colorado, drove home her points with a jackhammer, although she says Flowers's bombshell came as a surprise to her."

"I mean," Hillary said, "if you had told me that six months ago I would have laughed. I would have said, 'No way.'"

"Well, but some people argue that all is fair in love, war, and politics."

"Some people would," Hillary agreed, "and some people would also say they would do whatever it took to be reelected and it was a dog-eat-dog campaign."

Those "some people" were the Republicans, since she specified that "they" were trying to get *"re*elected." She had managed to turn the issue of Gennifer Flowers into an item on the opposition's dirty-tricks agenda. By this action, Hillary had effectively removed herself from the limelight. She was a wronged woman who had been hit upon by politicians of the opposition party. Thus there was no need to forgive Bill Clinton. He had done nothing. The entire matter was simply the machinations of politicians trying to win an election.

Donaldson was not entirely convinced. He commented on the Clintons' appearance on "60 Minutes" the previous Sunday. He recalled that Hillary had answered her interviewer's question about why she was standing by her husband with the comment that she was not "just standing by her man like Tammy Wynette." Donaldson noted that Tammy Wynette was "hopping mad" at Hillary's putdown of her name and the phrase made popular in the hit song.

As indeed the singer *was.* There was a great deal more to "standing by her man" in the song she had made popular, which had to do with her stormy relationship with George Jones. It was about drugs and too much booze and moral decay and restitution, and it talked about tough choices and even tougher stances. And yes, Wynette was unhappy with the candidate's wife and her flippant use of the phrase.

"I'm sorry about that, and I apologize to Tammy Wynette if what I said offended her," Hillary said. "But I would not feel as strongly as I do that he is the right man to be President in this country at this time if I personally believed anything other than that. So my standing by him, or for him—"

Donaldson was quick to seize the reins. "But you *are* standing by him."

She stared at him as if he were crazed. "Well, of course. We're married."

As numerous other people had, Donaldson pointed out that Hillary Rodham had made a strange decision when she had opted out of the big-city swirl and decided to go to Arkansas and marry Bill Clinton.

"You're not from the South," he reminded her, "and a lot of your friends in those days said, 'Oh, she's not going to go down to Arkansas.' I mean, this is a woman on the go. This is big city." He was watching her now, carefully.

She sensed a trap. She knew she would have to rely now not on hard intellect but on her softer instincts. "I had to make a hard choice," she admitted, "but I also knew that I'd be real dishonest to myself if I didn't follow my heart and see where this relationship led, and, you know, make— you know, take that leap of faith."

"The Clintons," Donaldson said later, "were the golden couple, and in 1978, at the age of thirty-two, Bill Clinton was elected governor."

Hillary beamed. "Bill wanted to slay every dragon he could find. I mean, he took on every special interest group. He was ready to right every wrong that came his way. We were all young."

The discussion veered around to Clinton's run for reelection and his loss to his Republican opponent. Hillary's motives for abandoning her maiden name and adopting Clinton's was discussed, along with her cosmetic change in 1990 when she threw away her glasses and changed to soft contacts. Included was a clip of Bill Clinton intoning, "Our life is very much a partnership. Our public endeavors, we do in common. And I always say that my slogan might well be, 'Buy one, get one free.'"

The talk then moved back to the Republicans, whom Hillary now specifically accused of masterminding the Gennifer Flowers story. "I'll tell you what we know," she told Donaldson. "What we know is that a member of the Republican National Committee consulted with and advised Larry Nichols, a former state employee, on at least six occasions."

"Who was that?"

"He's a man named Bob Lesley, who was the counsel to the Republican party in Arkansas for years and now is a member of the Republican National Committee. We know that this woman has admitted that the Republicans offered her money to change her story and implicated my husband after having denied it repeatedly. And we know that the former Republican gubernatorial opponent has been out beating the bushes trying to stir this up for as long as he could since he was defeated, so—"

"Sheffield Nelson."

"That's right. That's right."

Donaldson explained. "Sheffield Nelson, the Republican who was soundly beaten in the 1990 governor's race, says he was on the verge of running ads about Clinton's alleged dalliances."

Hillary said, "Sheffield Nelson is a very bitter man because my husband beat him as he well should have, because he was a negative force in Arkansas politics. And he has now spent the last two years doing everything he can to try to get even, and it's a sort of sad spectacle."

What Donaldson was most interested in, he said, was whether or not Hillary Clinton felt that infidelity was important enough for the American people to make an issue of it when electing a President.

The lawyer in Hillary answered. "I think that's up to the individual. I would not presume—"

Donaldson interrupted, "I'm asking *you*."

Hillary considered. "No. I would not presume to say what an individual ought to or ought not to take into account. That's what elections are for."

She had sidestepped the issue. Donaldson had asked her what she thought. She said that she thought she should not set herself up as an example for others. Donaldson realized he would get no answer from her, and he let it go.

Hillary went on, "Bill Clinton has a record of accomplishment in a state that is a very small state. It's like living in a fishbowl, a very happy fishbowl, but nevertheless a small one, where people know him and they know him very, very well. And they've given him their trust and their confidence for eleven years in the highest position they could vote for him for."

"But he wants to play in a far bigger pond now," Donaldson pointed out. "There are some people who would say that if you cheat on one thing, you may cheat on something else, that it's a character problem."

"Well," Hillary mused aloud, "I think character is a lot bigger than that, and I think all that's really important is the relationship of honesty and openness and forgiveness between Bill Clinton and me. I would not be—"

"Have you forgiven him?" Donaldson asked quickly, taking advantage of this opening.

"We have—" Hillary paused. "If you're married for more than ten minutes, you're going to have to forgive somebody for something. And that's one of the things we've had to learn over sixteen years. There are a lot of big and little things that come up in a marriage that if you don't deal with right then and there, they can sink you."

Donaldson was leading her, asking her if she had forgiven Clinton for sexual transgression. If she had said yes, she would have tacitly admitted that he had had an affair. So she simply said that she had forgiven him for many things in the past, avoiding any specifics.

Donaldson explained that it was the candidate himself who had told his wife, the Thursday before, about the *Star* exposé featuring Gennifer Flowers. A clip of Bill Clinton appeared on the screen: "I just told her. I called her on the phone and told her. And, you know, we talked about it. We did what two people who have, you know, made a lifetime commitment do. We talked it through. And, you know, she is an incredible person. She's so strong and she's so good and so honest. I mean, it was a—you know, I really love her."

Then a clip of Hillary Clinton: "He should be the next President of the United States—Bill Clinton!"

To end the segment, Donaldson commented on the relative popularity of the two Clintons, pointing out that some people felt the "wrong Clinton" was running for President. Donaldson said that Hillary Clinton had never taken up the idea of running for office seriously. She was playing two roles, he explained: the roles of campaign adviser *and* wife. Even though she gave her husband the same wide-eyed look that Nancy Reagan used to give her husband, she was no Nancy Reagan.

The Clintons, he said, were both students of the law and understood the political system. They were used to winning. This time it was up to Hillary Clinton to play the hardest game she could in order to help her husband score enough points to win over the American people.

In Oregon in 1991 with Bill Clinton's half-brother, Roger, in the background. (Wide World Photos/Wesley Hitt)

Waving to a crowd during a stop in downtown Cleveland, Ohio, in 1992. (AP/Wide World Photos/ Mark Lennihan)

Baking bread in the Bronx. (AP/Wide World Photos)

Greeting commuters in the Chicago and Northwestern train station.
(AP/Wide World Photos)

Hillary visiting a family center at New York's Bank Street College of Education, 1992. (AP/Wide World Photos/Richard Drew)

Hillary and Tipper Gore display "Women of Steel" T-shirts at a rally for their husbands in the steel-producing town of Coatesville, Pennsylvania. (AP/Wide World Photos/George Widman)

Hillary shares the stage with Bill at her high school in Park Ridge, Illinois. (AP/Wide World Photos/Mark Elias)

Tipper Gore and Hillary Rodham Clinton embracing after their husbands' nominations for vice president and president of the United States. (Globe Photos, Inc. /Adam Scull)

Future First Family: Hillary, Bill, and Chelsea after candidate Clinton's acceptance speech at the Democratic National Convention. (Globe Photos, Inc./Adam Scull)

The Clinton family in a final victory appearance after the Democratic delegates sang Fleetwood Mac's "Don't Stop Thinking About Tomorrow." (Globe Photos, Inc./Adam Scull)

Bill and Hillary Rodham Clinton join their Hollywood friends Harry and Linda Bloodworth-Thomason at her surprise birthday party held at the Ritz-Carlton Hotel in Pasadena, California. Hillary is decked out in a gown that she had worn four years earlier at the Governor's Ball in Arkansas. (AP/Wide World Photos/J. Scott)

Barbara Bush greeting Hillary Rodham Clinton at the White House two weeks after Bill Clinton was elected president. (AP/Wide World Photos)

We did it! Bill and Hillary toast each other during a Congressional luncheon on Capitol Hill in honor of Bill Clinton's inauguration as forty-second president of the United States. (AP/Wide World Photos/John Duricka)

Down to work. Hillary Rodham Clinton participating in the economic tutorial held in Little Rock, Arkansas, a month before Bill Clinton was sworn in as president. (AP/Wide World Photos/Greg Gibson)

President-elect Clinton and Hillary salute the crowd at the Inaugural Gala held at the Washington Hilton Hotel. The Clintons conducted marathon drop-ins at four dinners culminating in Clinton's inauguration. (AP/Wide World Photos/Greg Gibson)

From left to right: John Scully, CEO of Apple Computer, the First Lady Hillary Rodham Clinton, Federal Reserve Chairman Alan Greenspan, and Second Lady Tipper Gore applaud President Clinton as he addresses a joint session of Congress. (AP/Wide World Photos/Ron Edmonds)

CHAPTER SEVENTEEN

The Interim Report

W ithin the confines of the Clinton campaign, Hillary Clinton remained tagged as one of the basic problems, if not *the* basic problem. Although Gennifer Flowers had provided the most drama and the most excitement, it was Hillary's quick-witted responses, off-the-top-of-the-head quips, and snappish wisecracks that were remembered.

Yes, she had stood by her man. But in doing so, she had compared herself to Tammy Wynette, who also had stood by her man, and compared them in a way the singer found demeaning. That had offended not only the singer but many other voters in the country-music world as well. That kind of sophisticated wit was not what the Clinton camp wanted.

They warned her. She tempered her remarks. Her speeches were gone over and defanged where necessary. But Hillary was an excellent extemporaneous speaker, and her extempore persona could not be edited in advance. She could only be chastised after the fact.

Clinton's fortunes continued to rise.

And then, on March 15, 1992, trouble struck again. This time it appeared in a *Washington Post* article positing a possible conflict of interest between the professional life of Hillary Rodham Clinton and the professional life of Governor Bill Clinton.

Michael Weisskopf and David Maraniss wrote, "Clinton rivals say that the very listing of the governor's wife as a partner [in the Rose Law Firm] gives Rose's client undue leverage in their dealings with state government. . . . The Rose Firm offers the full range of representation before the government, from getting environmental approvals from the state Pollution Control and Ecology Commission, to lobbying to protect the poultry industry from strict regulations on animal waste, to writing the rules by which corporations treat their shareholders."

It was inevitable that an opponent would pick up this tidbit and use it against Clinton, as Jerry Brown did on March 16 during the Democratic presidential candidates' debate. Brown zeroed in on Tyson Foods, a poultry-products corporation and Rose client.

The attack came over poultry pollution. Brown said, "It's not only corruption. It's an environmental disaster, and it's the kind of conflict of interest that is incompatible with the kind of public servant we expect in a President."

Moving out from behind the lectern as if about to attack his opponent physically, Bill Clinton shouted, "I don't care what you say about me . . . but you ought to be ashamed of yourself for jumping on my wife. You're not worthy of being on the same platform with my wife."

Brown was amused. "Wait a minute, Bill! You're always trying to attack. You never answer the question."

But Clinton did. "I'm saying that I never funneled any money to my wife's law firm, ever!"

Hillary was in Chicago the next day. Reporters dogged her everywhere. Finally, they caught up with her on a street corner. A campaign aide who was following his instructions grabbed her by the arm to pull her away. But Hillary gave him a fiery look, as much as telling him to back off.

The questions were about Bill Clinton's defense of her the day before. Hillary was quite happy to make a statement.

"I thought it was sort of desperate and sad," she said, referring to Brown's attack on the two Clintons. She smiled. "You know, every time Bill Clinton gets ahead, the people that are running against him attack him, and I think that that's because the issues in this campaign really will cause change in this country."

Following this plug for the "change" issue that the Clintons were flogging, she did not dispute any facts in the *Washington Post* story. Instead, she chose to discuss the pressures that faced modern women and her own efforts to ensure that women had the opportunities to make their own choices in life.

The controversy over conflict of interest was the result of one of the choices she herself had made, of course. It was not *necessary* for her to go to work for a law firm once she was married; she could have stayed in teaching. Or, as she put it, "I suppose I could have stayed home and baked cookies and had teas, but what I decided to do is fulfill my profession, which I entered before my husband was in public life."

Syndicated columnist Ellen Goodman had a succinct reaction to the cookies-and-tea remark: "Ouch!"

Hillary was getting wound up. "This campaign is about issues that I've worked on for more than twenty years," she said. She had done "everything I know how," she said, to avoid any conflict of interest between her law practice and her husband's political career. The real issue, she said, was "women making the choices that are right for them.

"This is uncharted terrain," she went on, as if she could not stop. "There is no road map. How to avoid the appearance of conflict while still allowing the spouse to pursue the work of their lives is going to be the issue" for the entire group of politicians coming to national prominence.

"And the kind of choices that women have to make today are tough choices. I'm a big believer in women making the choices that are right for them. And the work that I have done as a professional, as a public advocate, has been aimed at trying to assure women can make the choices they should make.

"Part of what this campaign is about is empowering people to be able to make good choices, particularly women, who have had a disproportionately negative impact in the 1980s. The biggest increase in poverty in the 1980s is poverty among women and their children.

"You've got to remember that I have tried the best way that I know how to be as careful as possible. Now, in hindsight, I suppose people can say, 'You should have done this, you should have done that.' I didn't presume that anybody would presume anything other than that I was trying to do the right thing all the way down the line."

She said that she had done legal work for Madison Guaranty but that it was not related to the S & L dealings with state regulators. Letting some exasperation show, she remarked, "For goodness' sake, you can't be a lawyer if you don't represent banks."

According to a Little Rock political observer quoted by Charles F. Allen and Jonathan Portis in *Bill Clinton: The Comeback Kid,* the truth of the matter about the connection between Hillary Clinton's law work and state business was as follows:

"Most of the senior partners at the Rose Law Firm make more than

$500,000 a year; but Hillary Clinton only made a little more than $100,000 last year. It's clear she could have made a lot more money by taking on state projects, or by devoting less time to pro bono work such as the Children's Defense Fund, but she chose not to do that and took the economic loss. Now, for all of her good intentions, all she receives is bad press."

The Clintons' 1991 income tax records showed that Hillary made $109,719 from her law practice and $70,200 from fees and honoraria. Bill made $35,000, the salary of the Arkansas governor, $3,166 from a "public relations" fund, and $5,500 in honoraria.

Because of the increasing media interest in Hillary, she was drawing more attention whenever she appeared anywhere. Not all of it was positive. When she and Bill Clinton were walking in a St. Patrick's Day parade in Chicago just before the primary, there were a number of obscene comments from the crowd.

"Where's Gennifer Flowers?" someone wanted to know. "Adulterer!" others shouted.

Nevertheless, Clinton scored in Illinois on March 18, winning 51 percent of the vote. Tsongas came in second, Brown third. Clinton now had amassed a total of 949 delegates, with 2,145 the number that would put him over the top.

Still the turmoil over Hillary's image would not go away. It concerned not only Democrats who wanted Clinton to win but others who might be happy with a Clinton victory. William Safire, a Republican anomaly on the staff of the *New York Times,* wrote a column about Hillary.

He said that this "successful lawyer and feminist" was coming across not as a politically cunning animal but as "a political bumbler"—largely because she was exhibiting a great deal of contempt "for women who work at home."

Safire wrote, "Her first gaffe, derogating the Tammy Wynette stand-by-your-man pose, can be excused as an unfortunate choice of words under incredible pressure." But her second mistake—"I suppose I could have stayed home and baked cookies and had teas"—showed a complete lack of understanding of fundamental campaigning strategy. "You do not defend yourself from a conflict-of-interest charge by insulting a large segment of the voting public," he wrote.

Safire then listed a few suggestions for Hillary:

"Stop defending yourself by what you're not. Self-definition by exclusion is needlessly defensive, as is claiming to be quoted out of context when you were not."

He urged, "Press your strength, which is not articulation but realism." Her "60 Minutes" remark that people who didn't like the Clintons' explanation shouldn't vote for them was on target. "That was straightforward. Honest people like such realism."

Safire advised, "You don't need 'face time'; fish where the fish are." He suggested Hillary go after George Bush's strength, Republican women, by taking a "permit-but-discourage middle ground on abortion" and never knocking women who work at home.

Safire could not mention Hillary's third major gaffe, inasmuch as it had not yet happened. It occurred in her long interview with Gail Sheehy for a *Vanity Fair* article. In it, Hillary explained how annoyed she became when the media pilloried Bill Clinton because rumors of an affair with Gennifer Flowers had surfaced, while President George Bush allegedly had escaped having media scrutiny trained on his private life.

Hillary was referring to the fact that during the 1988 presidential campaign, various news organizations had investigated rumors then prevalent that Bush had a longtime romantic relationship with an aide. The rumors were never substantiated. During the same campaign, a top aide to Governor Michael Dukakis was forced to resign after suggesting to reporters that Bush had an extramarital affair. Bush and the woman mentioned flatly denied the rumors in 1982 when he was Vice President.

The *Vanity Fair* article quoted Hillary as saying, "I'm convinced part of it is the establishment—regardless of party—sticks together. They're gonna circle the wagons."

Hillary was then quoted, "I had tea with Anne Cox Chambers (head of the Cox newspaper empire) and she's sittin' there in her sun room sayin', 'You know I just don't understand why they think they can get away with this—everybody knows about George Bush.'

"And then (Chambers) launches into this long description of, you know, Bush and his carrying on, all of which is apparently well known in Washington."

When the story appeared, Hillary immediately apologized for discussing the rumors about Bush. "It was a mistake," she said. "Nobody knows better than I the pain that can be caused by even discussing rumors in private conversation," she said. "And I did not mean to be hurtful to anyone!"

She explained, "I shouldn't have been drawn into a discussion under any circumstances. It was in a private conversation, but that's not the point. After what my husband and I have been through, I don't think the media should go after anybody."

It was obvious that something would have to be done. Although Clinton was clearly the front-runner, he would lose unless his extramarital affairs were neutralized, his impression of wishy-washiness and indecision counteracted, and his untrustworthiness somehow buried. There were also similar appraisals of Hillary, including rough edges that would have to be sanded down and polished up.

A worried top echelon met in late April. The think-tank trio included Frank Greer, the Clinton media consultant, James Carville, the campaign's chief strategist, and Stan Greenberg, the organization's polling expert.

They reviewed the feedback they had been painstakingly gathering throughout the early months of the primaries. The basic facts were scary at best, damning at worst.

The memo that later came out of the appraisal said, "Bill Clinton is viewed unfavorably by a sizable minority of Democratic primary voters (about 30 percent) and a plurality of general election voters (about 40 percent). The questions about personal morality matter, but their larger impact is contained in the general impression that he will say what is necessary and that he does not 'talk straight.'"

It went on, "The impression of being the ultimate politician is reinforced by Clinton's presentation (evasive, no clear yes or no, handy lists, fast talking, and all that political analysis). Clinton's political nature leads voters to a number of critical and debilitating conclusions."

The conclusions were absolutely terminal, at least for the campaign:

1. Clinton is not real.
2. Clinton is for himself, not the people.
3. Clinton cannot stand up to special interests.
4. Clinton cannot be the candidate of change.
5. Clinton's message/ideas are discounted.
6. Clinton is privileged like the Kennedys.

The book on Hillary Clinton was not much better. In general, the committee found that Hillary was perceived as a successful career woman who did not particularly care for her homemaking chores. She was seen as an outspoken, obstinate individual, very intelligent, very opinionated, very sure of herself. She also appeared overwhelmingly obsessed with power and career.

She was thought to be domineering, cold, harsh, and defiant. Her attitude toward her husband was perceived as distant at best and glacial at worst. There seemed to be very little softness or feminity about her. She pursued her own ends tenaciously, without thought of anyone else.

Hillary was all business, in charge. She appeared to be the opposite of Barbara Bush. She was sharp-tongued, witty, and funny—but she habitually let loose barbs that could eviscerate. Besides that, she was short-tempered sometimes, unaffectionate, and certainly did not suffer fools lightly.

That was the bad news.

The good news? There wasn't any.

The trio recommended a general campaign strategy. There should be an overall theme, with tactics to back it up, and a specific message not only for Bill Clinton but for Hillary Clinton as well.

On the personal level, both Hillary and Bill should be perceived as more husband and wife. In American terms, with people who viewed sitcoms every night of the year on their television sets, that meant more lovey-dovey photo opportunities.

Bill Clinton should come across as high-minded, aggressive, oriented to the middle class, a youthful agent of change who could stand up to special-interest groups. Hillary should come across as a serious-minded but fun-to-be-with woman, a person dedicated to her family as well as to her professional goals.

The basic objective, as conceived by Greer, Carville, and Greenberg, was not to present false pictures of Bill and Hillary but to replace their current, distorted images with more accurate ones, presented in ways likely to appeal to voters. The strategists offered a number of specific suggestions to aid the candidate and his wife in effecting the changes that would cast them in a better light for the American people.

Clinton's untrustworthiness was the worst aspect of all. To replace the idea that Bill was "not real" but was a result of false packaging created by skilled enemy image distorters, the memo urged that he be presented as "a human being who struggled, pulled his weight, showed strength of character, and fought for change."

In addition, it was important to remind the public of his difficult childhood: His father had died before he was born; his mother had been forced to work and struggle to make ends meet; he had been obliged to intercede "to stop an alcoholic stepfather who abused his brother and mother." Emphasis should also be given to his achievements as governor. He had battled teachers' unions, opposed institutionalized racism, and challenged the perpetuation of a failed welfare system.

The memo gave examples of TV appearances in which Bill Clinton had scored. Responses of focus groups suggested that Bill Clinton had an extraordinary power when he talked about his mother and his alcoholic stepfather (example: a Gabe Pressman interview), when he talked about education and what he and Hillary had done for the Arkansas school system (example: a Maryland debate), and when he showed dramatically exactly what he really cared about (example: an ACT UP confrontation).

As for the fact that the character of Bill Clinton seemed always to be in doubt, the memo suggested an aggressive scheduling of the candidate on the popular talk shows, where he could project the real Bill Clinton they wanted the voters to see. "These shows must introduce these elements of the biography, our principal message and the human side of Bill Clinton"—such as his sense of humor and his musicianship.

The memo's criticism of Bill Clinton's appearance on talk shows included a remark that they hurt the candidate because they "too often suggested compromises to organized political support." It was recommended that Clinton be involved in "challenge speeches," addresses that would directly focus on specific interest groups in order to "draw in the press." There Clinton could appear as a "leader who lacks strings and is strong enough to challenge powerful interests."

The trio found that Hillary contributed to "a remarkably distorted" view of the Clinton marriage and family. "Bill and Hillary need to talk much more of their own family, including Chelsea, and their affection for each other." Perhaps Bill and Chelsea could surprise Hillary on Mother's Day, and the family might vacation at Disneyland.

The advisers' main goal was to make Clinton appear less "wishy-washy," less the fast-talking career politician, less the typical politico who did not "talk straight." As for Hillary, she should look less as if she were in the race for herself, less as if she were strictly "going for the power," and less like a wife intent on "running the [whole] show."

The memo, called the "General Election Project—Interim Report," reached the desks of Bill and Hillary shortly after it was drafted. Before long the Clintons had digested the material, discussed it at great length between themselves, and set about implementing the improvements that had been laid out for them.

Soon the force of the memo began to manifest itself in their images. The changes were so subtle and so well crafted that they did not immediately appear to the public at large. But the changes were there, and they would help bring victory.

CHAPTER EIGHTEEN

Return to Wellesley

Through most of the next four or five weeks, Hillary Clinton managed not to commit a verbal faux pas or utter a statement that cried for national excoriation, and the Hillary bashing diminished in intensity. Of course, there were stories about her, but they were mostly harmless recaps of her bio and assorted assessments of her current stand with the voters.

The reshapers of the Hillary Clinton image had been working quietly behind the scenes. Hillary herself had purposely adopted a low profile, appearing at her scheduled campaign stops, delivering speeches that had been written deliberately for those whose taste for politics ran to the bland.

Soon enough, though, she was plunged back into controversy. The Clinton campaign people had suggested to Wellesley College that Hillary Rodham Clinton be selected as the 1992 commencement speaker.

Instantly the sensitive antennae of the faculty and the administration quivered in horror. A political spouse in a political year? The college would instantly be compromised as backing a particular candidate!

At the same time, there was strong support for Hillary in the college itself. She *was* a graduate. She *had* given the first commencement speech ever delivered by an undergraduate. And besides, two years ago, in 1990, Barbara

Bush, the nation's First Lady, had been the guest speaker. Could the college turn down a woman who might indeed be the *next* First Lady?

The fires of dissent were finally quenched, and the absolutely impeccable Wellesley-ness of Hillary prevailed. The speech was scheduled.

In stories about the upcoming event, some journalists recalled the 1990 commencement. Not only had Barbara Bush spoken, but Raisa Gorbachev had come to visit the same day. There were so many reporters covering the two First Ladies that it was almost like a political event rather than a college graduation.

That was exactly what Hillary's 1992 speech turned out to be. But after all, it was a campaign year, and hardly anyone could have expected Hillary to ignore the fact that her husband was running for President.

The crowd assembled for the graduation was curious to see what attitude Hillary would adopt in view of her past struggles with the media and the public. The journalists assigned to cover the event were just as eager to assess this unpredictable, always exciting, always controversial figure.

On May 29, 1992, a Friday, propitiously warm and sunny, Hillary Rodham Clinton mounted the podium at Wellesley and began speaking. From the start, she tailored her speech for a political statement, but it was a softer approach than she had used in 1969. Yet it was definitely going to be a speech for Bill Clinton—as well as for Hillary Rodham.

She reminisced about her 1969 speech. After it was over, she said, she had changed clothes and headed for her favorite spot on campus, the lake. There she stripped down to her swimsuit, put her clothes in a pile on the ground, "took off those coke-bottle glasses that you've now seen in a hundred pictures and publications from one end of the country to the next," and went wading.

A security guard who happened by picked up her clothes and glasses and took them away. "Imagine my surprise when I emerged to find neither clothes nor glasses and, blind as a bat, had to feel my way back to Stone Davis." She visualized the headlines in the paper: "Girl offers vision to classmates and then loses her own." Or the tabloid version: "Girl swimming blinded by aliens after seeing Elvis."

Her light tone was a significant departure from her previous, more serious efforts, possibly in response to the Interim Report she had seen in late April. She certainly came across as less controversial, less aloof and detached, warmer, and more personally involved with her audience.

Next, she turned to the sixties, mentioning her own emergence from an "Ozzie and Harriet" suburb of Chicago into life at Wellesley. She remembered her class's inability to make up a decent cheer: "One-nine-six-nine Wellesley, rah, One more year, still no cheer." Then she talked seriously about civil rights, the Peace Corps, JFK's assassination, and the war in Vietnam.

"I was here on campus when Martin Luther King was murdered," she said in a low voice. "My friends and I put on black armbands and went into Boston to march in anger and pain—feeling as many of you did after the acquittals in the Rodney King case." Linking the two Kings and the two widely separated events was a skilled political maneuver, a tribute to Hillary's ability to construct logical sequences in her court presentations. But the tone was not high-decibel. It was moderate, almost mainstream.

She segued to the problem of all-women's colleges and the education of women. "What better time to speak about women and their concerns than in the spring of 1992?" She was interrupted by applause. It was only natural that she should be, because this topic was close to her listeners' hearts.

She gave a short summary of her travels during the campaign, stressing that she had seen the plight of all manner of women—shrinking welfare, no jobs, escalating violence, worries about children.

"But you know, women who pack lunch for their kids, or take the early bus to work, or stay out late at the PTA, or spend every spare minute tending to their aging parents do not need lectures from Washington about values." This blatantly partisan remark, obviously a response to Vice President Quayle's attack on the popular TV-sitcom character Murphy Brown, earned her more applause.

Then she moved along to her own personal relationships. "When I stood here before," she said, "I could never have predicted—let alone believed— that I would fall in love with Bill Clinton . . . and follow my heart to Arkansas."

Here was a perfect example of the Interim Report at work. Hillary used the phrase "fall in love with Bill Clinton," reinforced by the phrase "follow my heart to Arkansas," to present the picture of a pair of lovers rather than simply Mr. and Mrs. Bill Clinton. She was taking the opportunity to promote the idea of an adoring couple, as they could now be seen more and more often in the print media and on television.

"You may choose to be a corporate executive or a rocket scientist, you may run for public office, you may choose to stay home and raise your children— but you can now make any or all of those choices—and they can be the work of your life." More applause. The backlash of criticism she had weathered after making her "cookies and teas" crack about homemaking mothers had obviously taught her a lesson. She would never again be caught segregating homemakers from "working" women.

Children were still her main professional and personal concern, she said. Her words presented the profile of a care-giving woman to the graduates of Wellesley as well as the people of America. She was showing herself as a woman whose mission in life was to make the world a better place for its children.

"I remember one very long night when my daughter, Chelsea, was about four weeks old and crying inconsolably. Nothing from my courses in my political science major seemed to help at all. Finally, I looked at her in my arms and I said, 'Chelsea, you've never been a baby before and I've never been a mother before. We are just going to have to help each other get through this together.' And so far, we have. And for Bill and me, she has been the great joy of our life, and watching her grow and flourish has given greater urgency to the task of helping all children.

"There are many ways of helping children. You can do it through your own personal lives by being dedicated, loving parents. You can do it in medicine or music, social work or education, business or government service. You can do it by making policy or making cookies." She got another hand for that remark.

"Not for one more year can our country think of children as some asterisk on our national agenda," she warned, and her audience applauded.

"How we treat our children should be front and center of that agenda, or I believe it won't matter what else is on it. My plea is that you not only nurture the values that will determine the choices you make in your personal lives but also insist on policies that include those values to nurture our nation's children.

" 'But, really, Hillary,' some of you may be saying to yourself, 'I've got to pay off my student loans. I can't even find a good job, let alone someone to love. How am I going to worry about the world? Our generation has fewer dreams, fewer illusions than yours.'

"And I hear you and millions of young women like you all over our country. As women today, you do face tough choices. You know the rules are basically as follows:

"If you don't get married, you're abnormal.

"If you get married but don't have children, you're a selfish yuppie.

"If you get married and have children but then go outside the home to work, you're a bad mother.

"If you get married and have children but stay home, you've wasted your education.

"And if you don't get married but have children and work outside the home as a fictional newscaster, you get in trouble with the Vice President." That got another laugh. The score was Hillary 2, Quayle 0.

"So you see, if you listen to all those people who make those rules, you might conclude that the safest course of action is just to take your diploma and crawl under your bed. But let me end by proposing an alternative.

"Hold on to your dreams whatever they are. Take up the challenge of forging an identity that transcends yourself. Transcend yourself and you will find yourself. Care about something you needn't bother with at all. Throw yourself into the world and make your voice count."

This was straight talk from one graduate to another, right out of the book of commencement exhortations.

"Look forward to the challenges ahead," she said, beginning to wind things up. "And if you'd like to meet me for a swim later, don't tell the security guards—just find me. And I hope that over the next years, you will look back at this day as a truly unique opportunity to transcend and forge an identity that is uniquely your own.

"God speed."

There was no question about it. The Hillary Clinton who tended to jam her foot in her mouth when she spoke had vanished. A new Hillary Clinton had taken her place. This one was modeled more on the precepts of the Interim Report than on Hillary's own ideas of what made a good speaker.

Even so, equitable as the speech was, there were some murmurs of discontent from the audience and from the media.

"But was it a Bill Clinton campaign speech or a commencement speech for Wellesley College?" asked Elizabeth Ross, a staff writer for the *Christian Science Monitor*.

Sarah Cashin, a New Jersey member of the graduating class, thought Hillary's speech was too political. "Why did she mention husband Bill in the speech, and why did she talk about an agenda for America? Couldn't she have directed her talk more to the Wellesley Class of 1992?"

"Why should I have?" Hillary might have answered her. In 1969 she had talked about an agenda for America. Was 1992 that much different?

CHAPTER NINETEEN

Nothing Too Hillary

In spite of all the valiant efforts to act on the Interim Report and remodel Hillary Clinton into a more acceptable version of a candidate's wife, many people still did not know what to make of her. Was she the "Lady Macbeth of Little Rock"? Was she the "Yuppie Wife From Hell"? Or was she a viable spouse cast in the mold of the Baby Boomer generation?

"She confused them," Martha Sherrill wrote in a *Washington Post* story. "She wasn't just a mother or a wife or a lawyer. She made people uneasy, nervous." As Sherrill put it, "People had feelings about strong women and wronged wives."

Sherrill traced much of the confusion to the headbands Hillary wore. She had taken to them when she had first colored her hair because, as well as keeping her hair back, they tended to obscure the dark roots. Wearing them had nothing to do with her political stance at all. They were not hippie trademarks, or a secret code for a flaming liberal, as many suspected, or even symbols for a crypto Junior Leaguer.

Still, whether velvet, tortoiseshell, or red, these headbands came to mean a great deal to the public and particularly to the media. Hillary's hair was blurring her image, sending some unclear message. That was the reason the headbands were taking such a beating.

"No matter what feminists say, the way you look—if you're a woman—is still an overriding factor," Sherrill pointed out.

When George Bush had decided to run for President in 1988, his campaign strategists had suggested that he have his wife, Barbara, spruced up. Her response was pleasant but firm. "I'll do anything you want," she told Roger Ailes, the campaign media adviser, "but I won't dye my hair, change my wardrobe, or lose weight."

Hillary Clinton, who was as stubborn as Barbara Bush about ethics, morals, and other rigorous things that really mattered, threw up her hands and surrendered when it came to cosmetics. In 1980, when she tinted her hair for the first time, she had done the same thing.

Hairstyling was not among Hillary's many talents. One of her closest advisers said, "To tell you the truth, Hillary is kind of incompetent in that department." So the Hollywood connection was enlisted again, in anticipation of a brutal summer campaign. Linda Bloodworth-Thomason called in her own specialist in hair to do what he could for Hillary.

Cristophe Schatteman, usually known simply as Cristophe, was a former hockey player from Belgium who had become a hairdresser in Hollywood. He got the job done. The remodeling, intentionally subtle, would not be noticed overnight by the public and, especially, the media. Cristophe studied her carefully before making some important changes. Then he cut her hair shorter and sheared off some of the bangs.

"I felt she needed something with more style to it," Cristophe said. "Her hair is not her priority. She knows that she has to look good, but she needs something that she can take care of herself in two or three minutes." His careful changes seemed to help. Hillary's hair did not give off the same conflicting subliminal message it had before.

Linda then sent her to Cliff Chally, who did the clothes on "Designing Women," for a new look. He, too, refused to make radical changes but muffled her tendency toward loud colors in an effort to subdue her wardrobe. She began to wear more pastels, even neutrals.

Hillary's features were strong, matching her provocative personality, so there were makeup changes, too. To mute her tendency to dominate, she now wore smaller, less obvious earrings.

Hillary was taking another look inside herself as well. She was thinking about her position and how people were reacting to her points of view. "I want people to know me and all the dimensions of my life," Hillary said. "I probably made too many assumptions about what people would know [about me]."

"They may still decide that, you know, they don't like me because I wear headbands on occasion, or whatever the reason might be. But at least I want them to know that I think my experience as a woman growing to age in the last two decades is very much like the experience of most of the women I know. . . . I hope that will come across."

By July, when the Democratic Convention was scheduled to take place in New York, the refurbishing of Hillary Rodham Clinton was well on its way to being accomplished, inside and out. She was now more a combination of mother and homemaker and career woman than totally a cool, calculating, tough professional. Her hair was softened, her makeup lightened.

The makeover was not blatantly obvious to the media experts who saw her from day to day. And yet there was *something*. For example, *Newsweek* took a long, hard look at her in July and called her "a burned-out, buttoned-up automaton compared with the vibrant woman who strode purposefully onto the national scene last January."

Roger Ailes, the Republican campaign consultant, said, "Hillary Clinton in an apron is like Michael Dukakis in a tank."

According to *Newsweek,* the word "Hillary" had come to mean something special to the young women of America. "To do a Hillary" now meant offering a husband or male friend advice on the hard choices in life, sexual and otherwise.

A *New Yorker* cartoon depicted a typical cosmopolitan woman shopper searching for just the right jacket in a posh store. "Nothing too Hillary," she advises the salesclerk.

But not everybody agreed with the media. People who were close to the family said that Hillary was no "ambitious careerist" at all. "Her law career gets too much attention," her friend Susan Fleming said. "She is certainly a tenacious, multidimensional person. But she is also a compassionate and loyal friend and a great mother. There are people who don't want to believe a woman can play all those roles so well."

Skip Rutherford, a Little Rock businessman who worked with Hillary on health-care and desegregation issues, recalled once asking her about how to deal with his own daughter and her problems with elementary school math.

"First of all, she told me not to worry so much. Then she said to work on ways to build her self-esteem by focusing on things she did well. Finally, she suggested that we buy a calculator and work with it. She still calls back to ask how we are doing."

In fact, that very month, *People* magazine ran a story on the Clintons, and the focus of the article was a huge closeup of Hillary and Bill very much together: Bill looking down into Hillary's eyes and Hillary smiling up at him intimately.

Hillary was playing a trailblazing role, the spouse of the first presidential candidate to come out of the Baby Boom generation. It afforded her an in-depth education in mass communication.

However, she admitted to an interviewer that she had never expected to be viewed under the same microscope as her husband or subjected to such endless speculation about every detail of her life.

"What I didn't realize when we started," she said, "was that the changes that took place ten years ago at the state and congressional level really had not taken place yet on the Presidential level." She was referring to the electorate's acceptance of political candidates wives as professionals in their own right and not simply appendages of their more powerful husbands.

Hillary went on, "I didn't realize that because this is a transition period there would be so much focus on who and what and why as applied to decisions that millions of women, including myself, have lived with all these years."

She admitted that she had failed to understand early in the campaign that an unguarded remark taken out of context could easily be misconstrued and used to attack her in ways she had never suspected.

Referring to the notorious off-the-cuff remark she had made about staying home and baking cookies and having teas, she said: "I really was naive about things like sound bites. The remark presumed an understanding that Jerry Brown had attacked me totally unfairly." Unfortunately, the fact that most people who heard it had not been following the intricacies of the verbal exchanges between the Clinton and Brown camps quite escaped her at the time.

And Hillary had learned a great deal about communicating through the media, too, since leaving the relatively rough and tumble playing field of Arkansas. "In Arkansas," she said, "you have to deal with people's real problems. You can't run from them. . . . You're stopped on the street. People call you at home."

As for Hillary's conflicting roles of professional and wife, she had certainly managed to view all of her individual roles in their proper perspective and to utilize them when it was necessary to.

Betsey Wright, Bill Clinton's longtime campaign chief of staff, said, "She is a professional who has made a professional reputation in her own right and who also had an advocacy record, particularly for children, that is separate and apart from her husband's public service." Her old friend from Wellesley, Eldie Acheson, noted that Hillary's "own experience and her own intelligence didn't quite prepare her for what she was going to get when she took the same behavior [the way she behaved at home] on the road."

Hillary still blamed Republican politics for much of the flak. Back in February, she remembered, Richard Nixon had observed that Clinton should "manage [Hillary] carefully" because a strong wife "makes the husband look like a wimp. You want a wife who's intelligent, but not too intelligent." At the time he said that, Hillary recalled in July, "I thought it was pretty odd. But now I see it as part of a pattern. Tear down Bill Clinton by saying he's got this smart wife."

During the first hectic months of 1992, Hillary learned that campaigning up front in the limelight was different from campaigning in the background out of sight.

"What I have learned is you have got to give people a chance to know you." She compared campaigning to moving into a new neighborhood. "People may be glad to see you, but they are initially standoffish, waiting to find out who you are. Well, Bill and I just moved into America's neighborhood. I want them to know as much about me and all my different roles as possible.

"Part of why I think this election is so important . . . is [that] so many challenges facing families now really are different. You almost cannot fault George Bush for not understanding the importance of something like family and medical leave. It is not part of his experience."

She continued, "If all you do is give lip service and rhetoric to families but you don't do anything . . . to make the rearing of children a primary national priority, it's a farce."

Americans, she said, "need to quit moaning and whining about the Europeans and the Japanese and just say, 'My gosh, let's get out there and get the job done.' Get the country to pull itself together."

In July, a USA Today–CNN–Gallup poll showed that 45 percent of the voters had a favorable opinion of Hillary Clinton. That was way up from 36 percent in April, just before the Interim Report came out and the reshaping of Hillary and Bill began. The remodeling exercise was certainly working for her.

She was getting passing marks from the media as well. Eleanor Clift, writing in *Newsweek,* even commented positively on her use of pronouns. "She does not talk easily about herself and hardly ever says 'I' in connection with anything personal. She has learned to turn probing questions into policy discussions. A query about what surprised her in the campaign turned into a lament about reporters' lack of knowledge about Vietnam and world history."

On June 2, when California had gone for Bill Clinton on primary day, he had secured the 2,145 delegates he needed for nomination. Any suspense as to what candidate would be running for President had been eliminated. Yet the Democratic Convention began with a great stir of excitement not only on the streets of New York but on the television screens that broadcast it throughout the country and in the newspapers that were covering the convention from every conceivable angle. The drama implicit in any election caused a tingle of excitement to stir in even the most cynical.

There *was* suspense, of course, about who Clinton would select as his running mate, and that was played for all it was worth. When Sen. Albert Gore was anointed, everything was over but the cheering and the shouting. And in the cheering and shouting, another element worked its charm.

That element was the Hollywood connection. Linda Bloodworth-Thomason and Harry Thomason wove show-biz magic into the proceedings by orchestrating, directing, and then producing a promenade from Macy's to the Convention Hall in Madison Square Garden the night before the acceptance speech.

More important, Harry Thomason made a filmed biography of Bill Clinton titled *The Man From Hope.* When it premiered at the convention, it proved to be a skilled piece of dramatized character building, a riveting image maker of the *real* Bill Clinton. In its own way it was a brilliant extrapolation of the material in the Interim Report, and it was right on target.

In May and June 1992, Clinton's image had been nebulous and distorted, like a face seen through a badly cut prism. "He had been introduced as a caricature of himself because of the various scandals," said Mandy Grunwald, a campaign media strategist. Additionally, most people had the idea that Bill Clinton was as privileged as a Kennedy; who else could spend two years at Oxford on a Rhodes Scholarship after graduating from college in the United States?

Harry Thomason's film had an electrifying effect on the audience. It went further than anything had in the past toward defining the real Bill Clinton for the world.

"The net effect of the convention," Grunwald said, "was that the before-and-after knowledge of [Clinton's] personal life and his personal story was extraordinary." She felt that "a lot of the most powerful imagery of the convention was [the Thomasons'] idea. . . . It was a large part of what propelled [Clinton] into such a big post-convention bounce."

Bill Clinton's selection of Albert Gore as his running mate was unusual. It violated the unwritten law that said a party ticket should be balanced—geographically, psychologically, even financially. This time it was as if an attempt had been made to produce twins. Both men were southerners. Both men were liberal Democrats. Both men had proved themselves in local politics before moving out into the national stream. Both were articulate, personable, and persuasive politicians in their own right.

More than the men, their wives were look-alikes. Tipper Gore and Hillary Clinton could almost be exchanged face for face, body for body. Luckily, they took to each other easily and comfortably.

TIPPER: I always missed the fact that I didn't have sisters. I wanted a sister like her.

HILLARY: Tipper is a real partner, somebody I can talk to, somebody who sees the world as I do.

The press was still concerned about Hillary. Reporters who understood where she was coming from doubted that she was going to stay in the low-key role she had been assigned by the image makers on the Clinton campaign team. In fact, she had let it be known that she was deliberately playing the "designated wife" for purposes of electing Bill Clinton.

It was a foregone conclusion that the Republican National Convention would endorse George Bush. But before that happened, a particularly nasty attack was first mounted on the Democrats. Its main target was not a candidate, but a candidate's wife.

The assault was launched by a virtual unknown, Rich Bond, the chairman of the Republican National Committee. At the very beginning of his speech to the convention, he unleashed a scathing denunciation of Bill and Hillary Clinton. Bond criticized Clinton for taking advice from a wife who, Bond said, would "liken marriage and the family to slavery."

Here was a continuation of the Republicans' "family values" theme struck earlier in Dan Quayle's remarks about the sitcom "Murphy Brown."

"She has referred to the family as a dependency relationship that deprives people of their rights," Bond went on, citing Hillary's article "Children Under the Law."

"This [campaign] is not a contest between two men," Bond said. "This is a battle, a long, continuing struggle. It's a battle between their view of

America and our view of America. Their values versus our values."

The idea behind Bond's attack was to raise questions about Clinton's character and apparently about Hillary's as well. During the speech, Bond referred to Clinton as "Slick Willie" and to Hillary as "that champion of the family who believes kids should be able to sue their parents rather than help with the chores as they are asked to do."

To her credit, Hillary did not make any attempt to answer Bond for his jibes or attack him on her own.

"I don't like it," Barbara Bush said when asked what she thought about Bond's attack. "I'm not going to lie to you about that. I don't like attacking. I think he's got a great candidate to push, and I hope he will. . . . I'm devoted to Rich Bond, but . . . if you're going to knock [someone] you ought to knock the other person running." Asked if she had told Bond how she felt, she favored the reporter with a faint smile. "I don't have to. I'm talking about it to you."

At the convention, Patrick Buchanan raised the cudgels where Bond had laid them aside. He took Clinton to task for supporting abortion rights and gay rights, and then he turned on Hillary. Buchanan declared:

"Elect me and you get two for the price of one, Mr. Clinton says of his lawyer-spouse. And what does Hillary believe? Well, Hillary believes that twenty-year-olds should have the right to sue their parents, and Hillary has compared marriage and the family as institutions to slavery—and life on an Indian reservation.

"Well, speak for yourself, Hillary," Buchanan said, pointing at the television cameras. "This, my friends, this is radical feminism."

This time, unlike earlier times when Hillary had been laid open to ridicule, the press did not descend on her like vultures. Instead, the media either refrained from adding to the carnage or actually defended her.

Mike Royko, a *Chicago Tribune* columnist, wrote that "the Republicans have found their new Willie Horton" in Hillary Clinton. "I've heard right-wingers describe her as a Nazi, a pinko, a baby-snatcher, and a vicious, ambitious, grasping man-hater."

He concluded, "If the Republicans really believe what they've been saying about Hillary Clinton and children, maybe they ought to include something about it in their platform. That would be the first time a political party came out in favor of child abuse."

Dick Lehr of the *Boston Globe* wrote about the articles used in the attack on Hillary: "They are scholarly pieces, jammed with footnotes, in which Clinton assumes the role of legal scholar and theorist promoting the emergence of the legal doctrine of children's rights and arguing for a legal system that would take greater account of a child's point of view."

Lehr claimed that she had not "likened" and "compared" marriage and family to slavery and life on a reservation. "The content is her analysis of the dynamics of family life in relation to society—describing first the dependency of children on parents and emphasizing the presumption that society acts in their best interests."

All these attacks on Hillary Clinton did not rejuvenate the Bush campaign as much as had been hoped. In fact, it did not give it any life at all.

Charles Black, the President's senior political adviser, told Bush that he was concerned the sustained attack on Hillary Clinton had backfired. Black advised the President not to target her anymore. Polls showed a majority of working women were offended by the attacks. Women were deserting the Republican ticket in greater numbers than men, and they were going over to the Democratics.

Another Bush campaign consultant, Glen Bolger, said that the Republicans had erred by going so far in pressing "family values." "The important suburban vote cares about family values," he said, but the Republican Convention "may have beaten the issue into the ground."

James Pinkerton, another of Bush's advisers, said that attacking Hillary "was a way of energizing the audience." It was a necessary ploy to "get the campaign moving again."

Richard Wirthlin, a Republican pollster, said, "If you overplay values, you create backlash. In most cases values can be communicated more effectively by symbol, through anecdote, by nonverbal communications, and they have little political worth unless they are rooted in something that is concrete: policy or the attributes of an administration.

"When you persuade by reason and then motivate by emotion you can use values to change behavior. That is one of the things left undone" by the Republican campaign.

Black was questioned about the Republican Convention's attacks on Hillary Clinton. Asked why Rich Bond had made a point of attacking Hillary, Black responded: "You didn't hear him say that again."

Meanwhile, Hillary Clinton, the object of all the abuse, was going about her business, campaigning for Bill Clinton and faithfully adhering to the tenets of the Interim Report. In September 1992 she took full advantage of the chance to elucidate her own attitude toward family values in an interview in the *Boston Parents' Papers,* a periodical published by Dr. Betsy Weaver. In the interview, conducted by Dr. Weaver herself, Hillary talked about the roles of men and women in a family, family obligations, religion, and the family in general.

Hillary told Dr. Weaver, "I feel very lucky that I had a family that stressed a lot of values and the importance of responsibility and the right combination of love and discipline. That kind of parental guidance combined with religious faith were really the building blocks of my life." The church, she stressed, had always been one of her most important anchors in life.

She talked about the times when she and her husband were together with their daughter, Chelsea—"family times," she called them. "I think that probably there wasn't a night that went by until [Chelsea] was about ten or so that we didn't read to her before she went to bed." It was Bill Clinton who took Chelsea to school every morning. They kept dinner periods free and worked hard to keep Sundays free for church and for family activities in the afternoon.

Hillary said that "a woman's role in the family is that of the primary caretaker, and I think that is a role most women feel comfortable with and which their husbands are most supportive of and feel comfortable with as well."

Turning to the man's role, she said, "Typically a father has to be a support system for the entire family, including the mother. He has to assist in the primary caretaking, but also to serve as a fully engaged partner in the caring for and the planning for a child's life."

Fathers today, she said, were trying harder to perform the various tasks associated with the care of young children. But many of them were more comfortable in the playful, activity-oriented role fathers traditionally filled. Hillary said, "I think that is very important. I think children need that. They respond well to it, that kind of male role model that in a sense carries messages to and from the outside world to the child—whether it's talking to a little boy or girl about sports or teaching a child how to engage in some activity that's fun for the father."

According to Hillary, "the primary obligation of both parents is to take whatever gift God gave you in the person of that little boy or girl and pay attention to that child's needs, to respond to that child, to stimulate that child, to be there for that child, and to learn the kind of personality your child has so that you're allowing your child to flourish."

It was a tribute to the Interim Report and the team that had put it together—and to Hillary and Bill Clinton as well—that by the time Election Day 1992 rolled around, the negative images of Hillary and Bill had largely been erased from the public mind and replaced by more positive ones. In particular, Hillary had succeeded in clarifying her own ideas about "family values." They were quite at variance with the views the Republican attacks had assumed she held.

The campaign strategy called for Hillary to fly about the country with her staff of five women in her own small jet, on a rigorous schedule that sometimes included up to seven events in three cities in one day. This was all grass-roots stuff, with the emphasis on pressing the flesh and "being there" for the constituency.

Sometimes she met up with Tipper Gore, who was performing similar tasks, or with Al Gore, or even with Bill. But the fun times came when she saw "the boys"—her two brothers, Hugh and Tony. Both of them were now living in Florida and working for Clinton's campaign.

After getting two advanced degrees in education at the University of Arkansas in Fayetteville, Hugh had obtained a degree from the law school, where Hillary had taught.

Tony had opted out of college life after spending a year at Fayetteville with Hugh. He got a job with a metal-marking-equipment company in Texas. When he tired of that, he took up selling insurance in Chicago, back home.

In 1983 he rejoined Hugh, who had moved to Miami to take a job as a public defender. The city's *"Miami Vice"* reputation was not totally un-deserved, so it was a challenging place to practice law. Tony got a private investigator's license and offered his services to his brother and Hugh's fellow lawyers.

In 1989, Hugh became one of several officials of the Dade County Drug Court. He also joined an experimental group that helped addicts who had rehabilitation problems to work their way back into the mainstream. "We've processed almost nine thousand people, with a 93 percent success rate," he told Hillary with a smile.

In 1992, "the boys" were both living in Coral Gables. Hugh had met and married Maria Arias, who was also a lawyer, in 1986. All three threw them-selves into Clinton's campaign for President with their usual ebullience and enthusiasm. Hillary scheduled them for work in Florida, their home base, Pennsylvania, and Illinois, for old time's sake. They gathered people together wherever they could and gave ad-lib speeches on Clinton's behalf.

Their biggest problem was keeping their tempers when Hillary was being attacked by the opposition and the media. "She handled it better than we did," Hugh sighed. "She'd say in a big-sisterly way, 'It's just politics.' "

Hillary called her all-woman campaign entourage "Herc and the Girls" "Herc" came from her initials, HRC. During the long rides on the plane, they laughed and sometimes even sang old, familiar songs. To Brooke Shearer, a friend from Hillary's Washington days and now a campaign aide, it was a lot like being back in school.

She once said, "At seven in the morning we would all gather in Hillary's room, and while she was on the phone talking to a local radio station, somebody was doing her hair, somebody else was ironing her dress, and the press person was dialing the next radio station."

At the end of the day, when Bill Clinton always telephoned Hillary, they would sometimes all be laughing so loud, carrying on and kidding each other about the day's flubs, that he would say enviously, "You guys sound like you're having a lot more fun than I am. Can I come campaign with you?"

It *was* fun in some cases. At one stop in Denver, Representative Patricia Schroeder introduced Hillary to the audience, pointing out that those who believed the President's wife should be seen and not heard would do well to remember Valley Forge.

There, she said, Martha Washington camped out with George for three grueling winters to try to rally the demoralized Revolutionary Army. In spite of her service to her husband and her country, she was criticized for wearing cotton dresses rather than silk. She was also taken to task for speaking English, because French was more fashionable; besides, the French were helping the Americans, and they were both *fighting* the English.

When Hillary took the podium, she laughed, "You left out the most important part—when Martha Washington was pilloried by the press corps for wearing headbands at Valley Forge." Hillary beamed at the laughter that wafted over her.

By October, Hillary felt that, in those long, grueling months of campaigning day after day across the broad expanse of the country, she had won her battle for a softer, more gentle image. Clinton was in the lead, and the troublesome parts of her own persona were submerged so deeply that they were almost invisible to the public.

She appeared on the "Regis and Kathie Lee" show one morning, bringing along one of her old headbands. With a smile, she handed it over to Kathie Lee Gifford. "I don't need this anymore," she said, "and thought you might want it for Halloween."

She had emerged from her own Valley Forge with a self-possession that even her closest friends had never seen before. Her confidence had grown so much that when Bill Clinton won the election, thus propelling Hillary into the exalted role of First Lady of the land, she seemed not a bit surprised—only excited and looking forward to her next challenge.

CHAPTER TWENTY

Zero Margin of Error

Election Night in Little Rock was a blast. Everybody was there. A group of Hillary's classmates from Maine South High School—the new one, built after Maine East proved too small to accommodate the Baby Boomers—came down to Little Rock to celebrate. The crowds were unbelievable. Thousands of people milled about in the governor's mansion, the hotels, and the streets.

Hillary's mother-in-law, Virginia Kelley, held a victory party at the Camelot Hotel, with a few hundred involved in the celebrations. Dorothy and Hugh Rodham went there, along with Hugh Jr. and Tony, who were referred to as "the Brothers Karamazov" or "the bookends" among the campaign staff. Hugh Jr.'s wife, Maria, the Cuban edition of Hillary Rodham, was there. So was Mike Conway, a classmate of Bill's and Hillary's at Yale.

In the din of the celebrations, the Chicago Friends of Hillary surrounded Conway and made him "an honorary graduate of their high school," Conway recalled. He described the atmosphere as "mass euphoria."

"The person I am today is due to all the influences in my life," Hillary said. "And I like where I am. I like the kind of life I have, and I am very grateful for all the lucky breaks I've had and for the challenges I've had, because I think that's what life's about."

In the morning she woke up to the realization that she was going to be First Lady of the USA, not just of Arkansas. Bill Clinton woke up to the realization that he was President of the most powerful country in the world. And the two of them lay there and began to laugh.

"We did it!" the President said.

Indeed they had. But the President-elect and the First Lady—elect did not assume similar roles in the days that led up to Inauguration Day in January. Bill Clinton was all visibility; Hillary was still all invisibility. It was as if she were not there at all.

There was a reason. The campaign staff was not yet satisfied with the public perception of Hillary Clinton. Almost immediately Hillary was assigned to a job on the transition team that was busy making over the campaign team into the White House team. The most important assignment of the transition team was that of filling cabinet posts and other appointed positions. Because of her position so close to the President-elect, Hillary was probably the most influential of the transition group. In late December 1992, the fruits of the transition team's work was presented to the country at large when the cabinet selections were announced, along with the domestic and foreign policy teams of the new White House staff.

There were familiar faces everywhere. Hillary had gone to school at Yale with Robert B. Reich, the designated secretary of labor, and Reich had been Clinton's close friend during their Rhodes scholar days at Oxford, as well as at Yale. Hillary was also a close acquaintance of Donna E. Shalala, the designated secretary of health and human services. Shalala had succeeded her as chairperson of the Children's Defense Fund when Hillary had resigned to work on her husband's presidential campaign.

It was obvious to insiders that Hillary was having direct influence on the selection of those who would surround her husband in the White House. It was also obvious that she had almost as much say as he did, especially to insiders. However, only once in a while did her power become visible to the public eye.

During the Clintons' New Year's vacation in Hilton Head, South Carolina, Bill and Hillary took a bicycle ride on the sandy beach. When they left their rented house, Hillary saw a pair of pickup trucks loaded with journalists getting in position to follow them on their ride. This excursion had been worked out by the staff and the media, following tradition that had been years in the making.

But Hillary called to the Secret Service agent in charge. "No trucks!" she snapped.

The painstaking arrangements for coverage of the couple's bicycle ride were immediately canceled. If Hillary wanted privacy, she got it.

A Republican strategist, Edward Rollins, noted, "My sense is that Hillary will get brushed back a bit. She's got to be careful not to overexpose herself or to play bad cop to Bill's good cop. She can't overshadow him or be perceived as manipulating him."

Sheila Tate, Nancy Reagan's press secretary, agreed. "No matter how careful the Clinton people are to point out how qualified Hillary is, there could be trouble. People don't like the wife mucking about in the husband's affairs. She wasn't elected and they just don't like it."

Linda Bloodworth-Thomason thought differently. "Hillary feels like she's walking into Washington with her arms wide open and smiling, but she's watching on both sides. She's not a fool. She knows that Washington is treacherous. Hillary is not someone who feels the overwhelming need to be understood and validated by everyone. She will do everything she can not to be misunderstood. Then she will be who she is and let the chips fall where they may."

To get back to the bike ride; at the end of it, Bill Clinton stopped to play a game of touch football with daughter Chelsea and forty or fifty others, surrounded by cameras and reporters for a happy-family-at-play shot.

Hillary pedaled on home without wasting a glance on the photo opportunity behind her.

Chelsea was never far from her mother's mind. She had always been close to home—and in the coming four years home would be the White House. Her schooling had to be considered. Both Hillary and Bill were public school people. In fact, it had been the public school system that had benefited most considerably from the governor's actions in 1983 when he appointed Hillary to head the educational reform commission in Arkansas.

The environment in Washington, D.C., was going to pose problems to the Clintons and to Chelsea. The obvious thing to do would be to enroll her in the Washington public school system.

The last presidential child to go to a public school in Washington, D.C., was Amy Carter. Every school day in 1977 she attended her fifth-grade class at Stevens Elementary School near Washington Circle, surrounded by Secret Service agents. The next year she transferred to Hardy Middle School on Foxhall Road, another public school. Before Amy Carter, no presidential child had ever attended a public school since 1906.

The District of Columbia's Board of Education President R. David Hall had written a letter to Bill Clinton saying, "I met you here in Washington several years ago when you visited Jefferson Junior High School. My two daughters who were students at Jefferson still remember how exciting it was for them to meet you and shake your hand.

"If you and Mrs. Clinton are desirous of finding a public school in the District of Columbia . . . I would be pleased to assist you in that regard."

Franklin L. Smith, the school superintendent, seconded Hall's desire to have Chelsea attend a public school. "When you get the President moving to town with a child of school age, if he enrolls his child in a public school, it sends a strong message. It says he has confidence in that system and he has confidence in urban education."

During Clinton's gubernatorial years, the Clintons frequently mentioned how happy they were that Chelsea attended a public school in Little Rock. Yet some Washingtonians in the know suggested that the Clintons might take a leaf out of Al Gore's book and send Chelsea to a private school when they moved into the District.

The prestigious school Georgetown Day was also interested in recruiting Chelsea. A school catalog about the school was sent to the Clintons in Little Rock. Gladys Stern, head of the school, told a reporter, "We sent some material . . . I don't remember the name of the person who asked us for it. We were very careful not to do anything except answer the request."

There were those commentators who predicted that the Clintons might decide to enroll Chelsea in the politically correct Sidwell Friends School on Wisconsin Avenue NW, a Quaker institution founded in 1883. Sidwell's director of external affairs, Ellis Turner, told a journalist, "We don't have any idea whether they have any interest in the school because we haven't been contacted by them. We haven't sent them anything."

The public school for the White House area was Francis Junior High. Superintendent Smith noted that Chelsea would not be forced to go there if she should opt for a public school. Something could be worked out if she didn't want to attend Francis. Smith said, "It's safe to say we would work with the President to have his daughter go to the school of her choice."

While campaigning, Bill Clinton paid a visit to Jefferson Junior High, south of the Washington Mall. The school was known for its science and math departments and would be a good bet for Chelsea, what with her interest in becoming a scientist or aeronautical engineer. Or Chelsea could attend Deal Junior High School in North Cleveland Park or Hine Junior High on Capitol Hill. Choices of schools abounded in Washington, D.C. There was speculation that Hillary might select Hine Junior High, as she had delivered a speech to an assembly there in 1992.

In the end it was Sidwell Friends School that won out, and a White House announcement was issued before the news leaked out on January 5, 1993:

"After many family discussions and careful consideration, we have decided that our daughter, Chelsea, will attend the Sidwell Friends School in Washington, D.C. As parents, we believe this decision is best for our daughter at this time in her life, based on our changing circumstances."

Though not as tony as the National Cathedral School attended by the Al Gore children, Sidwell was still one of the most expensive schools in the country and would cost the Clintons over ten thousand dollars a year in tuition alone.

There *were* protests. During the campaign, the Clintons had repeatedly pointed out that their daughter attended public schools in Little Rock. This was the argument that backed up Clinton's attack on George Bush's "choice proposal" that would permit parents to use federal tax breaks or vouchers to help finance their children's private school educations. In the end, most of the protests were from ordinary citizens; the teachers' unions, which would have seemed to be the most disturbed by this about-face, did not protest at all.

"Let's face it, Chelsea Clinton is no longer a normal school kid," said Keith Geiger, president of the National Education Association. "I think anybody who has seen the life of the child of a President cannot be surprised by a decision like this."

Anne Millman, spokesperson for the United Federation of Teachers, the New York local of the American Federation of Teachers, echoed his sentiments: "Certainly, it would be symbolically nice if he could send Chelsea to a public school. But we're interested in what his policies will be. I think that this is really a private decision on the family's part."

As Inauguration Day drew near, Washington turned into a beehive of speculation about the new First Couple. With the Clintons still operating out of the governor's mansion in Little Rock, journalists had to get their hard facts from stringers on the road.

There was a great deal of guessing in Washington about whether Hillary or Bill was the managing partner of the Clintons. Sidney Johnson, president of the Arkansas Education Association, was asked for his opinion. "We always considered Bill and Hillary as one working unit," he responded. "Something would come down and you wouldn't know which one of them thought of it, where Bill stopped and Hillary began. That's why we called them 'Billary.' "

The conventional political wisdom was that the Clintons were best described as "classic liberals," devoted to societal solutions that rested on taxing and spending and on central planning in Washington. They were also political pragmatists, natural compromisers who would settle at times for victories of symbolism over substance rather than risk losing everything. But there was not a hint of what would really be happening once Bill Clinton became President—especially concerning Hillary. John Brummett analyzed the silence of the media on her. "I think there's a large percentage of the electorate . . . that thinks she's a scary radical and opposes her, but this is sort of a time to cease fire."

Media interest did begin to return to Hillary after an extended absence as inauguration week approached.

But Brummett was right. It centered on what she would be wearing at the inauguration week events. Demands for information about her wardrobe were so persistent that a special press release was issued:

"Mrs. Clinton will wear a full-length coat designed by Connie Fails done in olive green moiré with a portrait collar of black faux fur. The back of the coat is constructed with a series of pleats, creating a fan effect from the shoulder to the floor, helping to enhance the elegance of the train embellished with numerous appliqués."

Interest had focused once again on Hillary's appearance, not on her policy attitudes. "Nobody's going to care [about her policies] until somebody's ox is gored," said Patricia Aufderheide, a communications professor at American University. When that happened, she would be forced to shoulder her share of the blame. "Insofar as she's taken seriously she'll be taken seriously by her political enemies."

Her clothing stole the inagurational show. Much of it was supplied by her old friend Connie Fails, who had sold Hillary her wedding gown and later refurbished a look-alike into the dress she wore at her first inaugural ball as the governor's wife.

On Sunday, Hillary wore a black cashmere greatcoat with silver and gold appliqués, a printed lining, and matching long scarf. That was from Fails. She wore Fails's olive green moiré coat with a fake fur collar and an appliquéd train, the gown in the press release, on Monday evening. On Tuesday afternoon, she wore a multicolored parrot-print coat with fake fur collar and cuffs.

But of them all, the ensemble she wore for the inauguration received the most response. Some critics of women's fashion thought the bright blue, princess-shaped overcoat with the full skirt that brushed the top of her mid-heel pumps was too long and overpowered her. Others criticized her for the gray scarf she had knotted under the coat's high collar. But from the fashion industry came only smiles and encouragement; after all, she was wearing the new long length the designers had been pushing for months.

The most controversial item was the matching hat. It was blue velour with a wide brim turned up in front and turned down in back. A band in the same color surrounded the crown, which was fastened in the back with a big hatpin.

Some said that the hat dominated her face and made her look like a chipmunk under its brim. She wore it even after she had removed her coat. There was speculation that perhaps she kept the hat on because it would take too much time to redo her hair if she took it off.

Not all the statements about the hat were negative. "I think Hillary looked good and she looked happy," Darcy Creech said. Of course, she was the Southport, Connecticut, milliner who made the hat. "She's not trying to be Linda Evangelista or Jackie Kennedy. She made a statement that you can wear a hat inside or out. It was great for everybody in the hat industry."

It had been thirty-one years since a hat—Jackie Kennedy's pillbox—had generated anything like so much talk in the fashion world. Elaine Armstrong, a New York hat designer, called Hillary's a "very flattering, off the face, simple style." Lou Boulmetis, owner of Hippodrome Hatters in Baltimore, described the hat as a feminized version of two men's styles, the gambler and the derby.

Her tweed suit, which appeared reddish brown on television but actually was a mélange of fuchsia, yellow, blue, black, and white, was a Connie Fails. "When she first came out we thought she didn't have it on," Fails said. "But when she finally stood up, I thought she looked stunning." Fails was stunned when she saw Hillary coatless on Pennsylvania Avenue. "What is she doing without her coat?" she wondered. "I asked her to put on silk underwear with everything, so maybe she felt warm enough."

It was the Sarah Phillips blue-violet lace dress with the mousseline overskirt that Hillary wore to the Wednesday night inauguration balls that won overwhelming approval. There was one jarring note, however. White gloves had been tied to her beaded shoulder bag. "You couldn't see the bag!" howled Judith Leiber, who had designed and constructed it. The presence of the gloves was a puzzlement. Even Lisa Caputo, Hillary's press secretary, said she had no idea where they came from.

"One thing is for sure," said Anne-Marie Schior in the *New York Times*.

"Hillary Clinton made a fashion statement this week that she was willing to experiment with clothing and hair styles." But then, she had always done that.

Hillary's basic hairdo was now a smooth shoulder-length style with wispy bangs, which Cristophe had created for her. She swept it up into one of a variety of glamorous arrangements each evening. The most successful, most people agreed, was the swept-back confection whipped up for Wednesday night's inaugural balls by Gabriel DeBakey, a Washington hairstylist.

Some fashion experts thought Hillary overdid the colors a bit. "I just think less is more," said Grace Mirabella. "I'm such a fan, and one just wants to see her keep the pace and the smarts and the good style she's got without surrounding it with swatches of fabric."

"I'd like to see her in pants and a sweater, perhaps," murmured Anna Wintour, editor in chief of *Vogue* magazine. "Not so uptight and done, a little bit looser, a little more simple, and a little more modern."

"She's going to influence fashion," Wintour added. "Whatever she puts on her back is going to be of enormous interest to millions of women. She could be the epitome of American style. She's the ideal customer that every store and every designer is trying to reach."

But to Hillary Clinton, what she was going to wear was not quite so important as what she was going to be called in Washington. That was made resoundingly clear when she had herself announced at the inaugural balls as "Hillary Rodham Clinton." Not Mrs. Clinton. Not Ms. Hillary Rodham. Hillary Rodham Clinton.

Inauguration week was a memorable one for Chelsea Clinton. She was scheduled to enroll at Sidwell Friends School on Monday, January 25. She had all week to do what she wanted, with her parents operating squarely in the eye of the inauguration hurricane.

Sunday, the day preceding inauguration week, Chelsea was seen with a camcorder videotaping the crowds around the Lincoln Memorial. On Monday she was mostly out of sight, attending events with her parents.

Tuesday night she went to the hugely successful entertainment gala mounted for the new President. Chelsea did not get back to Blair House, where the family was staying until the White House was vacated, until 1:30 in the morning. "Quite a night for a twelve-year-old," commented the *New York Times*.

The next morning, at the Metropolitan African Methodist Episcopal Church, she seemed about to fall asleep and yawned a couple of times during the invocation. Later on, she got her second wind. When her father delivered his Inauguration Day peroration, she listened bright-eyed, with obvious interest and attention. Later on, she could be seen picking up the pressure-sensitive shoe marks that had been placed on the inauguration platform to inform speakers where they were to stand during the ceremonies. Chelsea could be glimpsed several times during the long schedule of events curled up catnapping in the back of the bullet-proof limousine that had become the official parade car for the Clintons.

The Clintons themselves had never been allowed a real honeymoon, even when they married—*that* affair was a honeymoon for six—nor were they to be allowed one with Congress and the media after the inauguration. Even during those exciting days of inauguration week a time bomb was slowly ticking away, set to explode at a most inappropriate moment—January 22, two days after the Clintons' installation in the White House.

It was labeled "The Attorney General Post."

From the beginning of the cabinet selection process, both Clintons were determined to find a woman for attorney general in order to produce a cabinet that in its makeup was not in any way weighted with males. This designee would be the first female attorney general in history. And the Clintons meant to get the right person for the job.

Several changes were made in the preferred-candidate list during the last days before the Christmas 1992 deadline. Clinton had at first settled on Pat Wald, a judge on the D.C. Circuit Court of Appeals, a court generally conceded to be the second most powerful in the land. Pat Wald was well known to Hillary Clinton. In her early Yale days, Hillary had worked with her on a chapter of Kenneth Keniston's book *All Our Children*. There was no question but that she was also Hillary's number-one choice.

When Wald turned down the appointment because she wanted to spend more time with her grandchildren, the Clintons went through a short list of names until they reached the last one—Zoë Baird, counsel to Aetna Life and Casualty Company, a protégée of Secretary of State designate Warren M. Christopher. And so finally Zoë Baird was called in for an interview. She had been frank with transition aides about hiring illegal aliens to do household chores in Connecticut, and the President was favorably impressed by her manner. She was named for the attorney general slot.

During inauguration week a number of cabinet appointees were approved, but storm clouds began forming over the head of the Justice Department designee. The public, having read about the hiring of the illegal aliens, was annoyed that the person who would be in charge of justice in the United States had knowingly violated a law she would now be responsible for upholding.

"Average working mothers don't make nearly what she makes, and yet we are obligated to follow the law," said Shelley Gates, the mother of two small children. "It's kind of unfair. This certainly diminishes her credibility."

Members of Congress were restive, too. Alan K. Simpson, the senator from Wyoming, who was the Republican whip and coauthor of the law against hiring illegal aliens as household help, opposed her confirmation. So did others.

When the storm broke, the Clintons did not resist. It was Zoë Baird herself who decided to quit. The President withdrew her name later the same day. And the Clintons determined to take a harder look at future nominees.

After reviewing a long list of new names, they finally came up with a viable candidate. She was Judge Kimba Wood, of New York, interviewed by the President the first week in February 1993. They sat in the Oval Office for forty minutes while Clinton went over the details of her career point by point. He asked her whether or not she had "a Zoë Baird problem" with her own child-care situation. She said she did not and she had the documents to prove it.

No alarm bells rang. Clinton was satisfied. He sent her upstairs, where she spent fifty minutes talking to Hillary Clinton. Hillary, as *Newsweek* put it, was the person "whose political network and personal views had helped her get in the door to begin with." Hillary saw no flaws in Wood's background.

Judge Wood was never actually nominated. Word soon leaked out that she would get the job. The media picked up the name, and her appointment seemed to become a fait accompli without action of any kind. However, during the week of February 8, the story of how she had hired an illegal alien in 1986 got into print, and by Friday, February 12, she, too, had withdrawn her name from consideration. *Technically* she did not have a Zoë Baird problem, because she had paid Social Security taxes and she had hired the alien before the law against hiring was passed.

Yet the parallel was too much for the public to stomach. And she was gone. Charles Peters, the editor of the *Washingtonian Monthly,* said that the cases of Baird and Wood were highly instructive:

"In both instances, you had a tremendous number of lawyers who fooled around and missed the main point. Isn't that a symbol of what happens when you've got all these lawyers running things?"

It seemed obvious that Peters was not attacking Clinton specifically but was targeting *another* lawyer—Hillary Clinton—who was in on the selection process as well.

"The basic philosophy of lawyers is that there is no morality, only legality," commented filmmaker Robert Altman. "My own lawyer, who is one of my very best friends, drives me crazy with his endorsement that anything legal is acceptable, even if it isn't moral."

In the case of Judge Wood, Clinton asked her if she had a Zoë Baird problem, and she answered in a strict legal sense that she did not have a problem exactly like Baird's; she neglected to sort out the broader political implications that were obviously part of the President's question.

In muted discussions among the inner circle of White House aides about the process of selecting cabinet members, the name of Hillary Clinton kept surfacing. Perhaps it was a mistake to include her in these discussions. The President understood the tenor of the talk. The media heard unsubstantiated rumors about these comments.

Eventually the name of Janet Reno, a prosecutor in Miami, came up. When asked by the media if her selection involved any input by Hillary, the President was reported to have said unequivocally, "None."

And yet a week later, as the name was being prepared for nomination, the *New York Times* was being provided background information on Janet Reno, the State Attorney of Dade County. And that background indicated that Hugh Rodham, Hillary's brother, worked as a public defender in the same courtroom as Janet Reno.

Meanwhile, during the extended confusion over the selection of an attorney general and in spite of her close inside involvement in this fiasco, the personal status of Hillary Rodham Clinton visibly rose, enhanced by an enormous amount of unseen yet powerful clout. Hillary's true position in the White House hierarchy was established in three distinct phases, each of which involved a clear-cut indication of position and power on a rapidly escalating scale.

The first part of the answer came on the very day after the inauguration, when she joined the new President in the Oval Office.

That was a break with precedent, since a First Lady usually spent her first day—as well as all of her days—in the East Wing, where the social staff worked. Unlike other First Ladies, said Dee Dee Myers, the White House press secretary, Hillary would have two offices. One would be in the traditional East Wing; the other, her primary office, would be in the West Wing.

That office in the West Wing sent out messages of status to those in the know. The West Wing itself is anchored by the most important office in the

White House—the Oval Office, located at the southeast corner of the first floor. Insiders could see that Hillary's office was the most strategically located on the top floor, on the south side in the middle. It allowed her to see any member of the domestic-policy staff heading downstairs to see the President.

"If you do domestic policy, you have to pass her door on the way any-where, and anyone on the way to her will pass you," a West Wing occupant noted.

The press secretary explained, "The President wanted her to be there [in the West Wing] to work. She'll be working on a variety of domestic-policy issues. She'll be there with other domestic-policy advisers."

George Stephanopoulos, the White House communications director, told the press, "I think she'll be closely involved in developing health-care policy with the President, and she'll be part of those discussions. We don't have any final decisions on structure right now, but I'm certain that she'll be involved."

The health-care group included Donna E. Shalala, the secretary of health and human services; Alice M. Rivlin, deputy director of the Office of Management and Budget; Carol Rasco, assistant to the President for policy development; Ira C. Magaziner, another policy adviser to the President; and Marina Weiss, an aide to Treasury Secretary Lloyd Bentsen. They had worked very hard in the transition months to develop a health-care proposal but had been unable to come up with anything that pleased the Clintons.

"We're stuck in the mud," one adviser admitted. "Everybody is panicked. There is a very short window of time to get something done here." He was referring to the fact that the President had promised to put a health plan in place within the first hundred days of his administration.

Although Hillary's expertise in health care had been restricted to Arkansas, it was the consensus among the White House staff that she could handle that kind of work if necessary. Ed Rothschild, a member of the public interest group Citizen Action, said, "Hillary Clinton doesn't have to be an expert [in health care]. She's a generalist who knows how to put together policy, and she has the President's ear."

Some were critical of the possibility of including Hillary on the health-care roster. If the President was turning to his wife, Robert Moffit of the Heritage Foundation said, "it indicates they don't have their [health-care] act together."

Hillary's West Wing office had been the first clue for those interested in observing and assessing her clout. The second came four days later, on Monday of the week following the inauguration. On that day the President called a press conference in the morning and announced that he had appointed Hillary to head a committee that would prepare legislation for a new health-care system for the nation.

"It is the most powerful official post ever assigned to a First Lady," the *New York Times* noted in a front-page story by Thomas L. Friedman.

The President then said that the task force charged with creating this legislation would be chaired by his wife because she was "better at organizing and leading people from a complex beginning to a certain end than anybody I've ever worked with in my life." He also reminded the press that Hillary had chaired a task force in Little Rock in 1983 to reform the Arkansas educational system.

Clinton named the members of the commission she would be heading, including the secretaries of health and human services, treasury, commerce, defense, and veterans affairs, as well as Leon E. Panetta, director of the Office of Management and Budget.

Throughout the press conference, Hillary did not say a word. It was clearly noted by those present that she was wearing a black velvet headband. It seemed to be a statement by the First Lady that she was back to normal after all the shifts and alterations of her public persona during the difficult months of the campaign.

Capitol Hill was impressed by the appointment. "It can only be a plus," said Representative Henry A. Waxman of California, who led a House Energy and Commerce Committee subcommittee on health and the environment. "This move shows that health care is going to be a very serious priority for the Clinton administration."

The President said that Hillary would be working "day and night" out of what he called a "war room" in the Old Executive Office Building to deliver the health plan on time. She would not be paid for what she did, and he expected her to share "some of the heat I expect to generate." She would start, he said, immediately.

The President's action was generally applauded in Washington. "I'm delighted," said Senator John Rockefeller of Virginia. "Hillary will be the ferocious advocate that health-care needs. Her appointment signals that the administration understands the urgency for fast action."

Paul Costello, Rosalynn Carter's press secretary, said, "This is a great opportunity for Hillary Clinton to come out and lay to rest the issue of her role."

Sheila Tate, Nancy Reagan's press secretary, wondered, "Who's going to tell the President his wife's doing a lousy job?"

Columnist Gail Collins of *Newsday* ended a piece with this thought: "It's not that [Hillary Rodham Clinton] isn't up to [the job of preparing health-care legislation]. It's just that if she doesn't pull it off, I have this terrible feeling the rest of us will never hear the end of it."

The *Toronto Globe and Mail* mused in an editorial: "Should she have a leading policy-making post in her husband's administration? . . . Let Mrs. Clinton do all she can to remold the archaic role of First Lady. . . . Let her speak out openly on the power of feminism and the virtues of education. But, after her hundred-day health posting is over, let her do it outside the official ranks of her husband's administration."

Vince Breglio, a Republican pollster, said, "It has every potential for disaster." He added, "Politicians are most frequently hoisted by their own petards, and that's where she's going to end up, I suspect."

By now Hillary's new use of three names had been tested in public. A *Wall Street Journal*–NBC News poll found that 62 percent of those polled thought the First Lady should be known as "Hillary Clinton." Only 6 percent thought "Hillary Rodham Clinton" was proper. The others said that it did not matter or that they were not sure.

The same poll asked whether she should be involved in the development of major policy positions. Yes, said 47 percent; 45 percent said she should not be.

Karl E. Meyer, a *New York Times* editorial writer, discussed the roles of previous First Ladies, then moved on to Hillary Clinton. "Her more formal role is less a radical break than a logical evolution of earlier developments in a society where women are seen as partners and coworkers, not simply homemakers. Moving her office to the West Wing formalizes that change in status. The argument that she was not elected is only half true, since she was clearly as much a running mate as Al Gore. Did anyone doubt that she would play a policy role? Need anyone really mind?"

On February 4, 1993, Hillary ushered in phase three of the unveiling of her new persona—what might be called the Total Twenty-First-Century First Lady.

Knowing the importance of preparing legislators for new legislation, Hillary planned a precedent-breaking trip to Capitol Hill to hold discussions with various important senators. Her lobbying trip was an extraordinary manifestation of her growing influence in Washington.

She met first with the Senate majority leader, George J. Mitchell of Maine, then with twenty-eight more Democrats and two Republicans, Bob Dole of Kansas, the minority leader, and John H. Chafee of Rhode Island.

Her visit to Capitol Hill proved no surprise to the media. From the beginning it was a high-profile appearance, listed on all the public schedules and advertised by press aides for days ahead of time for maximum attention. It was a signal from the First Lady that she would not only be the shaper of the important health-care proposal but would shepherd the legislation through Congress herself.

When the door to the Lyndon Johnson Room opened, Senator Mitchell strode out. Hillary Clinton joined him at the microphones. There she stood beside him and answered all the questions asked by reporters.

Later, she sat at the head of a horseshoe-shaped table, with Mitchell on one side and Senator Edward M. Kennedy of Massachusetts on the other. She spoke for five minutes about her task force's legislative goals and her desire to work closely with the leadership in Congress to attain them. The meeting lasted for an hour, after which she answered questions one by one.

She stressed her interest in working with congressional leaders to devise legislation that would "respond to the very real needs that Americans have to make sure they're secure in the health care that is given to them.

"People who have been denied health insurance because of a preexisting condition, who cannot change jobs because if they do, they lose the insurance for their spouse or their child, people who are laid off and lose their benefits, people who are in the 100,000 Americans a month who lose their health insurance, people who have to wait in long lines to immunize their children—I think Americans know we have a problem."

Senator Howard M. Metzenbaum of Ohio said, "She's sharp, she's on the ball, and I can't tell you what a real pleasure it is to be able to sit there with the wife of the President and have an open, warm conversation—to be able to sit there and talk about your concerns with her and call her Hillary."

Said one White House aide, "She has already taken the lead in speaking to members of Congress. It's all well and good to work with the committee to fashion a health-care plan, but if Congress won't pass it, that won't do much good."

The clout was there. Was it going to work for the good of Bill Clinton's administration?

"She's a pacesetter," said Thomas Cronin, a political science professor at Colorado College and an expert on the presidency, "and I kind of like it. But the change from her image in the campaign is so stark that there's almost an element of 'Too bad for you guys: we won.' She's walking on the edge."

At the *New Republic,* Mickey Kaus, a senior editor, wrote that he was worried about what he called "creeping Rodhamism." He called her a "false feminist" and concluded, "Nepotism is not feminism."

James Carville, the Clinton campaign strategist, said, "If the person that has the last word at night is the same person who has the first word in the morning, they're going to be important. You throw in an I.Q. of a g'zillion and a backbone of steel, and it's a pretty safe assumption to say this is a person of considerable influence."

A Republican lobbyist, Tom Korologos, said, "A White House with lots of voice is not conducive to good legislation. She has to be careful of what her mandate is. The political danger is that she might go say something that makes Dan Rostenkowski think she has cut a deal, and then Pat Moynihan and Bob Dole might get mad. This is the most sensitive of all places when people feel they have been slighted."

"Why level with Hillary?" one lawmaker wondered. "If you disagree with her, she'll just go back and say to her husband, 'This guy is all wrong.' And then I'll get a phone call from Bill Clinton and he'll say, 'You just don't understand.' "

William Kristol, who was chief of staff to Vice President Dan Quayle, asked, "What ever happened to Al Gore? Remember when we had a real Vice President who occasionally made news and was more than just a pretty face?"

Al Gore shrugged off the comment, appearing unworried that Hillary Rodham Clinton might be usurping his place. "I'm in every meeting," he said.

"The White House is going to want to make Hillary look good, and that ratchets up the stakes of the game," one congressional aide said. "So the question becomes, how much is the White House willing to give away to the Hill to make her succeed?"

No matter how many different opinions there were about the transformation of Hillary Clinton, she had clearly become far more than a First Lady. She came into the White House with her own established network of associates and friends. The network stretched across the country and went deep into the new administration. It had Hollywood connections and business connections. By the time Hillary arrived in Washington, she had more senior-grade aides assigned to her than Vice President Al Gore.

One White House aide was quoted in *Newsweek* to the effect that Hillary Rodham Clinton was not just in the loop, she *was* the loop. The Clintons were known to employ what could be termed "team survival strategies" that served to give her unprecedented clout.

She was learning to juggle all of her various roles: as mother, hostess, First

Lady, and consummate politician. For example, as a mother, she went to her daughter Chelsea's new school to watch her daughter's soccer team play. They won, 4–1. On another occasion, according to Linda Stasi of the New York *Daily News,* Chelsea, who had just turned thirteen, asked to see the nurse at her new school, Sidwell Friends. When the nurse offered to call Hillary, Chelsea reportedly replied: "Call my dad. My mom's too busy."

Nevertheless, Hillary took the time to be with an defend her daughter. She belabored the television show "Saturday Night Live" for a skit it ran about Chelsea Clinton. Hillary was annoyed at the meanness of the people who wrote it and who played in it.

"I think it's sad that people don't have anything better to do than be mean to a child," she told Roxanne Roberts in *Redbook.* "My attitude is that I'm going to do everything I can to help Chelsea be strong enough not to let what other people say about her affect her. In her particular situation it's obviously much bigger, but it happens to children all the time. Unkind and mean things are said by people who are either insecure or going for the laugh or going for the nasty remark—whether it's on a playground or on a television set."

Hillary said that she did not mean she wanted to *control* what someone else said. "The only thing [Bill and I] can do is to try to develop our own values and our own sense of who we are. That's what Bill and I were raised to believe about ourselves, and that's what we're going to try to do for our daughter. And I think that's the best gift you can give a child. Some internal compass. It's not pleasant when people say or do things that are cruel, but that's more a reflection on them than on my daughter or me or my husband. And that's what we're trying to help her understand."

The skit in question went in for boffo laughs through insult. The big joke was that Chelsea wasn't nearly as pretty as Vice President Gore's three blond daughters.

Another role Hillary played was that of White House hostess, and in fulfilling her obligations there, she attended several funerals and spent time fussing over a menu for her first White House dinner. In that role, as an au courant First Lady, she banned smoking at the White House and added a lot of fruits and vegetables to the menu.

Lisa Caputo explained: "She is representative of what a majority of women are doing today. And that is balancing career with family and entertaining." But it was her trip to lobby on the Hill that got all the ink.

Her network was formidable. Called FOHs by insiders—"Friends of Hillary"—her friends included at least six powerful individuals:

Marian Wright Edelman, who had been Hillary's mentor and friend for twenty years, now had a prime seat in the First Lady's "kitchen cabinet" on children's issues.

Donna Shalala, secretary of health and human services and a Children's Defense Fund colleague of Hillary's, would lead the Clinton domestic agenda.

Brooke Shearer, the White House program director, had been a friend and campaign aide and would be running a White House internship program for young political talents.

Susan Thomases, a longtime friend of Hillary's, had become an informal adviser, in spite of her tough-talking and often abrasive ways.

Linda Bloodworth-Thomason, part of the Hollywood connection, brought a show-biz appeal to Hillary's image—new clothes, new hair—and the inaugural.

Mickey Kantor, who staged Bill Clinton's Little Rock economic summit, had regained FOH status after apparently losing it for a period and was now White House trade representative for the President.

Whatever happens in the Clinton administration, the office of First Lady has been changed forever by the presence of Hillary Rodham Clinton in the White House. At a time when the role of husband and wife as equal partners has become widely accepted by the entrance of women in the work force, she has made the role of First Lady equivalent to an equal partner in the office of the Presidency by being both wife and mother, by playing a key role in the decision-making process, and by contributing significantly to the carrying out of the Clinton administration's programs and policies.

Newsweek summed up Hillary's position. "She's box office. She now outpulls Princess Di as a newsstand draw for *People* magazine. Most Americans, polls show, view her as a positive role model. Nervous Clinton aides profess to be pleased with her prominence. The White House's internal polls show her with a higher approval rating than her husband."

One aide who decried the image of Amateur Night produced by the administration's bungling attempts to select an attorney general confessed, "Right now, she's the best thing we've got going for us."

But all that could change. The stakes are getting higher and higher for Hillary Rodham Clinton.

"The whole world is watching," said one Republican strategist. "The margin of error is zero."

CHAPTER TWENTY-ONE

The Politics of Her Heart

"Her sense of purpose stems from a world view rooted in the activist religion of her youth and watered by the conviction of her generation that it was destined (and equipped) to teach the world the error of its ways. Together, both faiths form the true politics of her heart, the politics of virtue."

—Michael Kelly, from "Saint Hillary,"
in the *New York Times Magazine,* May 23, 1993

The three years from Bill Clinton's inauguration in January 1993 through the end of 1995 was an eventful period for Hillary Rodham Clinton, a time that may have as its singular defining gestalt the First Lady's sense of naive surprise that some Americans did not completely and unequivocally embrace her aggressive, feminist, intellectual style and express gratitude that someone of her caliber wanted to help change the country.

In retrospect, it is obvious that Hillary Rodham Clinton's "reign" as First Lady has been a work-in-progress—marked by controversy and clamor. Initially viewed by the American people as a visionary and pioneer, she diminished her status and popularity and triggered a major "reinvention" of her image through the failure of her health care proposals.

Hillary Clinton is unlike any First Lady this country has ever known.

The January 31, 1994, issue of *U.S. News and World Report* revealed that one of the problems facing White House staffers welcoming the new Clinton administration was how to address the new President's wife.

This had not been a problem with many of the former First Ladies. Most had been Mrs. "Fill-in-the-Name-of-the-President." But it was a little different with a First Lady who had boasted on the campaign trail that if the American people elected her husband, then they would get her as part of the deal in a political "two-for-the-price-of-one" bargain.

So the staffers weighed the merits of the various possible titles: "Mrs. Clinton," they felt, was too sexist for such an independent woman. "Ms. Clinton" sounded phony. "Mrs. Rodham Clinton" took much too long to say. They finally came up with the perfect compromise: "We call her Hillary," admitted a high-ranking White House aide.

The First Lady who came closest to Hillary Rodham Clinton's activist agenda and self-possessed independence was Eleanor Roosevelt, a woman who has been Hillary's role model since she was a young girl. As Eleanor did, Hillary champions the poor and underprivileged and, also like Eleanor, Hillary has become a newspaper columnist with her 1995 weekly syndicated column "Talking It Over."

Hillary acknowledged Eleanor Roosevelt's prodigious output when she told a gathering of newswomen in 1995, "I don't know how she did a daily column. I am going to do a weekly column, and I think that, in itself, is a rather big stretch for me on some weeks." Hillary has also talked about how she keeps a collection of Eleanor Roosevelt's columns on her night table, drawing strength and inspiration from them.

Hillary acknowledged Eleanor Roosevelt in an even more direct way in October of 1995 with a column about the former First Lady that began, "One thing I've learned since becoming First Lady is that wherever I go, Eleanor Roosevelt has surely been there before me."

Since her husband's inauguration, Hillary Rodham Clinton has been associated with a veritable smorgasbord of issues and interests.

America's health care crisis was her first and most important focus, and when she failed to successfully implement her monumental roster of changes, she withdrew a bit and downplayed her role as a senior administration policy adviser.

Hillary has had to contend with an array of disturbing developments during the Clinton administration, including defending her husband (again) against adultery charges; the Whitewater investment scandal; Vince Foster's suicide and her own role in the subsequent investigation; a plane crashing into the White House; being burned in effigy by tobacco growers; protecting her teenage daughter Chelsea from the insatiable national media; being called a bitch by Newt Gingrich's mother; and perhaps most upsetting, the deaths of her father and her mother-in-law.

Since 1993, Hillary has traveled to Tokyo for the Group of Seven economic summit; South Africa for Nelson Mandela's inauguration as President; Pakistan, India, Nepal, Bangladesh, Egypt, and Sri Lanka as goodwill ambassador and advocate for women's and children's rights; Warsaw, Poland, to visit World War II memorials; Copenhagen, Denmark, to call for worldwide weapons cuts; and Beijing, China, for the International Conference on Women; Russia; Martha's Vineyard (for Mary Steenburgen and Ted Danson's wedding); Jackson Hole, Wyoming; the Grand Teton National Park; and New York City for Jacqueline Kennedy Onassis's funeral.

The first quarter of 1993 was a settling-in time for the new President and First Lady that was marked by standard public relations moments as well as groundbreaking and revolutionary decisions that literally rewrote the role of the First Lady almost overnight.

In mid-January 1993, media reports indicated that Hillary, not Bill, had made the decision *not* to have a big inaugural party celebrating her husband's election. A few days later, Hillary visited JFK's grave, thereby offering a symbolic link (and classic photo opportunity) between her husband's nascent presidency and the slain iconic hero the sixteen-year-old Bill Clinton had been photographed shaking hands with thirty years earlier.

And as previously noted, one of the truly bold changes a very self-assured Hillary made was to move her office into the West Wing of the White House, the area where the major administration players were situated.

Shortly after the inauguration, around the end of January 1993, the President announced that he was naming Hillary head of the President's Task Force on Health Care Reform, a twelve-member commission that would be composed of Hillary Rodham Clinton, six Cabinet secretaries, Leon Panetta (the Office of Management and Budget director), and four important White House aides. This appointment made Hillary Clinton the most influential and powerful First Lady in American history.

Under Hillary's command, the Task Force would eventually propose a plan of "managed competition" for the country's gargantuan health care industry. This plan, which was originally conceived during the Clinton campaign by the

Clintons, Ira Magaziner, Bruce Reed, and Joshua Weiner, was an alternative to the rejected "single-payer" plan prevalent in many other countries and it epitomized classic American capitalism at its best (or its worst, depending on who you listened to): Universal medical coverage would be provided, but market forces, including supply and demand and regional medical rivalries, would keep costs down.

An ABC News *Nightline* poll in late February 1993 showed that 64 percent of women and 59 percent of men approved of Hillary's appointment as head of the Task Force. (And interestingly, a whopping 73 percent said they did not care what Hillary called herself. The poll had also surveyed Americans as to their feelings about Hillary deciding after the election on using "Hillary Rodham Clinton" as her official name.)

Later in February of that year, President Clinton, with Hillary's participation, proposed a national vaccination program for America's children; Hillary's longtime friend Peggy Richardson was named IRS commissioner; and a U.S. District Court ruled that Hillary's Health Care Task Force could continue to hold its meetings in secret, much to the consternation of Clinton opponents.

On Thursday, March 11, 1993, Hillary met with several prominent female senators for a friendly, get-acquainted gathering.

The Friday of the following week, March 19, Hillary's eighty-one-year-old father, Hugh Rodham, suffered a devastating (and ultimately fatal) stroke. He was hospitalized in Little Rock and Hillary immediately flew to Arkansas to be by his side. The President arrived later.

For the next three weeks ("the work-stop phase," as some of Hillary's team described it), not much progress was made on health care reform. Hillary flew back and forth to see her father many times and was obviously distracted and emotionally distraught. She was unable to do any kind of substantive work on something as complex and demanding as her health care initiatives.

With her father's grave condition on her mind, Hillary left Little Rock to deliver a speech in Austin, Texas, on Tuesday, April 6, the day before Hugh Rodham died. This speech, one of the most memorable of her career, was notable for its impassioned didacticism and crusading theme. There was poetry and metaphor in her words, and when she spoke of "hopeless girls with babies" and "angry boys with guns," her ferocious anger at the societal deterioration and cultural decay she was clearly tired of seeing blistered the sensibilities of her listeners.

She spoke of a "sleeping sickness of the soul" and sadly defined America in the Year of Our Lord 1993 (an apt way of putting it for a woman quickly dubbed "Saint Hillary" by the media) as being a nation terminally ill with the diseases of "alienation and despair and hopelessness."

Here was a First Lady giving a seminal—and blatantly spiritual—speech that was a true call to arms for a more moral country. It was obvious that her father's stroke and impending death had moved her to an existential attempt to find some meaning in the senseless violence decimating our cities from within.

Not everyone, however, was won over by Hillary's evangelical fervor. As one would expect, certain factions of the media, as well as the "anti-Hillary" Republicans, savaged her and took her to task for what Michael Kelly in his "Saint Hillary" piece in the *New York Times* described as "vaulting ambition" inadequately realized due to "intellectual incoherence." Kelly went on to declare that the Austin speech was the direct descendant of Hillary's notorious 1969 Wellesley commencement address (the one that got her profiled in *Life* magazine), and that both were marked by "the adolescent assumption that the past does not exist and the present needs only your guiding hand to create the glorious future."

In response to these attacks, Hillary told *Working Woman* magazine, "[The liberal media doesn't] know what to do with religion or faith. They don't know what to do with spirituality. And so they try to denigrate it or poke fun at it because they're scared of it. You have to feel sorry for people like that. But most people, in their private selves, knew what I was talking about. I wasn't trying to be a theologian or a moral philosopher . . . but it's something I feel very deeply . . . that both on a personal level and a social one, there has been a turning away from some of the deeper values that are part of the human experience in our culture."

Hugh Rodham was at times blunt and brusque, but he taught his daughter Hillary how to make it in a brutal and unforgiving world. There is an oft-told anecdote about Hillary's childhood: Her mother always told her that learning was valuable "for learning's sake." Her father would then chime in with his opinion that learning was even more valuable "for *earning's* sake."

On Wednesday, April 7, 1994, Hillary's father Hugh died.

Bill Clinton was shaken by Hugh Rodham's death and told *Parents Magazine,* "I must tell you, I miss Hillary's father a lot. I really love her parents. They've been wonderful to me. And that's been one of the great blessings of our life together. You know, the parents of one person are often skeptical of the other in the marriage. (Laughs.) I used to write sort of mental marks in my mind when I knew I was making progress with Hillary's father—marks toward worthiness, you know."

On Friday, April 9, Bill and Hillary attended a memorial service in Little Rock for Hugh Rodham and they then flew to Pennsylvania on Saturday for his funeral.

Hillary traveled to Tokyo in July 1993 to attend a world economic summit, representing the President and the United States in a way no First Lady had ever done before. Combined with the powerful statement her appointment as head of the Health Care Task Force made, this trip showed the world that Hillary Rodham Clinton, while perhaps not exactly a "co-President," was nonetheless a force to be reckoned with on the global stage.

On April 15, 1993, Bill and Hillary released their 1992 tax returns. Later in the month, Hillary previewed a key element of her health care proposal when she went public with her backing for health care price controls. But the sneak preview was for naught: On May 6, the scheduled release of the health care proposal was delayed. At the end of May, Hillary again appealed directly to the American people, urging them to support her and her commission's efforts to reform health care.

On July 20, 1993, Deputy White House Counsel and Hillary's longtime friend Vincent Foster was found dead in Fort Marcy Park in Virginia. It appeared that he had shot himself in the head.

Questions quickly arose about the conduct of the White House staff, particularly former White House counsel Bernie Nussbaum, regarding the removal of documents from Foster's office and what connection, if any, there was between Foster's untimely death and the ongoing Whitewater investigation.

Whitewater files were eventually removed from Foster's office and transferred to the Clinton family quarters at the White House. An October 1995 Senate Whitewater Committee report revealed that phone records may be meaningful in an attempt to implicate Hillary Clinton in a cover-up involving the restricting of access to Foster's records on the day of his death.

Hillary continues to deny any wrongdoing and has said that she would only testify before the Senate Whitewater Committee under subpoena. Persistent grilling of Hillary's chief of staff Margaret Williams and Hillary confidante Susan Thomases failed to establish any credible evidence of deliberate attempts by Hillary to hide documents or prevent acquisition of files by government authorities.

Senate Whitewater Committee Republicans expressed doubt about the truthfulness of Thomases and Williams, but Chairman Senator Alfonse D'Amato, according to White House spokesman Mark Fabiani, said that he had "no basis for taking the extraordinary—and wholly unprecedented—step of seeking the First Lady's testimony" in the Whitewater investigation. Through November 1995, however, rumors persisted that D'Amato might be preparing a subpoena to force Hillary to testify.

As 1996, the year in which Bill Clinton hoped to be reelected, began, the Whitewater situation and travel office matter (called Travelgate by the media) continued to plague Hillary and the Clinton administration.

In January 1996, just as Hillary was preparing to begin an eleven-city book tour for *It Takes a Village and Other Lessons Children Teach Us,* a newly discovered 1993 memo from White House aide David Watkins seemed to implicate Hillary in the travel office firings, although she has denied having very much at all to do with the travel office as First Lady.

In a January 15, 1996, interview with *Newsweek* magazine, Hillary was asked about the part of the memo which said, "Foster regularly informed me that the First Lady was concerned and desired action—the action desired was the firing of the Travel Office staff." Hillary responded, "I just don't have any memory of that." Critics jumped on this variation of "I can't recall" as evidence that she had abused presidential power just to put her cronies into positions of financial gain.

The heat on Hillary was also turned up when a box of Rose Law Firm billing records was discovered by her personal assistant, Carolyn Huber. These records showed that Hillary had billed Madison Guaranty for sixty hours of her time, at $120 an hour. Hillary explained that these bills were for a period of fifteen months and that it netted out to about an hour of work a week for Madison. In that same *Newsweek* interview, Hillary said, "There is no way that I think of an hour a week over fifteen months as being a significant amount of work."

As for Whitewater, Mark Fabiani, special associate counsel to President Clinton, in an editorial in the January 10, 1996, *USA Today,* summed up what the White House saw as definitive exoneration:

> In the waning days of 1995, a major national law firm—one with strong Republican ties—issued its final Whitewater report for the Resolution Trust Corp.

This independent inquiry, prepared over two years as a cost of $4 million, concluded, in the words of the *Wall Street Journal*, that "President Clinton and Hillary Rodham Clinton had little knowledge and no control over the Whitewater project in which they invested, and they weren't aware that any funds that went to Whitewater may have been taken from Madison. In addition, there is no firm evidence that the Whitewater project harmed Madison."

Fabiani concluded, "In short, this final independent report concluded that what the President and First Lady have said all along about Whitewater is true."

Nevertheless, the Republican accusations and charges continued and generated countless editorial columns and opinion pieces, none of them causing any uproar—until an article by *New York Times* columnist William Safire appeared.

"Blizzard of Lies" ran on Monday, January 8, 1996, and began:

Americans of all political persuasions are coming to the sad realization that our first lady—a woman of undoubted talents who was a role model for many in her generation—is a congenital liar.

Drip by drip, like Whitewater torture, the case is being made that she is compelled to mislead, and to ensnare her subordinates and friends in a web of deceit.

Safire went on to state that Hillary was "in the longtime habit of lying; and she has never been called to account for lying herself or in suborning lying in her aides and friends."

Such vicious rhetoric aimed at his wife did not sit well with the President of the United States.

"Presidents have feelings, too," Clinton responded, and went on to threaten action: "If I were an ordinary citizen, I might give that article the response it deserves." And what would that response be, Mr. President? Presidential spokesman Mike McCurry explained: "The President, if he were not the president, would have delivered a more forceful response to that on the bridge of Mr. Safire's nose."

Newspapers across the country had great fun with the President's new "forcefulness," and one paper, the *New York Post,* went so far as to run the subheadline, "He'd sock Safire in the nose." They even provided a "Tale of the Tape" comparing Clinton versus Safire in a series of humorous ways.

Whitewater was an Arkansas land development deal that Bill and Hillary Clinton invested in in 1978. The investment was directed by a savings-and-loan manager in Little Rock, and the Clintons ultimately lost money on the deal. It had been thought that the savings and loan may have covered some of the Clintons' losses, at taxpayer expense, and the Clintons took justified tax deductions for the remaining, unreimbursed losses. These tax deductions became an issue for the new President and First Lady—irregularities were suggested—and Vince Foster was working on the case when he is supposed to have killed himself. Reports indicate that he had expressed some "concern" about the Clinton Whitewater files.

In March 1994, under increasing pressure from the media and the public, Hillary met with two *Time* magazine reporters to talk about Whitewater. She told them, "We made an investment decision that lost money." She also said that she and her husband had been completely "straightforward" and that they had "fully cooperated with the grand jury; with the special counsel." She painted a picture of two people who had taken the advice of trusted friends and advisers and had gone along with their investment suggestions. "We did not run the company, we did not make its decisions," Hillary said. "We made lots of mistakes," she admitted. But she again adamantly insisted, "We didn't do anything wrong."

When asked how the accusations and innuendo were affecting her, Hillary replied, "I feel, on most days, good about what I'm doing, but on other days I get down like anybody else. People can lie about you on a regular basis and you have to take it. That's very hurtful. [Now] that we're in public life at the level we are, we have no protection against any of that."

Hillary also told *Time* that she thought that the whole Whitewater debacle "was a Republican plot to discredit her." The magazine described Hillary's role in the White House as "rather like a queen on a chessboard," which is an apt and accurate metaphor. "Her power comes from her unrestricted movement; but the risk of capture is great, and a player without a queen is at a fatal disadvantage."

Immediately after Foster's death, White House lawyer Bernie Nussbaum prevented police and investigators from examining documents in Foster's office. In August 1995, Nussbaum testified before the Senate Special Committee on Whitewater and defended his actions, claiming that even though he would, in hindsight, do some things differently, "on the big calls . . . I was right," and said that he was proud of his conduct. He told the committee that no files had been destroyed and that he was simply trying to "preserve the right of the White House—of this president and future presidents—to assert executive privilege, attorney-client privilege, and work-product privilege."

On July 23, 1993, Hillary attended Vince Foster's funeral. The initial belief that his death had been a suicide was officially confirmed in early August—and later *re*confirmed.

A few days after Foster's death, a despondent note was found in the bottom of his briefcase. The note detailed issues that seemed to have been upsetting Foster and investigators considered it an explanation of his suicide. Conspiracy rumors sprouted immediately, and to this day there is talk that the note was a forgery. There has also been speculation that the orders for the transfer of Foster's files to the White House came from Hillary Clinton herself.

(Satirists and comedians have had a field day with Hillary Clinton and the whole Whitewater–Vince Foster conundrum, going so far as to allege criminal activities involving the White House and the President and First Lady. One magazine, *Slick Times,* a journal devoted to blistering attacks on the Clintons and the administration, published a vicious list called "Ten Ways to Piss Off Hillary" that included "Refuse to commit suicide when she orders you to." The Whitewater affair, while not thought of by most Americans as greatly important or lastingly significant in the annals of politics, nonetheless has its own newsgroup on the Internet: "alt.current-events.clinton.whitewater").

August 19, 1993, was Bill Clinton's forty-seventh birthday, and he and his family decided to spend it on Martha's Vineyard, a tiny island populated by the intellectual and artistic elite; a place that is called home by Beverly Sills, Art Buchwald, Carly Simon, and, before her death, Jacqueline Kennedy Onassis.

The First Family stayed through August 30, residing in former Defense Secretary Robert McNamara's guesthouse. Thanks to Clinton administration attorney Vernon Jordan, workaholic Bill Clinton actually seemed to slow down and truly relax for a bit. Vacation activities included a birthday party during which the President was serenaded by the likes of author William Styron and *Washington Post* chairwoman Katherine Graham, and toasted by both his wife *and* daughter. The First Family also enjoyed an outing with Jacqueline Kennedy Onassis and Maurice Tempelsman aboard Tempelsman's yacht, the *Relemar.* The President, riding a horse named Jack, toured the Scrubby Neck section of the island with his daughter Chelsea. They also visited the annual agricultural fair in West Tisbury, Massachusetts. Bill and Chelsea were mobbed by fairgoers, which kept the Secret Service busy the entire time the President and First Daughter were walking the fairgrounds.

During their vacation, the First Family also played miniature golf. In one game, the President came in first; Chelsea, second; and Hillary was a distant third.

With the summer officially over, Hillary and her team worked feverishly to complete the preparation of their health care reform plan.

On Wednesday, September 22, 1993, the final version of the plan was wrapped up, and for three days Hillary testified before five congressional committees on the details of the plan.

One of the charges she addressed was that her plan had been concocted in secret and that politicians and the media had been excluded from the process of putting the massive bill together. Hillary later told James Fallows of the *Atlantic Monthly,* "Some people say they were excluded because in this case we didn't agree with them. But I think that a fair assessment is that we listened to everybody—and then made recommendations based on what we thought made the most sense."

Hillary did acknowledge, however, that she and her team had made "a major mistake" in imposing a news blackout on the specific details of the developing plan. "Even though we had a process unlike any other that has drafted a bill," she told Fallows, "—more open, more inclusive—we got labeled as being secretive because of our . . . failure to understand that we should be more available to the press along the way. That was something we didn't do well. . . . We were not aware of how significant it is to [shape] the inside story in Washington, in order to make the case . . . for whatever your policy is."

Nevertheless, the response to her personal appearance and presentation— both by the politicians and the public—was nothing less than spectacular. Hillary Rodham Clinton bipartisanly seduced entrenched and jaded Washington politicians with a winning mix of intelligence, charisma, confidence, respect, and sheer charm that had them literally tripping over their own tongues hunting for ever more words to praise and compliment her. Dan Rostenkowski, chairman of the House Ways and Means Committee, even went so far as to voice what many Americans might have been thinking: "In the very near future, the President will be known as your husband," he gushed.

With one amazing and bravura "performance," Hillary had shifted the attention away from her hated headbands and perceived hubris and had successfully redefined herself—by using the forum of a daily, national TV appearance (CNN covered most of the hearings in their entirety)—as a woman who could run a corporation, rebuild and simplify the labyrinthian health care system into something more complete and more equitable, and perhaps, just perhaps, even run the greatest nation in the world, all while successfully finding time to raise a "good kid" daughter and attend all her soccer games.

Hillary's testimony on Capitol Hill about health care did more to redefine her image than any number of photo ops or visits to soup kitchens could have done.

Shortly after the hearings, a poll showed that the American people thought Hillary was smarter than her husband.

Bill Clinton likes to joke about it. "There's a poll saying that forty percent of the American people think Hillary's smarter than I am," he begins. "What I don't understand," he continues, "is how the other sixty percent missed it."

This joke speaks volumes about the American people's persistent perception of Hillary Clinton, and what's not so funny is that in all probability, the underlying premise—that Hillary *is* actually smarter than her husband—might just be true.

At the end of October 1993, it was reported that Hillary's former partner James McDougall was under investigation for his role in the Whitewater investment deal.

In early November, Hillary impulsively lambasted the medical insurance industry for their pricing policies, outrageous practices, and campaign to discredit her reform attempts.

Also in November, Hillary went on record as supporting the reelection campaigns of James Florio, Democratic governor of New Jersey, and David Dinkins, Democratic mayor of New York City. Both lost. Later in November, a court ruled that the withholding of records by Hillary's health care Task Force should not have been allowed to happen.

Hillary's public statements and presence in the last two weeks of November 1993 might provide the quintessential example of her ability to focus on several issues and duties at once. On Friday, November 19, Hillary the seasoned politician publicly blasted the spending cuts proposed by Republicans in the House. The following week, Hillary the dutiful First Lady hosted the first official Clinton state dinner at the White House; and finally, on

November 23, an astonishingly sexy Hillary appeared in glamour poses in a Donna Karan gown in the December issue of *Vogue.*

Mixed signals? Who *was* Hillary Rodham Clinton anyway? Was she a policy wonk who wanted to communicate her husband's administration's messages and help implement Clintonian programs? Or was she the socially flawless First Lady who could entertain world leaders in her home with charm and élan? Or was she an egotistical fame hound who delighted in the celebrity and acclaim gorgeous fashion photos of herself would bring?

Now we believe that the single answer to all these questions could well be yes.

Hillary has said, perhaps a bit disingenuously, "I'm not one of those Energizer bunnies," and yet the truth cannot be denied: She has a razor-sharp intelligence and a remarkable ability to do many things at one time— and to do all those things well. Her intellectual authority may have come from her father's childhood influence. The story is told that when Hillary brought home straight A's on her report card, her father would crack, "You must go to a pretty easy school."

Bill Clinton has said of his wife, "[We] have a First Lady of many talents, but who most of all can bring people together around complex and difficult issues to hammer out consensus and get things done." A Washington lobbyist once told *Mother Jones* magazine that Hillary is so adept at reading and completely understanding long and complex documents that "it really freaks [people] out."

In December 1993, Hillary again found herself having to dutifully defend her husband against allegations of marital infidelity. And then, just before Christmas, an alleged link was once more suggested between Vince Foster's death and the Whitewater investigation.

One of the first major events in 1994 in the lives of Bill and Hillary Clinton was the death of Bill's mother, Virginia Kelley, from breast cancer. In a 1994 interview, Hillary told *Parents* magazine, "[One of the things] I would say about Bill's mother, which was really remarkable, is that she was able to love lots of people unconditionally. Sometimes I would say to her, 'How can you stand that person?' And she'd say, 'Oh, he's good to his mother,' or 'She's good to her dog.' She had a capacity to find something good about people. And that love enabled her to reach so many people and to give them the gift of her spirit."

In mid-January 1994, Hillary traveled with her husband to Russia.

When they returned, Bill Clinton focused his attention on his upcoming State of the Union address, a speech that had substantial input from Hillary (they even discussed it late one night in the Kremlin) and which Hillary later publicly praised.

In the speech, Clinton talked about bringing a sense of community back to the lives of American families. According to *U.S. News and World Report,* Hillary sat in on "top-level meetings" concerning the tone and format of the address, and she had come up with the idea of a "pre–State of the Union" address (which was ultimately canceled because of frigid temperatures) that would focus on the achievements of Bill Clinton's administration.

At the end of January, Hillary received an AIDS awareness award for her efforts to educate the public about how to prevent the spread of the HIV virus.

In early February 1994, Hillary continued to sell her health care reform package by lobbying a professional organization known as the Business Roundtable. Her sales pitch fell on deaf ears, however, and the Roundtable rejected the Clinton plan and endorsed a rival plan as the proper place to start with reforming health care. The group criticized what it described as an overreliance on government regulation and arbitrary price controls.

In February 1994, Hillary and Chelsea attended the opening ceremonies of the Winter Olympics in Lillehammer, Norway.

During their stay in Norway, Hillary was interviewed on videotape by none other than David Letterman's mother, Dorothy. During a USA vs. France hockey game, Dave's mom chatted with the First Lady:

DAVE's MOM: When did you come to Lillehammer?

HILLARY: Oh gosh, we got here at about two thirty in the morning, Saturday morning. Who else have you interviewed?

DAVE's MOM: You're the first.

HILLARY: Oh, great! Well, I feel very honored then!

DAVE's MOM: Did Chelsea get to come with you?

HILLARY: Chelsea's here with me, and that's one of the reasons I've got to go back. You know, she can miss a little bit of school, but not very much.

After a brief conversation about United States downhill skier Tommy Moe, Hillary made a gracious offer:

HILLARY: You'll have to come visit us in the White House some time.
DAVE'S MOM: Oh, I'd love to!
HILLARY: And tell Dave to come on down and see us and bring you
   . . . or you come by yourself.
DAVE'S MOM: I'll tell him.

Just before she wrapped up the interview, Dave's mom, in an obviously planned, but nonetheless charming and funny moment, seized the opportunity to make a special request of the First Lady:

DAVE'S MOM: Oh, and I have a question I need to ask you from David.
   I jotted it down. "Is there anything you or your husband can do
   about the speed limit in Connecticut?"
HILLARY: (Laughs) That sounds like a very personal inquiry from your
   son! Has he gotten into trouble?
DAVE'S MOM: Oh, he has a heavy foot.
HILLARY: Does he have a heavy foot? So does my husband. What is it
   with some of these guys with heavy feet?
DAVE'S MOM: I don't know, but he has received more tickets from the
   Connecticut troopers than I think he cares to count!

After the segment, David Letterman complimented his mom on her efforts and made a few flattering comments about Hillary, which he had to conclude, of course, with a joke!

DAVE: Nice job, Mom!
DAVE'S MOM: It was wonderful, David! She's a charming lady!
DAVE: She's very, very nice, isn't she?
DAVE'S MOM: Yes, she is.
DAVE: Very pleasant and very smart and fun to talk to and I think you
   did a very nice job. Thank you very much. Were you nervous talking
   with her?
DAVE'S MOM: No! She put me so at ease. She was just great.
DAVE: Are you nervous talking to *me?*
DAVE'S MOM: (Laughs) No!

Hillary was genuinely engaged by the spectacle and excitement of the Olympics and reportedly stayed glued to the TV set watching the competition when she returned home.

In early March 1994, Hillary's past financial dealings and Whitewater activities once again took center stage. Hillary learned that a billing probe of her former employer, the Rose Law Firm, was being planned.

As previously detailed, Hillary agreed later in March to meet with the press and discuss the Whitewater "mistakes" made by the Clintons. On March 18, it was reported that in the two years from 1977 through 1979 Hillary had turned a $1,000 commodities investment into $100,000.

Near the end of March, the Clintons' 1977–79 tax records were released, and Hillary's losses in the Whitewater investment were revised.

Bill Clinton resolutely and publicly defended his wife for her past financial dealings, saying, "I have never known a person with a stronger sense of right and wrong in my life. And I do not believe for a moment that she has done anything wrong . . . If everybody in this country had a character half as strong as hers, we wouldn't have half the problems we've got today."

Hillary later explained that she trusted James Blair to make investments for her and that she "relied primarily on his advice." She also admitted that she had "never understood the furor over this failed land investment, and the kind of conspiracy theory people have tried to weave strikes me as kind of silly."

On March 26, 1994, Bill, Hillary, and Chelsea attended the wedding of Bill's brother Roger Clinton. The following day the First Family headed to California for a vacation that lasted through early April, after which Hillary made good on a year-old promise, by throwing out that first Cubs game pitch.

Mid-April the White House revealed that Hillary had made a profit of $6,498 on a 1980 commodities trading venture and had never reported the profit to the Internal Revenue Service. Soon thereafter, Bill and Hillary paid the IRS $14,615 in back taxes and interest, and they also released their 1993 tax returns.

Hillary met with Native American leaders at the end of April 1994, and then, in early May, flew to South Africa with Vice President Gore and his wife Tipper to attend Nelson Mandela's inauguration as President. Hillary used the media spotlight focused on the trip to lobby vigorously for domestic health care reform.

She later described the trip as "extraordinary" and said that she felt "privileged to witness history in the making." She told a group of women journalists, "There was much about that entire inaugural event that was beyond words, that moved me to tears and laughter, and made me believe that, in spite of the twentieth century, progress is, after all, possible."

She also spoke eloquently about the luncheon that followed the swearing-in ceremony:

> But probably the most extraordinary aspect of that visit for me took place at a luncheon after the actual inaugural ceremony. President Mandela had invited many of the representatives from the various countries who were there to come to the President's house where he was then residing and have a luncheon in a very large and beautiful tent on the grounds.
>
> So there we were with people representing nearly every single country of the world, strategically placed so that those who were fighting with one another and those who wouldn't talk to each other, and those who had severed diplomatic relations with each other were far enough away that no international incident would occur.
>
> When President Mandela began to speak, and in his speaking he referred to the fact that he had invited three of his former jailers to attend the inaugural—men who had watched over him, kept him imprisoned, who had been the symbols and reality of the oppressive regime against which he had fought and spoken out against for so many years—I was dumbstruck.
>
> I thought to myself, how could anyone even understand the depth of compassion and forgiveness that must reside inside that man for him to be able to do that. And how much better off we would all be were we able to replicate even a small part of that.
>
> We argue about so many things that don't amount to a hill of beans in our own country. We draw lines against each other. We demonize each other. We accuse each other and attack each other. And here we are living in the greatest country in the world without any of the kinds of true obstacles to democracy and freedom that people like Nelson Mandela lived with for twenty-seven long years.

A year and a half later, in October 1995, Hillary Clinton introduced Nelson Mandela at the New York world premiere of the Alan Paton–Miramax film *Cry, the Beloved Country,* the story of how two South African fathers, one white and one black, deal with a murder. Hillary said, "Thank you for making a movie like this out of a book like this, that was for many of us the first contact we had to apartheid, to South Africa, and to the struggle there. Why can't we, in the richest, most blessed country in the world, forgive one another? That to me is the message and the challenge of this movie to America." Later, Hillary had two words to say about the renowned former political prisoner: "He's saintly."

In late May 1994, Hillary attended her brother Tony Rodham's wedding and then, at the end of the month, she flew to New York City to attend the funeral of Jacqueline Kennedy Onassis.

On Sunday, June 5, 1994, Hillary marked the anniversary of D-Day by speaking to the Women in Military Service of America, an organization for which she is honorary chairwoman.

A little over a week later, Hillary revealed publicly for the first time that she had tried to enlist in the Marine Corps in 1975.

In late June 1994, Hillary *again* had to address charges of alleged infidelities of her husband. This time the charges were made by right-wing religious leader Jerry Falwell.

In early July, Hillary visited World War II war memorials in Warsaw, Poland. When she returned, she and her husband again tried to put out fires pertaining to questionable Whitewater loans in the eighties, all while Hillary continued to lobby for universal health care coverage.

One of Hillary's most controversial proposals for funding health care was to levy a forty-five-cent tax on all retail tobacco products. As can be imagined, this "sin tax" suggestion did not sit very well with tobacco growers. In late August 1994, Hillary Clinton was burned in effigy by the Kentucky Association of Tobacco Supporters.

In early September 1994, Hillary's health care commission's papers were released to the public. By the end of the month, after a year of public debate and political wrangling, it was clear that the Clinton administration's health care bill was dead.

James Fallows of the *Atlantic Monthly* summed up the health care reform debacle like this:

> The scheme was fatally overcomplicated. The proposed legislation, 1,342 pages long, was hard for congressmen to read and impossible for anyone except the plan's creators, Hillary Rodham Clinton and Ira C. Magaziner, to understand.

The Clinton plan would have imposed sweeping changes on one-seventh of the national economy, with consequences far greater than Congress could possible consider before casting a rushed vote. It represented a regulation-minded, top-down, centralized approach at a time when the world was moving toward decentralization and flexibility—and when the supposed health crisis was solving itself anyway. The more people learned about this plan, the less they liked it, and it finally died a natural and well-deserved death.

The jibes began immediately: The media attacked Hillary and Magaziner and sarcastically asked how Hillary would fill up her day now that "her" health care project was dead.

One of Hillary's immediate responses to the public failure of her pet project was to withdraw a bit from the public eye. (One alarming unrelated event during the fall of 1994 occurred on September 12, 1994, when a small plane crashed on the south lawn of the White House. The pilot was killed but no one else was injured. The plane was headed directly for the President and First Lady's bedroom, raising questions about the security of the air space around the White House.)

In November 1995, the General Accounting Office issued a report that said the final cost to the American taxpayers for the health care task force was $13.8 million. The original March 17, 1993, charter for the task force estimated total costs for the task force "to be below $100,000." Costs were spread across ten federal agencies, including Health and Human Services, the Office of Management and Budget, the United States Treasury, the White House, and the Defense, Education, Labor, and Justice departments. White House spokeswoman Ginny Terzano said that despite the original low estimate, it was "never our intent to mislead or misreport" the true costs of the task force. There was no public comment from Hillary Clinton.

Hillary did some limited campaigning in Florida for her brother Hugh Rodham's senatorial bid in early October, but basically laid low until after her brother lost in early November.

Hillary's next "cause" was to speak out against Newt Gingrich and his fellow Republican's cost-cutting proposals, suggestions that she saw as being "antipoor" and "antichildren." Hillary made a point of ardently blasting one of Gingrich's more cold-hearted ideas: That of putting poor children in orphanages.

In January 1995, Hillary Clinton and Newt Gingrich would again be linked in the media, only this time it was because of something Newt's mother said, specifically to journalist Connie Chung.

On Thursday, January 5, CBS aired an episode of Chung's magazine news program *Eye to Eye*. This installment featured an interview with Newt Gingrich's mother, Kathleen Gingrich, in which she told Connie Chung that her son Newt had once said that Bill Clinton was "intelligent" and that Hillary Clinton was a "bitch."

What was especially interesting about this incident is that the insulting slur took a backseat to the way in which the remark was elicited. At one point during the interview, when the two women were discussing Bill and Hillary, Kathleen Gingrich let it slip that her son had a very specific opinion of the President and First Lady. At this point, Connie Chung leaned forward and conspiratorially asked Mrs. Gingrich if she'd spill the beans, using the words, "just between you and me," implying that her secret wouldn't go any further than the ears of Ms. Chung.

"Off the record" still means something in journalism, and most reputable reporters and writers respect its boundaries. The best way to get blackballed in the industry is to reveal an off-the-record comment publicly. To high-profile people, such a betrayal brands a journalist as a pariah, and no one will talk to him or her after such a double-cross. There are many ways to indicate that specific comments are "DNQ" (Do Not Quote); one of which is for the reporter to say something like, "This won't leave this room," or "They won't hear it from me," or, perhaps, "Just between you and me." Because Connie Chung revealed what she essentially assured Kathleen Gingrich would be confidential, she violated the unwritten rules of journalistic integrity. "Just between you and me" takes on a whole different meaning when the person making such a promise is wired for sound. CBS also took the heat for deciding to air the remark, even though there was controversy as to how it was obtained.

To her credit, Hillary Clinton took the whole incident in stride, choosing to take the high road and not sink to the Gingrich level of name-calling. On Friday, January 13, Hillary gave House Speaker Gingrich and his mother a personal hour-long tour of the White House. Score this contretemps a win for a very gracious Hillary Rodham Clinton.

In the second week of January 1995, the *New York Times* reported that Hillary Clinton was deliberately seeking ways to make herself more "likable." She admitted that she had been "naive and dumb" about national politics and publicly accepted full blame for the failure of her health care overhaul plan. The *Times* reported that the normally confident and savvy Hillary actually invited suggestions and advice at a White House luncheon from a group of women reporters on how she could project a more "sympathetic" image to the American people.

Shortly thereafter the *Washington Post* published "First Lady of Paradox," a long feature story subtitled "After Two Years, Hillary Clinton Is Defined by Contradictory Perceptions." The piece profiled the various perceived personas of the First Lady—feminist, activist, administration leader, mother, wife, lawyer, etc.—and noted that because of the wardrobe of hats she had worn in the first two years of her husband's administration, she was often looked upon unfavorably by the American people.

These two articles acknowledged the conscious decision Hillary Clinton made in the aftermath of her failed health care plan to change her public image. It was now obvious that she had decided to "soften" it, so that she would be viewed as "Mrs. Bill Clinton" to the majority of Americans, rather than "Hillary Rodham Clinton," independent mover and shaker who just so happened to be First Lady of the United States.

Hillary's "makeover" continued when, on Friday, January 20, she called nine radio stations to talk about breast cancer.

In early March 1995, Hillary attended a summit meeting in Copenhagen, Denmark, in which she pushed the agenda of worldwide female literacy and called for global weapons cuts, both of which were nonabrasive, "no-lose" issues for her to support.

In mid-March, Hillary argued against $40 billion in cuts that Congress wanted to make in children's programs by the year 2000, and also spoke at the United Nations, asking the organization to do more for women and women's rights around the world.

A few days later, as she continued to argue against what she considered to be cold-hearted, Draconian, "punish the victim" cuts in social programs, she said that the Republican Party did have some "good people" in it but that the GOP also harbored a vocal faction of "extremists."

Acting as goodwill ambassador for the United States, Hillary and Chelsea Clinton traveled through South Asia from Friday, March 24, to Thursday, April 6, 1995. Among the places Hillary and fifteen-year-old daughter Chelsea visited were Pakistan, India, Nepal, Bangladesh, and Sri Lanka. Hillary's agenda for the trip was to promote the education of girls and women.

Upon her return, Hillary penned a two-thousand word article for the

Washington Post titled, "Investing in Sisterhood: An Agenda for the World's Women," which appeared on Sunday, May 14.

The article began with an evocative and vivid look at a bank in India owned and operated solely by women:

> The Women's Bank is a one-room building in Ahmedabad, a textile center in western India. The teller's counter is an old kitchen table covered with cloth. Bank clerks record all transactions by hand, on yellowed sheets bound in volumes that resemble worn-out telephone books. When I visited, I saw poor women who had walked 12 to 15 hours from their villages to take out loans—some as small as $1—to invest in dairy cows, plows, or goods that could be sold at market.

Hillary wrote movingly of seeing "women struggling to overcome poverty, illiteracy, inadequate health care, and deeply rooted cultural barriers by joining together to increase their earning power and improve their circumstances." She also used the wide-ranging forum of the *Washington Post* to remind Americans that "investing in people—especially women and girls—is as essential to the prosperity of the entire global family as investing in the development of open markets and trade." She cogently and passionately argued that "South Asia reminds us that social development and economic development go hand-in-hand. It reminds us too that women represent the soundest investment any nation can make in the effort to jump-start development."

She also addressed the charge that she had somehow abandoned the "harder" social issues (like economic concerns and crime) she had been focusing on earlier in her husband's administration for "softer" issues in an attempt at changing her image:

> I realize that issues such as education and health care are still regarded in many quarters as "soft" or marginal to economic growth. Often they are reflexively dismissed as "traditional women's issues" that do not rank high among the problems we will face in the 21st century. A growing body of research from the World Bank and elsewhere suggests otherwise; questions surrounding social development, especially of women, are at the center of our political and economic challenges.

Reaction to Hillary's very public embrace of a more traditional First Lady role was mixed. As the *Washington Post* had done earlier, the *Los Angeles*

Times likewise suggested that Hillary had now become "Mrs. Bill Clinton, for once and for all," and that it was obvious that she no longer viewed herself as America's "co-President."

Some Hillary-watchers thought her transformation too calculated and obvious. Others welcomed the changes, and the view was held in some quarters that it was "about time" that Hillary toned down her aggressive style and deferred a bit more obviously to the President and the Presidency. Since she had not been elected to any accountable office, many Americans were relieved when Hillary stopped acting like a senior administration official and policy-maker and started acting more like a mother and a wife.

In April 1995, the President and First Lady released their 1994 tax return. The First Couple had paid $55,313 on an adjusted gross income of $263,900 ($200,000 of which was Bill Clinton's salary as President). They had given $30,125 to charity, and they received a refund of $14,418.

At the end of April 1995, Simon & Schuster announced that they had signed a publishing contract with Hillary Rodham Clinton for a book to be titled *It Takes a Village and Other Lessons Children Teach Us*. (The title is a reference to the philosophical adage, "It takes a whole village to raise a child.") The book, the publisher said, would champion family life and the need for closer communities in modern American society. Hillary Clinton would take no money for the book, and all proceeds, after expenses, would go to children's charities.

It was also revealed that the book would actually be written by Georgetown University journalism professor Barbara Feinman, who would base the text on a lengthy series of interviews with the First Lady. Hillary would be involved in editing the final text.

It Takes a Village and Other Lessons Children Teach Us was another stage in the evolution of Hillary Rodham Clinton. The *New York Times* suggested that Hillary's "new book could help Mrs. Clinton recast herself in the traditional image of nurturing wife and mother," but Hillary's spokesperson Lisa Caputo denied any hidden motives, stating, "[Hillary] is someone who has talked and advocated for over twenty-five years on the behalf of children and families. These are issues that have been important to her throughout her entire life." Carolyn Reidy, president of Simon & Schuster's trade book division said, "[O]utside of a handful of articles and speeches, her thoughts on [family and children's issues] have not been available to everyone in an easily readable format. I think," she concluded, "it will be an inspiring book."

It Takes a Village and Other Lessons Children Teach Us was published on

January 12, 1996, with a first print run of 350,000 copies. Four days later, Hillary began an eleven-day book tour starting in her former hometown of Little Rock, Arkansas. All profits from her tour are to be donated to various children's hospitals.

In late April 1995, shortly after the Oklahoma City Federal Building bombing, Bill and Hillary Clinton held an Oval Office session that was broadcast live throughout the country. The get-together involved worried children and their parents and was designed to reassure concerned families throughout the nation that the Oklahoma City bombers would be caught and brought to trial.

During May and June 1995 Hillary Clinton spoke out on a range of issues, including breast cancer; the "Baby Richard" adoption/child custody case (she said it had greatly upset her); women's education; and funding for the National Endowment for the Arts. She blasted the GOP's efforts to cut funding for the NEA, saying art and artists had "helped transform communities" by allowing people to experience what she described as a "shared artistic heritage."

By mid-July Hillary was embroiled in the controversy over whether she should attend the Fourth World Conference on Women in Beijing, China. She had been named honorary chairwoman of the forty-six-member United States delegation to the conference and had said that she hoped to be able to attend.

In mid-August Bill, Hillary, and Chelsea vacationed in Jackson Hole, Wyoming, where they stargazed, hiked, played golf, and visited the Grand Teton National Park. During this period the Beijing controversy escalated.

The China debate began when Ching Lee Wu, the wife of jailed human rights activist and political prisoner Harry Wu, asked Hillary not to attend the Fourth World Conference as long as China continued to hold her husband in custody. In August, Republicans Bob Dole and Richard Lugar publicly cautioned Hillary against attending.

The prevailing opinion seemed to be that Hillary's attendance—if China was still holding Wu—would be viewed by the Chinese as tacit approval of the abusive human rights policies and dictatorial power structure of their oppressive totalitarian government.

In late August, however, the "Harry Wu problem" went away. The Chinese government, bowing to worldwide pressure, released the activist, thereby clearing the way for the Clinton administration to agree to Hillary

Clinton's attendance at the conference on September 5 and 6. Clinton administration officials pointedly acknowledged that Wu's release had played an important role in the decision to attend.

Many politicians and media analysts expressed doubts about Hillary's agenda in China and posed tough questions about her commitment and her willingness to boldly speak out against China's abuses—while on Chinese soil as a guest of the Chinese government.

On Tuesday, September 5, Hillary Rodham Clinton erased any and all doubts about her dedication to human rights and her personal capacity to express her outrage, regardless of whether her words were "politically correct."

She was passionate during her time at the rostrum:

> It is time for us to say here in Beijing, and the world to hear, that it is no longer acceptable to discuss women's rights as separate from human rights.
>
> It is a violation of human rights when babies are denied food, or drowned, or suffocated, or their spines broken, simply because they are born girls . . . or when women and girls are sold into slavery or prostitution for human greed.
>
> It is a violation of human rights when women are doused with gasoline, set on fire, and burned to death because their marriage dowries are deemed too small . . . or when thousands of women are raped in their own communities and when thousands of women are subjected to rape as a tactic or prize of war.

Conferencegoers were stunned by Hillary's fiery rhetoric and her words were met with applause and cheers, as well as loud banging on tables. "If there is one message that echoes forth from this conference," she continued, "let it be that human rights are women's rights and women's rights are human rights, for once and for all."

"Freedom means the right to assemble, organize, and debate openly," she continued. "It means not taking citizens away from their loved ones and jailing them, mistreating them, or denying them their freedom or dignity because of peaceful expression of their ideas and opinions."

Hillary's speech was a watershed moment in her "career" as First Lady. This might have been the first time a deliberate admonishment of a foreign government was delivered on the country's own soil, and not by a President, Vice President, or senior administration official, but by the President's wife.

It was obvious to the Chinese—and to the world—that Hillary's words expressed the beliefs and sentiments of the President of the United States and, by extension, the American people.

Hillary Clinton's appearance and speech in Beijing in early September of 1995 may very well have been her finest moment in the first three years of her husband's administration. Of course there had been domestic triumphs (her health care testimony, even though the plan failed, must be counted as a personal triumph), but this time, Mrs. Clinton was on a global stage, and she used it to make an impassioned plea for human rights and to speak out against the reprehensible actions of China's despotic government.

The Voice of America, an international shortwave radio service that broadcasts into countries where the media are censored, carried Hillary's speech live in English and then later translated it into Mandarin. Chinese citizens were not allowed to hear Hillary's words directly. Her speech was banned from the official airwaves by the Chinese government.

On her way home from China, Hillary stopped in Ulan Bator, Mongolia, where she visited a center for homeless children and spoke out in favor of American aid to places like Mongolia, a land where street children live in abandoned train cars and disease runs rampant: "I think most Americans, if they knew the facts, would be very proud of our country because of what we're trying to do around the world."

While in Mongolia, she visited a "ger," a movable dwelling that is similar to a tent, and she sipped mare's milk, which at first tastes like cow's milk but leaves a rancid aftertaste.

An interesting and revealing exchange took place between Hillary and a Mongolian reporter during her tour of a children's center. The *New York Times* reported that the journalist asked Hillary, "Will you run for President when your husband's term is completed?" She laughed and replied, "Reporters are the same the world over. It must be something in the water."

And then, the *Times* reported, "She changed the subject."

On Sunday, July 23, 1995, Hillary Rodham Clinton made her debut as a syndicated newspaper columnist, following in the footsteps of her revered role model, Eleanor Roosevelt, the First Lady who wrote a daily column called "My Day" for over twenty years.

Hillary's column, called "Talking It Over," now appears in more than one hundred newspapers and magazines worldwide, including English and translated versions in Japan, Germany, Italy, Scandinavia, Pakistan, and Saudi Arabia. In her first column, she wrote about trying to be inconspicuous at a

Washington, D.C., museum. She also acknowledged what she described as "the odd duality of my role as First Lady" but affirmed that "whatever minor inconveniences my situation presents, I wouldn't trade it for the world." She wrote that she "could never have imagined the range of activities that are part of my life today, such as defending public television, planning state dinners, and visiting the CIA with the President."

Even though "Talking It Over" will undoubtedly be used as a political tool, and has already been viewed as such by the media, Hillary's stated intentions regarding her weekly "say" are to write about subjects that mean a lot to her, including breast cancer, motherhood, marriage, adoption, childbirth, and even the mail she receives.

In her September 23, 1995, column, for instance, she took to task designer Calvin Klein for running graphic ads featuring young people in sexually suggestive poses, with their underwear in full view. In a blatant pitch for "family values," Hillary blasted the ads:

> The Calvin Klein ads are disturbing because they feed on the innocence and vulnerability of children. And the cynical message delivered to young people is that their value as human beings depends on looking sexy and acting cool.
>
> It's hard enough for kids these days to grow up feeling confident and secure about who they are. What we should be doing as a society is helping young people focus on schoolwork and other positive activities that build self-discipline and character—not adding to the confusion and anxiety that are part of growing up.
>
> If you care about your family's values, as I do, you have to be concerned about values in the marketplace. You have to be concerned about the messages conveyed through the things we buy and sell.

In her November 4, 1995, column about the United Nations, she spoke out in defense of the oft-beleaguered world organization:

> The United Nations is far from perfect. But it offers a forum where talking instead of fighting is valued. It provides assistance that helps people around the world and even here in the United States. And it holds out the promise of peace, prosperity, and democracy, which make the world safer for Americans.

Hillary comes up with the ideas for her column and then works up a draft with help from White House speechwriter Alison Muscatine. Hillary's column is one more milestone in the ongoing reshaping of her evolving image. It gives her a weekly forum (similar to her husband's weekly radio address) to discuss timely topics, and it also contributes to the reshaping of her persona into a "warmer and friendlier" First Lady.

Other 1995 "Talking It Over" columns included a blast at insurance companies who want to mandate how long new mothers can stay in the hospital after giving birth; meeting Mother Teresa; thoughts on her and the President's twentieth wedding anniversary; musings on Eleanor Roosevelt; the story of one of her staff who has breast cancer in the context of an impassioned "sales pitch" for mammograms; and memories of her trips to Mongolia and Beijing.

The last few months of 1995 found Hillary Clinton continuing to foster goodwill for her husband's administration and helping to lay the groundwork for the grueling reelection campaign that would begin shortly.

She traveled to South America in October, and an embarrassing incident occurred during her stop in Brazil. While standing chatting, she was unaware that her skirt had gotten stuck in her underwear, exposing her panties. A photograph of the "in flagrante delicto" First Lady was taken surreptitiously, and it wasn't long before a two-page spread advertising Duloren brand lingerie appeared in Brazilian magazines, with the tag line, "Mr. President of the United States, Your Excellency cannot imagine what a Duloren can do." Beneath that line, in smaller text, it said, "A tribute from Duloren to one of the most important women of the decade."

Lisa Caputo, Hillary's spokesperson, said, "In the interest of good taste and good sense, we have no comment." The ad agency's creative director, Silvio Matos, defended the ad, saying, "We're trying to take advantage of Hillary's image among Brazilian women, which is an extremely positive one. We weren't the ones who took the picture. We just added the phrase and made it into a tribute. In this case, we want to say that daring women don't mind letting their panties be seen."

Also in October, Hillary and Bill Clinton welcomed the King and Queen of Norway to the White House for dinner and an overnight stay. When King Harald and Queen Sonja arrived ten minutes early, however, the White House social secretary Ann Stock had to rush out to greet them—Bill and Hillary were still getting ready—and escort them into the White House. The perpetually tardy President made his entrance shortly thereafter and the three heads of state and the First Lady then posed for an official portrait.

In early November, Hillary led a Times Square rally in New York City to protest planned Republican cuts to Medicare and Medicaid. The march, which was organized by the Greater New York Hospital Association and hospital workers' unions, drew more than twenty thousand people. "This debate is about whether or not we will take care of our children," said Hillary, and she assured the crowd that the proposed harsh Republican budget was "dead on arrival when it reaches the Oval Office."

On Monday, November 6, 1995, Bill and Hillary Clinton attended the funeral of slain Israeli Prime Minister Yitzhak Rabin at the Mount Herzl cemetery in Jerusalem. Rabin had been assassinated Saturday, November 4, by a Jewish radical who was against the Arab-Israeli peace process. Hillary dressed all in black, including a black hat, as one would at the funeral of a beloved friend or cherished family member, so emphasizing the very close ties between the United States and Israel.

As 1995 came to an end, the "new" (and improved?) Hillary Rodham Clinton continued to stump for the social issues near and dear to her heart: women's rights, the well-being of children, breast cancer awareness, motherhood, health care reform, and literacy.

Her deliberate personality "makeover" had not been wholeheartedly welcomed by all: *New York Times* columnist Maureen Dowd, in a scathing column titled "The Two Mrs. Clintons," blasted what she called Hillary's "white-glove femininity," suggesting that "One of the smartest, strongest, most complicated women in Washington history" had retreated behind a Picasso-like duality. Dowd said that Hillary's reflection was "cubed and surreal" and that the First Lady had "a talent for taking on the aspects of those she once scorned: Richard Nixon, Ronald Reagan, and the women who bake cookies."

Nonetheless, much of the American public embraced the new Hillary. People seemed almost unanimously more "comfortable" with this less abrasive First Lady. Hillary still had problems, though, that disturbed some Americans. Election Day 1995 came and went, and the Whitewater hearings continued. Rumors about Hillary's involvement in the travel office firings and the Vince Foster investigation lived on. (There were even rumors floating around that Whitewater prosecutor Kenneth Starr was talking about exhuming Vince Foster's body.)

But as serious as these political hot potatoes might actually be to the

Clinton administration, to many Americans, these were, and are, nonissues: something politicians liked to play around with, but nothing that would affect the daily lives of most Americans.

No, what seemed to concern the American people were things like Medicare cuts, child care cuts, school lunch cuts, and other harsh measures that would change their lives, often for the worse. And it seemed to many that Hillary Rodham Clinton understood their concerns and spoke out for them. When the First Lady spoke out against the things she felt would hurt the poor, the sick, and the helpless, people sensed that she spoke with compassion, and from the heart.

Index